WOMAN'S EDUCATION BEGINS

The Rise of the Women's Colleges

BY

LOUISE SCHUTZ BOAS

ARNO PRESS & THE NEW YORK TIMES
*New York * 1971*

Reprint Edition 1971 by Arno Press Inc.

Reprinted from a copy in
The Newark Public Library

American Education:
Its Men, Ideas, and Institutions - Series II
ISBN for complete set: 0-405-03600-0
See last pages of this volume for titles.

Manufactured in the United States of America

Library of Congress Cataloging in Publication Data

Boas, Louise (Schutz)
    Woman's education begins.
    (American education: its men, ideas, and
institutions. Series II)
    Written on the occasion of the hundredth
anniversary of Wheaton College, Norton, Mass.
    Bibliography: p.
    1. Education of women--U. S.--History.
2. Women's colleges--U. S.--History.
I. Title. II. Series.
LC1756.B55 1971   376'.9'73   74-165705
ISBN 0-405-03694-9

WOMAN'S EDUCATION BEGINS

The Rise of the Women's Colleges

BY

LOUISE SCHUTZ BOAS

WHEATON COLLEGE PRESS
NORTON, MASSACHUSETTS
1935

PRINTED IN THE UNITED STATES OF AMERICA
BY THE PLIMPTON PRESS, NORWOOD, MASS.

THE one chief thing in this matter — which compriseth the beginning, middle, and end of all — is education and regular instruction; and that these two afford great help and assistance towards the attainment of virtue and felicity. For all other things are but human and of small value, such as will hardly recompense the industry required to the getting of them. It is, indeed, a desirable thing to be well descended; but the glory belongs to our ancestors. Riches are valuable; but they are the goods of Fortune, who frequently takes them from those that have them, and carries them to those who never so much as hoped for them. Yea, the greater they are, the fairer mark are they for those to aim at who desire to make our bags their prize. . . . But the weightiest consideration of all is, that riches may be enjoyed by the worst as well as the best of men. Glory is a thing deserving respect, but unstable; beauty is a prize that men fight to obtain, but, when obtained, it is of little continuance; health is a precious enjoyment, but easily impaired; strength is a thing desirable, but apt to be the prey of diseases and old age. . . . What indeed is my proportion of human strength, if compared to that of other animals, such as elephants and bulls and lions? But learning alone, of all things in our possession, is immortal and divine. . . . Yea, war itself, which like a winter torrent bears all other things before it and carries them away with it, leaves learning alone behind.

Plutarch

CONTENTS

INTRODUCTION

THIS study was undertaken as an attempt to understand the social conditions which brought about the education of women. The occasion is the hundredth anniversary of Wheaton College, Norton, Massachusetts. Founded in 1834, opened in 1835, Wheaton Female Seminary became in 1912 Wheaton College.

This book, however, does not attempt to solve the question of the "first endowed seminary," "first incorporated seminary," "first woman's college." It has been the tendency of anniversary volumes to make these claims for many institutions, some still in existence, others surviving only in loving memory. Questions of priority are almost impossible to settle satisfactorily. Often a school incorporated at its inception; often only after years of successful and honored existence. The date of incorporation is, therefore, misleading.

The matter of endowment is another puzzle. Did the gift of a house and the land on which it stood constitute endowment? or the gift of a sum of money sufficient to erect a recitation hall? or a recitation hall, a dormitory, and a laboratory? or, if income bearing endowment alone be considered, did the gift of one or five thousand dollars constitute endowment? how large an income from invested capital is to be counted as the minimum endowment?

Again, some schools started as co-educational academies, later excluding boys, and continuing as "female" schools. Are these to be dated from their founding? or from their change of policy?

A discussion of priority becomes a mere academic argu-

ment. The schools which have vanished, as well as the
fairly large number which survive, were all outgrowths
of the same impulses. Originally conceived as colleges
for women, the seminaries after a generation had to
choose between the change to colleges, new style, or to
preparatory schools for the young colleges. Hence the
history of the seminaries involves a consideration of the
changes in the character of education, and in the changing public attitude toward woman's education.

If the discussion tends to limit itself too narrowly to
Massachusetts and New York, it is because in these states
the most prominent educators lived and worked, and because in Massachusetts education was a more serious matter than in most states. It seemed more necessary to
Massachusetts to found schools, more necessary to regulate them; and, later, more necessary to restrict their
numbers. In 1879 Indiana and Missouri had each
twenty-three colleges, Iowa twenty-one, Tennessee twenty-
seven, Pennsylvania twenty-nine, and Illinois thirty
against sixteen in New York and seven in Massachusetts.

New Englanders are inclined to believe that their
schools and colleges have made more noise in the world
than those in other sections of the country. Certainly the
leaders of the movement toward higher education for
women were for the most part New Englanders: Joseph
Emerson, Emma Willard, Catharine Beecher, Zilpah
Grant, Mary Lyon. Though the Moravians and the
Friends both established schools in the eighteenth century,
they served their own groups rather than the public at
large. Joseph Emerson trained a long list of successful
teachers in Massachusetts, among them Zilpah Grant and
Mary Lyon. Emma Willard gained her first fame in New
England, before she was invited first to Watertown, New
York, and then to Troy. Catharine Beecher began her

work in Connecticut, later leaving a famous school to establish schools in the Middle West.

That the task of these so-called pioneers was to stabilize educational practice rather than to " invent " woman's education came as a surprise to one who had been brought up in the tradition that woman's education was the result of a tremendous self-sacrificing struggle against heavy odds of indifference and of active opposition. Evidences of opposition are much scantier than those of interest and co-operation. The men whose voices were heard and respected, whose influence moulded public opinion, were advocating educational advantages for women early in the nineteenth century, and even before. Emma Willard, Zilpah Grant, Catharine Beecher, and Mary Lyon were women who continued to educate themselves as long as they lived; but they had all received excellent educations at reputable schools.

This book, therefore, has no thesis. It is not an attempt to glorify a person or an institution. Wheaton is used only as a background, where an illustration is needed. The leading seminaries followed practically an identical program, with the rising hour, the textbooks, and the rules copied one from the other. In age Wheaton is younger than Bradford — if Bradford's age be figured from its opening as a co-educational academy, and not from the time of its existence as a school for girls only. It is younger than Albany Academy for Girls or than Emma Willard, but both of these are now preparatory schools. Younger as a modern college than Mount Holyoke, it is older as an institution. But " there were many brave men before Agamemnon."

As far as possible the book has been based upon primary sources. The Bibliography is not burdened with all the items consulted: school and college catalogues, textbooks, town histories, current newspapers and magazines, contemporary histories of the United States, histories of schools and colleges, alumni records (for information about young men teachers), students' notebooks and diaries, and many manuscript letters and diaries of people of the time.

To Miss Frances Vose Emerson of Boston and to Miss Clara Emerson of Beloit I am indebted for invaluable letters, diaries, and speeches of the Reverend Joseph Emerson which have now been placed, many of them, in the Wheaton archives. I am also indebted to them for transcripts of Mary Lyon manuscripts in their possession. To Mrs. Annie W. E. Macy and to Mrs. L. W. H. Weld I am indebted for important material obtained through their kindness in sending manuscript letters of Sarah Grimke, Angelina Grimke Weld, and Sarah Douglass. To Mrs. Bertha S. Hopkins of Mansfield I am indebted for the loan of old dictionaries, for early issues of the *Youth's Companion*, and for a copy of the anti-Masonic newspaper. Miss Jennie Copeland of Mansfield kindly gave me information about this region in the eighteen-thirties, including that about the coal mines of Mansfield.

Thanks are due many friends who ransacked attics for old textbooks, and my son who ransacked European bookstores for books on America. I am indebted to Miss Lucy Chapman for the loan of many textbooks; to Miss Katherine Burton for the gift of Emma Willard's *Guide to the Temple of Time;* and to Mrs. Norman Vaughn Ballou for the gift of ladies' annuals and old treatises on education, the fruits of her search in odd corners of New England.

To the principal of Albany Academy for Girls, Miss Margaret Trotter, my warmest thanks are due, for her material on this early female academy and for her kind offers of help.

From President Ricketts of Rensselaer Polytechnic Institute I have received much enlightenment, both from his letters and from material on Amos Eaton supplied by him.

The task was lightened by the researches of Miss Grace F. Shepard, as embodied in her History of Wheaton College.

My daughter has rendered much assistance in the compiling of the bibliography.

To President J. Edgar Park and to Mrs. Park I am deeply indebted for encouragement and for kindly criticism.

LOUISE SCHUTZ BOAS

NORTON, MASSACHUSETTS
December 1934

CHAPTER I

Colleges for Men; Seminaries for Ladies

"IN this day of innovation," began the speech dedicating " the new and commodious edifice " of the co-educational academy in Leicester, Massachusetts, in 1833. One year later Judge Wheaton founded Wheaton Female Seminary, now Wheaton College. Norton, favorably situated thirty miles from Boston and twenty miles from Providence, Rhode Island, was a prosperous town fast turning from an agricultural community into a beehive of industry. Copper furnaces, ploughs, baskets, soap, boots and shoes, bonnets and gravestones were among its manufactures. A fair sized township, it had not yet made any large provision for the education of its sons or daughters. The common school, for which a teacher was regularly provided, taught reading and writing and arithmetic, and the master was supposedly qualified to prepare for college such boys as were destined for Harvard or Brown, for the pulpit or the bar. No academy similar to that of Leicester or many another town had ever been suggested, but the establishment of the new institution for young ladies was a matter for pride.

Wheaton Female Seminary was not an innovation. Ever since the Revolution interest in education had been gaining force. Massachusetts, always the pioneer, had for the past decade rejoiced in a rapid increase of educational facilities. Between 1825 and 1835 there had been incorporated in Massachusetts sixty academies which, however inadequate for a growing population, compared favorably with the forty of the preceding forty-five years.[1] At this time there were sixty colleges in the United States, of which a few were notable, and of these, three were in Massachusetts: Harvard, Amherst, and Williams.

Although the young educational societies and journals were lamenting the million children without educational advantages — in the state of New York alone there were said to be eighty thousand, ranging from six years of age to fifteen, without schooling — yet so alive were Americans to the need of an educated people that few communities except those on the farthest frontier wholly lacked elementary schools. The country stretching westward through Wisconsin and Arkansas — even Minnesota had its sprinkling of settlements — started schools as soon as the presence of enough children made the need obvious. A small log cabin, the vestry of a church, the front room of a householder served whenever a teacher could be found.

The West had had little time to think much beyond the common school where the three R's were dispensed. Alarmed by statistics of illiteracy and urged forward by missionary zeal, Lyman Beecher's daughter Catharine left her already famous female

[1] Inglis, A. *Principles of Secondary Education.* Boston. 1918.

seminary in Hartford, Connecticut, to devote herself to the establishment of schools and to the importation of trained teachers to conduct them throughout what is now the Middle West but which then was fresh snatched from the wilds. Chicago itself in 1833 was a town of scarcely more than five hundred inhabitants, served by one mail a week. Villages, however, grew fast, and what was a mere cluster of log cabins soon became a thriving city with churches, newspapers, and schools.

The need of schools and teachers in this West, emphasized the need of education in the East from which the supply of teachers and textbooks would have to come. In the East and South there were already schools old enough to have traditions and histories. Not only the common school flourished, the school provided by the towns themselves, but all sorts of private schools, from the cluster of infants gathered about some genteel though impoverished elderly lady, to the elegant " finishing " schools where young ladies learned the arts and graces that were to win for them the regard of a probably handsome but certainly well established Prince Charming.

All through the East and South there were schools: the so-called common school, the grammar school either public or private, boarding schools, academies, and seminaries; schools privately owned and run for profit; schools supported by townspeople or by the town itself, sometimes with the aid of state funds; schools endowed by individuals, by bequests, or by groups of public-minded citizens. " He kepit a schule," said Boswell's father of the great Johnson, " an' ca'd it an acawdemy."

The name academy was very popular in America. Milton had applied the name to those schools established in England by the Dissenters of his day. When in America public spirited men like Governor Dummer left bequests to establish schools, or men like Samuel and John Phillips during their lifetimes established Andover and Exeter, the name academy was used probably to distinguish these schools from such as were established by the towns under the name of grammar school.

Now the grammar school, though required by law in Massachusetts, as often as not existed purely on the statute books. The grammar school was practically a Latin and Greek cramming school where a boy could acquire the heavy dose of classics required for entrance into the colleges. Academies were originally grammar schools, established by private benevolence, or sometimes by groups of townspeople, supported by endowments or by subscription, sometimes eked out by state grants of land or taxes or by lotteries. They were free in the sense that they were not operated for profit, and in that any boy properly qualified by a lower school education could enter. Tuition fees were charged, and for those who came from out of town, board as well. Generally speaking academies were placed in the country which was thought to furnish the quiet conducive to scholarly attainment. When in the early days of the Bay Colony Harvard was founded, it was set across the river in the scantily settled Cambridge, rather than in the already busy city of Boston in order that the students might enjoy that seclusion from the world necessary for scholarly pursuits.

As grammar schools, academies, then, prepared for college by teaching the classics. When self-willed girls forced their way into the academies, as occasionally happened, they followed the same narrow course, though there was as yet no college to receive them. Sometimes a girl would obtain a certificate testifying her ability and accomplishments, her qualifications often exceeding those of her male companions readily admitted to Yale or Harvard or Union. The number of co-educational academies where girls, if they chose, might imbibe as much Latinity as their brothers was by no means small.

It was soon apparent, however, that this inoculation of Greek and Latin after the English fashion was not particularly useful to those who did not intend to go to college. College was a vocational school, preparing for the ministry, for law, or for medicine. The need for all three professions was very large at a time when population was increasing rapidly, when the boundary lines of the country were being pushed farther and farther to the West. Yet not every boy wished to enter one of the professions. Should, then, his education stop with the common school? If not, he might find other studies than the classics more pertinent to his needs. Though Harvard, the arbiter of things academical, was loath to put the stamp of its approval upon the study of geography, the academies nevertheless began to widen their curriculum. And because the academies included the sciences, now fast capturing popular interest, because the academies considered the modern languages dignified studies, the colleges, however reluctant, were in time forced to include these subjects. For boys who went to college were, by the entrance requirements, held down to the prescribed classics, while their fellows not destined for professional life learned things far more apposite and more interesting to the adolescent mind. Moreover the academies had begun to recognize the right of higher education other than that which prepared for the professions.

When this course became established, it was, quite naturally, open to the girls in co-educational academies; and just as naturally extended to the girls' schools which, since there were no colleges accepting women, had developed a non-classical program. This non-classical course which, by the omission of Greek and Latin, permitted the introduction of the sciences and the modern languages, was known as the " English classical course." It afforded a serious curriculum for the girls' schools known usually as female seminaries.

" Academy " was ordinarily, but not exclusively, kept for boys' schools or for co-educational schools. " Seminary " was the name given to colleges. The Annual Report of the President of Harvard to the trustees in the eighteen-thirties begins regularly, " The President of the Seminary respectfully reports that the general state of the seminary, in respect to moral conduct and faithful attendance to studies, on the part of the undergraduates, has been, during the past academic year, in a high degree, satisfactory."

In his Phi Beta Kappa address at Yale in 1833 Edward Everett referred to " ' the two twins of learning,' . . . this most efficient and respected Seminary, within whose walls we are now convened, and my own ancient and beloved Harvard."

It was after hearing ministers pray regularly each Sunday for " our seminaries of learning " that Emma Willard first applied the name to her own school. In using the name seminary another educator, the Reverend Joseph Emerson, made a valuable distinction. In 1818 he conducted in Byfield, Massachusetts, a " seminary and school." The " school " was the preparatory branch, taught by his wife, qualified by her years as student and teacher at Bradford Academy to take full charge. The " seminary " consisted of a class of young ladies of more mature years — often well on in the twenties — who came to improve themselves in the profession of teaching which they had already practiced.

" To Superiors of Female Seminaries " is the heading of the preface of a volume published nearly twenty years earlier than either of these uses of the name. It was 1799 in Hartford, Connecticut, that a small volume with a large title appeared: *A Mirror For the Female Sex. Historical Beauties For Young Ladies Intended to Lead the Female Mind to the Love and Practice of Moral Goodness. Designed Principally For the Use of Ladies' Schools.*

" Original school " is the definition of seminary in the American edition of an English dictionary of 1788 [2] while " academy " is defined as " school of liberal arts and sciences."

In later American dictionaries the definition is " Seminary: a place of education from whence scholars are transplanted into life," [3] a definition identical with that in English dictionaries from Johnson [4] down.

Academy is defined as " an assembly or society of men, uniting for the promotion of some art; the place where sciences are taught; a place of education in contradistinction to the universities or public schools." A closely printed column is alloted in the American Walker's *Dictionary* to a discussion of the pronunciation of " academy " in which the compiler takes exception to Samuel Johnson's throwing of the accent upon the first syllable and justifies the practice of accenting the second syllable.

Whatever the pronunciation, American usage was giving the name academy to many schools, reserving that of seminary for those schools which, as colleges, prepared for the professions or which, while not preparing for the professions, nevertheless sent their graduates out into the world. Academies, whereas they did offer non-collegiate courses, seem to have been known chiefly as college preparatory schools.

[2] Perry, William. *The Royal Standard English Dictionary. The First American Edition.* Worcester. 1788.

[3] Walker, John A. *A Critical Pronouncing Dictionary and Expositor of the English Language.* New York. 1819.

[4] Johnson, Samuel. The first folio edition of the *Dictionary*.

But the names were in no way protected; and many an insignificant school might give itself the prestige of either name, or, if preferred, that of college.

Whether used for Harvard or for female schools, the term *seminary* in the popular mind meant a school which was preparatory for life; perhaps a life as a teacher; certainly a life of usefulness. Young ladies who attended the seminaries of Emma Willard or Judge Wheaton need not look forward to a gainful occupation — which meant teaching — but neither did they look forward to a life of elegant leisure where harp playing and lyric warbling would fill their hours.

Few women of the eighteen-thirties dreamt of colleges for women. Emma Willard herself felt that such a designation for her school would be presumptuous. It was recognized that the seminaries were the equivalent of college, as all foreign visitors carefully recorded, but the term itself was sedulously avoided. And not without reason. Lucinda Foote, Sarah Goodrich, Elizabeth Cady, following their brothers conjugation by conjugation, might rebel at the barriers suddenly thrown in their paths at the college gate, but they had no munitions with which to shatter the barricade. There was, indeed, no valid reason why Yale or Union should accept them as pupils. Colleges were not for women because colleges were vocational training schools, training for professions not open to women. In the eighteen-thirties women had not yet thought of becoming lawyers or doctors or ministers. To be sure Mary Wollstonecraft in her

Vindication of the Rights of Woman in 1792 had advocated the study of medicine for women, deploring the growing custom of employing male midwives, but Mary Wollstonecraft's views had never been received with much favor on this side of the Atlantic. America was far more amenable to the sermons of Fordyce and the flattering advice of Gisborne, both of whom emphasized the duties rather than the rights of woman.

It was not until 1849 that the first woman, Elizabeth Blackwell, received a degree in medicine. It was not until 1869 that Iowa became the pioneer state in admitting a woman, Arabella Mansfield, to the bar. Although the Quakers, who did not maintain a special group of ordained ministers, permitted all members of the Meeting, including women, to preach, other congregations remembered the admonition of Paul that women should be silent in the churches. No woman of the eighteen-thirties seems to have had ecclesiastical ambitions. Antoinette Brown and Lettice Smith forced their way into Oberlin's theological school in the eighteen-forties, graduating with the class of 1850 though it was long years before their names appeared in the catalogue of alumni. Even then Lettice Smith did not, like Antoinette Brown, seek ordination. And Miss Brown did not find her path to ordination lined with cheerleaders.

Oberlin had been caught in the net of its own liberal principles, and had had to abide by the quixotic terms of its foundation. When the Oberlin Collegiate Institute opened its doors in 1833 it was committed to a policy of admitting any one who was qualified to enter, male or female, black or white. The feminine triumph was considerably dimmed by the equal inclusion of negroes. With all its liberality, Oberlin kept the female department separate, emphasizing therein " the useful branches taught in the best female seminaries" (meaning probably Emma Willard's at Troy, Catharine Beecher's at Hartford, and Zilpah Grant's at Ipswich). It was not until the forties that the first degree was actually awarded to a woman at Oberlin. Until women began to demand admission to the professions for which the colleges trained their students, they neither requested nor daydreamed of degrees. College was not even for all their brothers; for some college, for some the academy. And in any case, colleges for men, seminaries for ladies.

It was customary to deplore the mere suggestion of degrees for women, as ostentatious aping of man. A woman with a degree would be unsexed, since by divine will woman was assigned to domestic duties. True womanliness required that a woman escape, not command, public attention.

To be sure there were in the South institutions for the education of young ladies calling themselves colleges, but the North was wary of Southern education. Even where these schools compared favorably with the masculine colleges in their vicinity, the North found their standards lower than its own. Since the North did not give degrees to women, it was a matter for jest that the South did. In the spring of 1834 the

Boston Transcript quoted with approval the *New York Transcript's* merriment over the " Young Ladies College " in Kentucky which granted degrees. Facetiously and, as it would seem, to the joy of the public, the gentlemen of the press suggested degrèes suitable for a female college: Mistress of Pudding Making, Mistress of the Scrubbing Brush, Mistress of Common Sense. Best of all would be the honorary degrees: R.W., Respectable Wife, and M.W.R.F., Mother of a Well Regulated Family.

However, girls of the North did not generally go South for their schooling any more than did their brothers; it was for the Southerner to come North for learning. Now and then parents sent daughters to Southern schools to acquire the languid grace and the perfection of manner of the Southern lady, but in general education meant Northern education, in the educationally advanced states. And in the North no seminary gave degrees.

Wheaton Female Seminary was planned for the needs of the North, and followed the customs of the North. It did not break the bounds of Northern propriety, but added itself to the growing list of schools which attempted to provide adequate facilities for the education of daughters. Not yet were there enough seminaries or academies to educate proportionally as many daughters as sons. The cities naturally provided more opportunities than the small towns or the country districts, save where these had acquired an endowed academy, but few cities in the public schools educated girls in the so-called higher branches.

Long since girls had won the right to attendance at the lower schools, either in schools specially established for them, or at the regular sessions of the boys' school. The day had passed, though recently, when instruction was offered girls only at odd times: during the noon recess, and in the afternoons after the close of the boys' session. Even then the summer term was open — less of a concession than it might seem, since in the summer the boys were safely out of the way, working on their fathers' farms. The girls owed the privilege of the summer term at first to Yankee thrift: since the teacher was frequently hired for the year, it seemed wasteful to let him loaf during the summer. The turning over of the summer session to the girls satisfied the just demands of the fathers as employers and of their daughters as eager learners. Many a father doubtless quieted the complaints of his daughters in the winter by the promise of a good long summer of instruction with the very same teacher the boys tormented.

There was, of course, the question of high schools. Various cities had come to provide high schools for such boys as could not afford to attend the already famous academies such as Dummer, Andover, and Exeter. In a democracy the right of the poor boy to an education was easily recognized, an education that should fit him for a career as high in the intellectual or social scale as his talents permitted. For girls, however, the case was different. Girls would never become printers or architects or clerks or politicians any more than they would become doctors or lawyers or ministers.

Yet in 1826, in response to popular demand, Boston opened a high school for girls. It closed after two years of riotously successful existence. It closed, not because girls did not attend, not because their parents were unwilling to educate them, but because to the town fathers even the modest outlay of eleven dollars a pupil a year seemed a wholly unwarranted expense — when the number of pupils was so large.

As the city fathers viewed the matter, higher education for girls was definitely something beyond their actual needs, and therefore something which the town was not called upon to provide. For girls who would have something of leisure and wealth in their lives it was permissible, but the taxpayers should not be responsible for the cost of the education of the daughters of the well-to-do. There was no question of preparing girls to earn their living, as there was with boys. Girls ordinarily were not expected to enter the competitive world; they married and were supported by their husbands; or they remained single and were supported by their fathers and eventually their brothers. It was therefore the part of wisdom to spend the taxpayers' money on schools for the boys who would be the breadwinners, the voting citizens of the future.

For the daughters of the poor, many of whom seemed inclined to take advantage of this free high school, such education was an anomaly. These girls were needed in the factories, where their labor would contribute to the support of their parents, or later of their children. This undemocratic view is more easy of comprehension when it is remembered that the tide of Irish immigration had begun to rise. Boston was without slaves. Boston ladies looked to the comely Irish girls for the work of their kitchens. To have what seemed a likely supply of housemaids snatched from them seemed a sad mistake of policy. Boston was not in duty bound to provide for the newly arrived daughters of Irish peasants an education which would be beyond their wildest dreams in the British Isles.

A few cities did maintain high schools, but in general, education beyond the common school was possible for girls only in private institutions [5] which charged tuition and board.

Though some of the established seminaries had endowments — none probably as large as that Judge Wheaton was about to give — none could offer free education. Some schools had no endowment, beyond their land and building, the gifts either of the town, of some philanthropic individual, or of a group of parents. Some schools were private, individual or group projects which optimistically hoped to make a profit for the owners. Adams, in Londonderry, New Hampshire, was endowed by a man's bequest; Abbot by a wealthy widow; Bradford was established by a group of parents; Albany by the ambitious parents of a little girl, aided by other parents; Hartford and Troy by those dynamic women, Catharine Beecher and Emma Willard. Some were partly supported by

[5] The Moravians had established a school for girls in Pennsylvania in 1750.

the town, some by the parents of the children attending; though the tuition charges were intended to carry the actual costs of teachers and care of the building.

As one reads of these groups of earnest parents who subscribed as large sums as they could to establish academies in their native towns, who later subscribed more money to erect larger and better buildings, acquire more and better equipment, who sometimes deluded themselves into believing that their " stock " would pay dividends — only to find that it was assessments they had to meet — one sees a close resemblance to the twentieth century parent who, not wishing to send his child to the overcrowded public school, subscribes money for new buildings for the private school to which he already pays a large tuition fee.   The modern private school, having ceased to be a money-making project, has become a co-operative undertaking not unlike the academies of a hundred years ago.   In New York City in the twentieth century the principal and owner of an exclusive school addressed the assembled parents of her pupils upon the need of incorporation and the need of new buildings and equipment.   The time had come, she said, when the children of the rich should have as adequate an equipment and as luxurious a building as the children of the poor.

In the eighteen-thirties the daughters of the rich seldom emulated the daughters of the poor, or the daughters of the middle class for whom the seminaries were primarily designed.   Frequently the daughters of the rich did not go to school at all, but had masters come to them to teach them such matters as seemed worthy of their attention: French, always, as the language of polite society, and music, the performance of which was necessary for displaying the graces of a lady. In the South more often than not " some impoverished man of good descent and education was a member of the household, and taught the youngsters — and in many cases was engaged in selling and shipping rice, corn and cotton, steers, and lambs, and other products of the plantation." [6]

In both South and North the daughters of the rich, and often of the near-rich, if they went to school, attended some private enterprise where deportment and embroidery took equal rank with French and music and drawing. A bill rendered in 1797 by a fashionable New York school to a Philadelphia father speaks for itself. Thirty-six pounds nine shillings from February eighth to April first included, beside board and tuition, one book, Thomson's *Seasons*; some drawing paper and pencils, a slate, printed music; French, music, and dancing lessons — always an extra. For the rest there was a " broad satin sash ribon," a " dress for a party," a pair of gloves, a pair of leather shoes, " flannel for two petticoats," medicine for a cold, dentist, theater, " hack hire for a lady's party," and a fine comb. [7]

Many of the schools which did attempt to give serious instruction — Miss Pierce's famous school in

[6] Mrs. Annie W. E. Macy in a private letter.
[7] Benedict, Clare. *Voices Out of the Past.* London. n.d. The bill approximated ninety dollars.

Litchfield, Connecticut, and Emma Willard's school in Middlebury, Vermont, later in Troy, New York — included as of necessity the " ornamental branches " which were to be rigidly excluded from such establishments as Wheaton Female Seminary and Mary Lyon's Mount Holyoke, which postdated Norton, opening two years later.

Miss Sarah Pierce,[8] a young woman of good family, in a town where a committee of women, including her own stepmother, had petitioned the school board in vain to extend to girls the same educational privileges as to boys, had established her school in 1792, starting with two or three pupils in the dining-room of her father's house. Incorporating in 1827, Miss Pierce concluded her forty-one years of increasing prestige by turning the school over to a board of trustees in 1833. Though the school day began at dawn, as did all serious schools and colleges, the régime was not so strict as to exclude the arts and graces. Along with as much Latin and Greek as they might elect, together with requirements in history, rhetoric, arithmetic, logic, Natural and Moral Philosophy, and chemistry, went fine sewing and embroidery, music and French. The diploma which attested the young ladies' proficiency was of twilled silk. And on exhibit at the close of each year were the elaborate embroideries often proving by their subject the erudition of their makers. The embroidery of maps was probably as pleasurable and possibly as profitable as the modern

8 Vanderpoel, E. N. *Chronicles of a Pioneer School (1792–1833)*. Cambridge. 1903.

pupils' basket-weaving, silver or copper hammering, painting or modelling busts. The emphasis upon embroidery and water colors was rather less than that of the modern school which stresses handicrafts or art. In the eighteen-thirties drawing and painting were " ornamental branches "; in the nineteen-thirties they are " self-expression."

Elaborate art works were not the exclusive accomplishments of young ladies. The law students at Litchfield worked with pencil and brush, too, though their art work doubtless was extra-curricular. To Judge Tappan Reeve's law school came many a young man destined to become famous. Judge Reeve was himself a famous person, connected with a famous family — he had married the daughter of the president of Princeton, and had had as pupil the president's son, Aaron Burr. The presence of his law school in Litchfield undoubtedly did much to convince parents of the wisdom of sending daughters to Miss Pierce's school. Of her pupils half were local girls, the others coming from various places near and far.

Perhaps the young gentlemen of the law school exercised their talents in drawing and painting when on stipulated evenings they were permitted to call upon the young ladies — or perhaps they stole hours from their law studies, bringing the completed product to dazzle the school maidens. George Catlin who, at the time of the opening of Wheaton Seminary, was living among the Indians, making the studies which were to bring him fame as the inter-

preter and recorder of Indian life, had earlier been
a law student at Litchfield. The pictures he drew of
" Love Carrying the World " and " Love's Fall " —
for one of Miss Pierce's pupils — rivalled for elab-
orateness any performance of the young ladies.

That many a young man, later a successful lawyer,
did his studying and his courting in the same years
did not harm the reputation of Miss Pierce's school.

Miss Pierce's was never an embroidery-deportment
school. The curriculum compared favorably with
that of the later seminaries, but the ornamental
branches were included, properly subordinated to the
more serious studies.

It was at Miss Pierce's school that Lyman Beecher's
children were educated: Catharine who was to gain
prominence as the founder of Hartford Female Seminary, of schools in the Middle West, and as author
of various books; Harriet who was to write America's
most famous and influential novel; and the sons who
became prominent ministers. The Beecher boys
prepared adequately for college at Miss Pierce's, and
later at their sister's school. One of these sons became
the minister of the Congregational Church in Poughkeepsie, New York, where his brother, Henry Ward
Beecher, frequently visited him. The Beecher interest in education may well have been influential in
the founding of Vassar College of which Henry Ward
Beecher was one of the first trustees, thereby linking
Miss Pierce's school with the new college.[9]

This, however, was far in the future. Miss Pierce's

9 Letter from President MacCracken of Vassar College.

school, in accepting boys, was following the usual custom. Just as girls were from time to time taught in schools for boys, so, when a local boys' school was lacking, boys prepared for college in girls' schools. In 1830 Miss Pierce's school had as pupils seventy-eight girls and sixteen boys, a larger proportion of masculinity than usual, but one may take it for granted that the boys preparing for Yale were less provocative of feminine flutter than the law students who counted the privilege of calling upon the young ladies an honor, the denial or restriction of that privilege a disgrace.

Wheaton Female Seminary was also to have its occasional masculine student, preparing young men of the town for Harvard or Brown, though few Norton boys seem to have had collegiate ambitions.

That boys could prepare for college at girls' schools speaks well for the Latinity of the teachers, who were for the most part women, though at Miss Pierce's John Brace, the nephew of the head of the school, had been trained especially for a place at the school. Mr. Brace later left Litchfield to conduct the school in Hartford founded by Catharine Beecher declaring with satisfaction in his inauguration address in 1832 that "seminaries now crowd our land."

Wheaton was directed by women from the start, which meant a steady succession of principals for some years because of the propensity of principals and teachers to marry and relinquish their positions.

The ability of women teachers to prepare boys adequately for any of the men's colleges had been amply demonstrated not only at the girls' schools but also by private individuals acting as tutors. Many a young man, including the Reverend Mr. Clark of Norton, prepared for Harvard under the guidance of Miss Hannah Adams who was known far and wide as a miracle of learning.

Her profundity of knowledge Hannah Adams owed partly to her own insatiable intellectual thirst, and partly to happy chance arising from unfortunate circumstances. Her father, who had been thwarted in his own desire for a college education, was sympathetic with his daughter's desire. When financial reverses made it necessary for him to seek new ways of making a livelihood he decided to take boarders, choosing for his paying guests young men either preparing for the professions or already entered upon them. Impressed by the young girl's eagerness to learn, these young men became her teachers. In Latin, Greek, and ecclesiastical history she rapidly distinguished herself. Herein she laid the foundation which later was to provide her with a better livelihood than that of making bobbin lace, a toil which she had been unable to avoid during the Revolution.

After the war was over she made good use of her learning in two fields: she tutored young men, sending them to college excellently drilled, and she wrote histories of religion which became enormously popular. At first the victim of rapacious booksellers, she learned to exact a good price for her toil; and so high was the respect of the community for her accomplishments that gentlemen of prominence set about securing her an annuity which should make her declining years serene. She lived a long life, dying in 1831 when she considered that " happily the time has arrived, when the cultivation of the female intellect needs no longer to be advocated or recommended." No longer, in her opinion, was a girl esteemed an oddity if she chose to devote herself to the classics instead of to the embroidery frame. With buoyant faith in the future a woman could say in 1831, " There are few branches, if any, in which boys are instructed, which are not now equally open to girls." [10]

It was not expected that all women should, like Hannah Adams, acquire greater learning than that of most men. Hannah Adams was an encyclopedia to be respected, not a woman to be loved. " Marry Hannah Adams! " exclaimed a worthy gentleman. " I would as soon embrace a Greek Dictionary! " In an age when it still seemed a reproach not to be married, Hannah Adams remained single. Gentlemen aided in the publication of her five foot shelves, interceded with publishers to gain profitable terms for her, and even subscribed generously to an annuity; but no one cared to marry her. They sent their sons to her to imbibe learning, but they had no desire to rear a race of intellectual Amazons.

That female phenomenon, Margaret Fuller,[11] did

[10] *A Memoir of Miss Hannah Adams. Written by Herself, with Additional Notices by a Friend.* Boston. 1832.
[11] *Memoirs of Margaret Fuller Ossoli.* Boston. 1852. And Bell, M. *Margaret Fuller.* New York. 1930.

eventually marry — an Italian count. Margaret Fuller's father had determined to make a prodigy of his
daughter and had himself instructed her, forcing her
beyond her years so that as a young woman she was
disqualified for the society of her contemporaries.
She became the friend and associate of the Transcen-
dentalists, those men of mental fire to whom Ideas
were more sustaining than food, to whom men and
women were Intellects. Emerson, Thoreau, Bronson
Alcott, — these were the companions of Margaret
Fuller instead of young women of her own age, none
of whom had been turned into so notable a pillar of
learning. In the year that Wheaton Female Seminary
opened its doors to young women of more ordinarily
inspired ambitions, Margaret Fuller was associated
with Bronson Alcott in his progressive school for
young children in Boston, at the same time conducting "conversations" for would-be intellectuals.
With her swift utterances, based upon a profundity
of knowledge, she astonished her little world, gaining
such prestige that she was engaged to teach in a school
in Providence, Rhode Island, at what was then a phe-
nomenal salary — one thousand dollars a year.

Many a young woman was overjoyed at one hundred and fifty dollars a year; many a woman teacher
was fortunate with two dollars a week, from twenty
to forty weeks constituting her whole working year.
At this time the president of Harvard received two
thousand two hundred and thirty-five dollars a year,
with fifteen hundred the salary of professors. One
tutor and one instructor at Harvard received a thou-

sand dollars, the rest from five hundred to six hundred and forty-five — but the larger salary here represented pay for extra teaching. Since in general a woman teacher received half the salary of a man — in co-educational schools exactly half for the same work, though she might be experienced and he fresh from college — this salary of Margaret Fuller's was indeed something to boast of. The school, to be sure, was a private venture; obviously counting upon Miss Fuller as an advertisement sure to draw pupils. Whatever the reason, Margaret Fuller did earn the salary, teaching under pleasant conditions, delighting in her classes of boys as well as girls. Parents, hearing of her success, began to see that learning might be profitable for a woman.

The *Lady's Annual Register,*[12] one of that host of popular yearly booklets which combined calendar, cookbook, encyclopedia of useful knowledge, and anecdotal amusement, felt it wise to take note of the growing interest in education. Under the heading SCHOOLS in the issue of 1838 it prints:

" Seminaries for young ladies are about being established under the natural progress of experience, which will produce an important effect over the whole country. The ephemeral character of schools heretofore, has been a tremendous evil. Our institutions should be on such a footing that a *system* may go on in case of the death or removal of a principal. Any information which may be received through the

[12] Gilman, Caroline. *The Lady's Annual Register and House-wife's Memorandum-Book For 1838.* Boston and Philadelphia.

year relative to such institutions, will receive due notice in the Lady's Register, which will endeavor to furnish a complete list of established seminaries for girls throughout the United States, hereafter."

Here is not only the beginning of the school service offered by modern magazines in the interests of advertising prosperity — in the *Lady's Register* there was no financial motive, since it carried no such advertisements — but also an explanation of the whole movement toward endowed seminaries. Schools had not ordinarily endured beyond the lifetime of their proprietors. There was a general tendency to regard incorporation as a partial safeguard against the discontinuance of a useful institution, but incorporation alone was not enough; there was need of an endowment sufficient to guarantee the income for the normal increase and repair of equipment aside from that which should provide the initial plant. Moreover a school directed by a board of trustees was likely to have more hope of permanence than one directed by an individual who might remove his residence at will, and who might die without having appointed a successor.

The argument of permanence helped to persuade a wealthy widow to establish Abbot Academy. Mrs. Abbot [13] saw at close range the advantages derived by young men from the endowed academy Phillips Andover. She had funds to dispose of which she was urged to give to her own sex since, in her part of the country, young men were amply provided for.

[13] Catalogues of Abbot Academy 1824–1879 and McKeen, Philena, and McKeen, Phebe. *History of Abbot Academy*. Andover. 1880.

Similarly Judge Wheaton, a man of eighty-two, was urged to give his wealth to a permanent school, a project considered at the time one of the most valuable outlets for benevolence. Judge Wheaton was interested in various businesses which returned an excellent income, and he had an accumulation of funds rather larger than the average, but he was not a person of great wealth. It was Judge Wheaton's young daughter-in-law who persuaded him to give as a memorial to his daughter not the monument he originally planned, but a seminary for young ladies. In this Mrs. Wheaton was acting against her own financial interests; she was directing into other channels large sums of money which would eventually have been hers; for a monument requires little beyond its initial cost, while the seminary was to be a constant drain upon the Wheaton purse.

It is doubtful if any other school was founded with motives more completely disinterested. Even the most altruistic founder of a boys' school, who gave of his substance during his lifetime, could expect a return in the glorification of his name, bestowed on the school, and in the recognition of those pupils who might enter public life. Famous men threw a luster upon the place of their education. Women did not usually become famous.

Moreover the motives for the establishment of other schools were frequently mixed. The founders, either individuals or groups of townspeople, had children to educate, or they had their livings to earn, or friends who were in need of positions as teachers, or educational theories to vindicate.

Very many schools were established as the means of making a livelihood. This was, probably, the most frequent occasion for the opening of a school. Fashionable schools were for many a long year a stepping-stone to a very comfortable living, sometimes to actual wealth. In the days when practically no equipment was necessary, even maps and blackboards being luxuries while rote learning from textbooks was regarded as education, it was not difficult for any one to put a few benches in the parlor, insert an advertisement in the local paper, and open the door to a small but profitable group of boys or girls. Newspapers tended to reserve a certain space on their pages for these school advertisements, which appeared regularly at the beginning of each school quarter, being continued day by day, since pupils were accepted for the most part at any time that they cared to enter. It follows that the friends of education, people who were interested in the development of youth, were eager to present the advantages of schools with some purpose other than that of an easy living for the owners. Hence Mrs. Hale, who edited the *American Ladies' Magazine* in Boston and later *Godey's* in Philadelphia, with painstaking care inserted notices of schools which she regarded as more serious attempts to instruct young women. Newspapers accepted advertisements from all, without editorial comment.

Fortunately for the cause of education the motives of those who established private schools or who taught in them were frequently far from venal. Though

many a teacher, in setting up a school of his own or
in securing a position in a private school, was in need
of making a living, there was definitely manifest a
strong desire to benefit both the immediate pupils
and the cause of education.

This held true for men as well as for women.
Often a teacher or proprietor was an idealist seeking
to serve a cause which he felt worthy of a lifetime of
striving, a cause that was bigger than the individual
but which could advance only through the services
of individuals, each working in a comparatively small
radius.

Many a young man hoped to combine the duties
of a parish and the headship of a school, but the
double burden usually proved too heavy. Many a
young man broke down under the strain of sermons
and turned to teaching as a less laborious profession.
Teaching had always been open to young men fresh
from college, and lawyers, ministers, politicians often
counted among their apprentice years a year or more
earning money for graduate school or travel. Academies frequently drew year after year from the same
college as Topsfield Academy did from Dartmouth.
Sometimes a young man instead of returning to his
own education, instead of entering upon the profession definitely or vaguely planned, remained in
the profession of teaching.

As for women, teaching was the most respectable
of female occupations, save writing. It was less lucra-
tive than writing in an age when annuals flourished,
when the demand for sentimental poetry and long

novels was insatiable; yet all could not become literary ladies. Even those who did write frequently omitted their names from the title pages of their voluminous works, lest they be thought overbold. Books abounded by letters of the alphabet, with or without dashes to follow, " by Mrs. — ," " by A Lady." After the first book, the way was easier: " By the author of . . ."

It was said at the time that only three occupations were open to women: domestic work, needlework, and the streets. Domestic work was servile. Northern women " did their own work " but did not normally hire themselves out to do housework for others. Needlework was respectable, in a humble way; it was, indeed, the only resource open to most widows, and to most girls whose fathers died without providing for them, or otherwise failed in the paternal duty of provision for daughters. Mrs. Hale, later the editor of *Godey's,* resorted to needlework when widowed. Finding this, however, a meager living for herself and her children, she took to her pen, which brought her comfort and fame.

There was always the resource of storekeeping, to which, however, few women resorted either from lack of business experience, or more likely, lack of initial capital. The mother of the abolitionist Lucretia Coffin Mott had conducted a store in Nantucket, but Lucretia, when her husband needed assistance, opened a school in Philadelphia. Though schools often made litle money, they gave a better return for less arduous labor than the poorly paid needlework.

Any woman who had had more than the mere rudiments of education could open a school for little children, thereby relieving overburdened mothers, and starting the children more gently than in the town school on the path of the three R's. Women who had had educational advantages could open schools of higher grade.

So Emma Willard, when her husband's finances became involved, opened a school. She had taught before marriage, and therefore when her husband needed assistance, she thought at once of a school. Now that teaching was to be her steady occupation, not the mere passing of the years before matrimony, she found time and energy to develop theories of education. At first her school in Middlebury included the " ornamental branches " and had no firmly outlined policy. It was merely a means of making a living respectably. In recalling Mrs. Willard's extraordinary achievements, one may still remember that the initial impulse was the necessity for earning money.

So another famous woman of the time, Catharine Beecher, dedicated her life to the cause of education after her plans for marriage were frustrated. Catharine Beecher was engaged to a Yale professor who was drowned. Though she inherited from him a fair sum for the times, two thousand dollars, she did not have an income sufficient for her needs. She had been educated with a view to self-support because her father, Lyman Beecher, was a clergyman with a very large brood of children and a not very large income.

Even with two thousand dollars capital she needed an income bearing position.

Lyman Beecher had been helped too much by female education to think aught but good of it. He educated his daughters, and encouraged them to educate others. His first wife, the mother of Catharine, had in the earlier years of their marriage opened a school to eke out his meager income of four hundred dollars a year. When he moved to Litchfield, Connecticut, he found further aid from female teaching. In Litchfield there was an already famous school, Miss Pierce's, to which he sent both sons and daughters. And there was another benefit from the school: it had no central " boarding house," distributing its out of town pupils among the families of Litchfield. Mr. Beecher was glad indeed to have his income extended by such paying guests. Since the atmosphere of a clergyman's home was obviously superior to that of any other home which received pupils to board, Lyman Beecher could charge more than others.

Had there been no such school in Litchfield, Lyman Beecher would probably have been interested in its founding either by his wife or by his daughters. A school was a respectable enterprise, the head of which held professional standing in the community.

It is, then, worthy of note that neither Judge Wheaton nor his daughter-in-law was in need of making a living. It was clearly understood at the outset that no profit would ever accrue; that, on the contrary, the initial gift would be supplemented. The

seminary was not even to serve as personal aggrandize-
ment since it was originally named not for its founder,
but for the town; a modest intent which yielded
shortly to the change into Wheaton Female Seminary.[14]

So far were Judge Wheaton and his daughter-in-law
from the need of providing situations for relatives or
friends that they were at a loss to find a lady principal and a staff of teachers. They turned in their
perplexity to the seminary whose reputation was the
highest in Massachusetts and hence popularly believed to outdistance any rival in other parts of New
England or in New York.

Ipswich Seminary was under the guidance of Zilpah
Grant (later Mrs. Banister) who at the time of
Wheaton's founding was on leave of absence. The
school was temporarily in charge of her assistant,
Mary Lyon, who, finding that the trustees would not
accede to Miss Grant's plans for a permanent endowment of some amplitude, had announced her intention of opening a new seminary. The Wheatons
therefore believed that Miss Lyon would best be able
to advise them. They may even have hoped that she
would find their school the fulfillment of her plans.
Giving her full authority they gladly accepted her
course of study, which, like that of her own seminary
later, followed Miss Grant's at Ipswich, and welcomed
her selection of one of her teachers, Miss Eunice
Caldwell, as the first lady principal. Miss Caldwell,

[14] Officially not so named for five years, the Seminary in its first
public notice appeared as Wheaton Female Seminary.

however, was merely lent to the Wheatons for a period of two years, after which she was to join Miss Lyon again.

In 1834 Mary Lyon's [15] plans for an endowed seminary in the western part of Massachusetts, an institution for women in the district served for men by Amherst and Williams, had already received wide publicity. Mary Lyon had no money to bestow; she was not interested in a humble beginning in a private home; her seminary was to spring full fledged, endowed with an unusually large sum, to be raised by personal solicitation among the rich and the poor.

Mary Lyon had been a country girl, whose father had died when she was very young, whose mother had remarried and been unable to provide for her daughter. Mary Lyon, with an insatiable thirst for knowledge, had advanced herself step by step from teacher of a district school — at a time when fourteen year old girls were thought competent enough for all its requirements — to substitute principal of a famous academy, associated with the foremost woman educator of New England, Zilpah Grant. By this time Miss Pierce had retired, Emma Willard had long since left New England for New York and was soon to retire, and Catharine Beecher had gone West. Zilpah Grant had met Mary Lyon at Joseph Emerson's Byfield Seminary, whither she had come at the age of twenty-four.

Crude in manners, careless in dress, with an intense eagerness to learn and an extraordinary vitality of

[15] See Bibliography.

intellect, Mary Lyon had catapulted herself through schools and academies, earning the necessary funds by teaching from time to time, attaching herself to any school or teacher offering opportunities to women. Born in 1797, she passed her childhood in those post-Revolution days when girls won securely the right to attend the village schools, and were pushing themselves into the academies. Legend has it that when, at the age of twenty, she managed to enter an academy, she remedied her deficiency in preparation by mastering the entire Latin grammar in a week-end. Her intense studiousness, which limited her to four hours sleep a night, did not then label her a " grind " since her fellow-students were also exceedingly earnest in the acquisition of knowledge not generally permitted women before this time.

Just as she swallowed Latin grammar, so she went about conquering various fields of knowledge, including the sciences, of which chemistry was always to be her favorite. Nor did she disdain the contemporary emphasis upon orthography, her teachers' insistence bearing fruit in her meticulously careful and minute script. In a day when postage was exorbitantly high, such handwriting was a virtue.

Both as pupil and as teacher Mary Lyon was rapidly given recognition. Zilpah Grant took her with her to Adams Academy in Londonderry, New Hampshire, and from there to Ipswich, Massachusetts. During Miss Grant's illness, while she herself was acting principal, Mary Lyon contended even more earnestly than Miss Grant with the trustees for those things which both felt were of the utmost neces-

sity for the well-being of the school. Income bearing
endowments, adequate equipment, and buildings of
sufficient size and stability for both schoolrooms and
living quarters, were the constant cry of educators,
the perpetual nightmare of prudent non-imaginative
trustees. Since the Ipswich trustees proved obdurate
Mary Lyon became more and more determined to
establish a seminary according to the plans she and
Miss Grant had matured together, in the western
part of the state; since her "dearest sister," Zilpah
Grant, was incapacitated, she would proceed alone.

By the time that Judge Wheaton turned to her for
advice, she had pushed her plans beyond those of Miss
Grant. Her seminary should not only fulfil the
dreams of them both for permanence, for equipment,
but should provide for poor girls, such as she had
been herself; she would offer them a chance to educate themselves, and to prepare themselves for teaching others, either as teachers or as missionaries.

For this charitable enterprise Mary Lyon solicited
funds, travelling about to knock at doors that were
sometimes hospitably flung wide, sometimes promptly
and rudely shut. The refusals strengthened her faith
no less than the kindly gifts. And every person who
gave her five or fifty cents, one or one thousand dollars, had a stake in her venture. Every donor was
a prospective student, not, naturally, in person, but
in influence.

In her lectures [16] to students at Wheaton Female

[16] Manuscript in Wheaton archives, also transcripts in students'
notebooks of 1835.

Seminary in 1835 she presented her views on teaching, decrying the pecuniary motive for women in general and for teachers in particular. Providence designed the care of money for men, of minds for women. " The love of making money in a lady is calculated to destroy all that is feminine, tender, and benevolent." Intelligent minds should shrink from the thought of hoarding up wealth. As the world went, few women in Mary Lyon's day had direct control of wealth; few women therefore could exercise the virtue of benevolence through the disposal of large sums. As teachers, however, women could exercise benevolence — by omitting to scan the terms of their contracts. That female benevolence encouraged masculine and civic parsimony seems not to have occurred to any one of the gentler sex as yet. Mary Lyon poured forth scorn upon those women who taught " just to get a little money, and taking care to please the parents so as to secure the school for the next summer."

In her projected seminary, teachers were to receive small salaries, and were to regard themselves as missionaries. To this scheme Catharine Beecher, daughter and sister of ministers, objected vigorously. " The profession," she wrote to Mary Lyon in 1836, " cannot be sustained by a missionary spirit — that spirit will send men forth as ministers and missionaries, but rarely as teachers." Mary Lyon was not moved from her belief that teachers should earn no more than sustenance.

Yet sustenance was more than physical needs. Beyond their meager pay teachers had definite compensations of more value than money. A motive there was to spur them on, " a love of being thought of consequence in the world. I do not mean by this that low ambition which is so common, neither do I think it so degrading as a love of money. There is a principle in the human mind which shrinks from the idea of being nothing in the world. Without energy of character a teacher cannot do much good, and those who have it and set their mark high, and determine to be well qualified will be of consequence."

It may, then, have been ambition which prevented Mary Lyon from accepting the offer of Abbot Academy to conform entirely to her plan if she would come to Andover to direct it. Abbot was already founded, through the gift of a widow who had sought for some object of benevolence upon which to bestow her wealth. Bearing her name, the school would always be known as her project.

Moreover, Mary Lyon had become interested in placing a seminary in the western part of Massachusetts which had schools but none meeting her requirements, none of such high repute as Ipswich. Though she personally supervised the opening of Wheaton, though she spent long periods in Norton, she did not seriously consider settling there. It is doubtful if, even had Mrs. Wheaton been sympathetic with all Mary Lyon's plans, the two women could have fitted into the same seminary. Though Mrs. Wheaton was not the nominal donor, though she never held an official position, she was the true head of the school for the seventy years following its inception.

Except for the town's early gift of fifty dollars for " philosophical apparatus " [17] all needs were met by the Wheaton purse. Mrs. Wheaton agreed with Mary Lyon that wealth entailed benevolence. Asking for money for her seminary was like asking it for herself. Always she deprecated any attempt to raise funds, supplying the immediate need herself.

The seminary was an outlet for benevolence, but it was not therefore regarded as a charitable enterprise. The endowment of educational institutions was recognized as necessary for the provision of land, buildings, and equipment. Teachers were not expected to remit their just fees — though they were always expected to be moderate in their demands — and students were expected to pay sufficient to carry the normal running expenses. In thus endowing an institution, in making it possible for it to start with suitable equipment for all current studies: for the teaching of geography, globes and maps; for the teaching of the sciences, a telescope and laboratory materials, a benefactor was performing a civic service.

The motive of providing an education for their own children, a motive present in the establishment of many schools, was entirely lacking. Judge Wheaton's son, a grown man long since graduated from Brown, was the last of his line.

A large number of the existing academies had been established by parents for the benefit of their own

[17] Equipment for physics.

children. It was a group of parents earnestly interested in the mental welfare of their sons and daughters who gathered to found Bradford.[18] Sometimes sons alone were the object of such meetings, but daughters had a way of forcing themselves in where they were not invited, as at Atkinson, New Hampshire. Four years after Atkinson was founded for boys (it was founded in 1787) the parson's daughter, Polly Peabody, announced firmly that she was going to the academy, and go she did with three of her girl friends. Atkinson continued co-educational. Bradford was co-educational until 1828.

In 1814 a prominent lawyer of Albany, New York, one Ebenezer Foot, joined with his wife in anxiety for the proper education of their daughter still in her first decade. Mr. and Mrs. Foot gathered about them a group of their friends who also had daughters, and Albany Female Academy was founded. Though the Foots' daughter was young, the plan was not confined to her immediate needs. The course would extend through the childhood years into the years of young ladyhood. Albany was to provide a complete education so that parents might, if they chose, keep their daughters at home instead of sending them away for their final schooling. There would be the advantage, too, of daughters' meeting girls from other places, since a good school would attract pupils from less favored towns.

The Wheatons had, however, nothing to gain for

[18] Pond, J. S. *Bradford, a New England Academy*. Bradford. 1930.

themselves, their family, or their friends in the establishment of the school. What is perhaps more re-
markable is that they had no axe to grind. Neither
Judge Wheaton nor his son's wife had any pet theories
of education to vindicate. Neither was an advocate
of old or new methods, of the Monitorial or any other
system then awakening enthusiasm or opprobrium.
Neither probably had heard of Pestalozzi, unless they
had read encomiums in the prefaces of textbooks
written by his disciples.

Mrs. Wheaton had never taught, or planned to
teach. She had been taught, however, by a man who
had the highest regard for the abilities of his female
pupils. Any one who doubts the sincerity of a
teacher's appreciation of the female mind, has only
to turn to the pages of Holmes's *Elsie Venner*. Discipline in the boys' schools was severe — and far more
difficult for teacher than for pupil. The ferule was
used freely until parents began to have their doubts
as to the value of its results. Schools in the eighteen-
thirties were already advertising that corporal punishment was not used, that gentler methods in which the
pupil co-operated were the proper system. That
willing co-operation so difficult to establish between
young men none too far from the schoolroom themselves, and unruly boys with a strong sense of fun,
was quickly and pleasantly established between young
men and their feminine pupils. Many a case is on
record of the marriage of a teacher and a former
pupil. The daughter for whom the Foots established
Albany Female Academy grew up to marry the prin-

cipal; James Mott married a pupil who became his
assistant teacher at Nine Partners' School. The list
of such marriages is fairly long. Between teacher
and pupil in girls' schools the relationship seems to
have been almost invariably free from strain.

One case is on record of a serious difficulty between
a teacher and a pupil. A Dartmouth graduate, Alfred Pike, teaching at the academy in Topsfield,
Massachusetts, was accused of illtreating a girl in the
school. The accusation was made by the *Boston Post*
which was immediately obliged to defend itself in a
libel suit. Mr. Pike won his case, but the trustees
of the school, though publicly expressing their confidence in him and their belief in his blamelessness,
felt obliged to ask for his resignation.

Quite a different tale was that of George B. Emerson to whom Mrs. Wheaton had gone to school up to
the time of her marriage.

George Emerson,[19] the son of a physician, had himself attended Dummer Academy and then Harvard
where among his classmates were Bancroft, the future
historian, and Samuel May, the future abolitionist —
and incidentally the uncle of Louisa May Alcott.

Emerson followed a custom, common enough during his day, of teaching school to help pay his college
expenses. College boys would absent themselves for
a term or two, frequently in the winter, and take
charge of a school in the country, applying the money
thus earned to another term or two at college. The

[19] Emerson, George B. *Reminiscences of an Old Teacher.* Boston. 1878.

winter term was the most difficult, since then all the boys released from farm labors were turned into the schoolroom.

At one time during his teaching days Emerson boarded with a sea captain whose invalid sister, a woman of forty, impressed the young man with the breadth of her reading and the depth of her critical insight. In this contact with a truly cultivated woman was laid the foundation of Emerson's belief in the education of women. His experiences as an educator of boys strengthened this belief.

The schools which George Emerson taught during his student years were sometimes co-educational, and he therefore had basis for the comparison he made between the male and female mind. His opinions were probably biased by the ease of teaching the girls, and by the difficulties of controlling the boys. Falling into the habits of the prevailing system he plied the ferule. Unlike many of his contemporaries who remained blithe and happy, Emerson, naturally averse to cruelty, revolted against the system. He could not honestly approve of the ferule, he could not observe the beneficence of its effects. If girls could learn without having knowledge pounded into them it seemed at least possible that so might boys.

Part of the difficulty, Emerson felt, was caused by the method of living. Many of the boys came from out of town, following the custom, used also by the girl pupils, of boarding about in families. Since girls were, even while getting an education, fragile artic'es, it was natural and fitting that the principal of a girls'

school should exercise supervision over these boarding places. No such supervision seems to have been
thought necessary for boys. Nor did the families
concern themselves unduly with their boy boarders.
Emerson came to believe, as did Zilpah Grant, that
pupils should be housed with their teacher. In the
endeavor to establish better relations between pupil
and teacher, and also to regulate the life of the pupil,
he at one time rented a large house entirely on his
own responsibility. He then found a family to run
the house, and there gathered all the boys from out
of town, living with them the two years he remained
at the school. This was in Lancaster, which he left
to become a tutor of mathematics and natural philosophy at Harvard. But he had made his point: it was
better for pupils to be in a central boarding house.
So Emma Willard had believed, gathering her pupils
into one building. So Wheaton, in the second year
of its existence, was to have a " boarding house " —
the homely name sufficed for many a long year. Common experience led schools to follow the custom thus
established.

Emerson, however, did not remain either at Lancaster or at Harvard although for a period he continued to teach boys. He declined a professorship of
mathematics at Harvard to become a master in the
English Classical School in Boston — so-called to distinguish it from the Latin School which was college
preparatory. This school was a new venture, opening in 1821 and offering a sound education for those
boys who did not plan to go to college. Here George

Emerson interested himself in the problems of discipline, evolving a kind of student government. He suggested that the boys attempt to rule themselves; if they would act as young gentlemen he would treat them as young gentlemen. He believed in strict discipline, administered not from above but from within — in classroom and on the playground.

That Emerson's path was not smooth is proved by his prompt acceptance of an offer to head a girls' school. The change meant a substantial increase in his income, but his motives were not mercenary. The sponsor of the new school stressed the importance of female education over that of the education of boys: the upbringing of children, who become the citizens of the future, would always be in the hands of women. Men seldom assumed this responsibility, but they might assume the responsibility of the education of those who would carry on this important duty. It was in 1823 that this new female school opened, with thirty-two young ladies, a registration considered large for a private venture, guaranteeing a good livelihood to its head.

Twenty years earlier a young theological student at Harvard had paused for a year to teach a young ladies' school in Framingham, Massachusetts, and was immediately impressed by his pupils' interest in geometry and Caesar. It seems not to have occurred to him or to other young teachers similarly placed that interest in the teacher may have stimulated this eagerness for Latin and mathematics. Back at Harvard as tutor this young man contrasted his present pupils with those of the preceding year. Not only were the young gentlemen less eager to learn, but their conduct was frequently reprehensible: they threw bread in the dining halls.

At the time that Wheaton opened the young gentlemen still had their moments of rebellion. Omitting the customary phrases anent the good conduct of the students during the past year the President of Harvard in his report to the trustees in 1834 explained the expulsion of a large group of students. The trouble had started in a Greek class. A student had refused to answer a question addressed to him by the instructor who, feeling that such open defiance could not be overlooked, took the matter to the authorities. At this point the friends of the student decided to make life truly pleasant for the instructor and for the college at large. They carried their warfare beyond the classroom into the chapel. By making " irreverent noises at chapel " until they drowned out the service, they created a major disturbance. More than bread was thrown from first to last, until order was restored by drastic action.[20]

It is small wonder, then, that teachers praised the female mind — and manners. It is easily understandable that the Wheatons preferred to establish in their home town, across the street from their own residence, a seminary for young ladies rather than an academy for young men.

Moreover, the field of men's education was thought

[20] *Report of the President;* and *Proceedings of the Overseers Relative to the Late Disturbances in that Seminary, August 25, 1834.*

to be overcrowded, at least in New England. Dummer, Andover, and Exeter, beside all the academies of the various towns, the high schools of the cities, could amply provide for boys. And with colleges boys were well supplied. Both Williams and Harvard protested the founding of Amherst. Williams could serve the needs of the western part of the state, Harvard the eastern; Maine, New Hampshire, and Rhode Island had colleges of their own; what need, then, of another college? The men of Amherst, however, persisted, pointing out that there were boys in and near Amherst who could not afford to attend either Williams or Harvard. They would be able to attend a college in Amherst.

Whether the protest or the defence was in the right, the protest did make clear to benevolently minded people that the field of boys' education was fairly well pre-empted. Though there were large numbers of girls' schools there were not yet many with anything like adequate endowments. Bradford, starting as a co-educational academy, had a few years since separated the two departments, and in 1836 was to close the boys' department as no longer needed. Such action emphasized the fact that new girls' schools were more likely to flourish than boys' — that is, if they were properly guided.

There was at this time a certain amount of publicity through Zilpah Grant's disagreements with the trustees first of Adams Academy in Londonderry, New Hampshire, and then of Ipswich Academy. Adams had fallen into difficulties and debt and the trustees were trying vainly to secure Miss Grant's return. Miss Grant's emphasis upon adequate funds to provide equipment had made the public, at least of the neighborhood, aware of the needs of such schools.

Miss Grant was trying to build up a school for the middle class; not a school for the daughters of the well-to-do, as Albany and Troy academies were often regarded; and not a school for the daughters of the poor farmers, such as Mary Lyon planned. Wheaton was to be such a school, a school for the daughters of those who were moderately, but only moderately, well off; for the daughters of ministers, doctors, teachers.

The new seminary was to be neither a charitable institution nor a fashionable school. It was to train some of its pupils to be teachers but its training would be mainly for those who would become wives and mothers. For them education was of the greatest importance that they might live their own lives intelligently; and intelligently guide the lives of those who would be entrusted to their care.

CHAPTER II

Educated Woman and Her Place

NO ulterior motive of feminism actuated the Wheatons. In the decade that Judge Wheaton lived after the founding of the seminary he evinced no interest in the first faint flickers of the woman's rights movement. His daughter-in-law lived on until 1905, a vigorous, alert woman to the end of her long life, but never did she ally herself with feminism.

Had there been anything radical in woman's education Mrs. Wheaton would not have suggested the founding of a female seminary to her husband's father. She did not regard herself as a torchbearer, or as the leader of a movement. She was a naturally conservative woman, one who was not set in her ideas, but who conformed to the prevailing ideas of her time. Brought up in a home of wealth, given the privileges which wealth gave, she had accepted her own education as a matter of course. Married at twenty to a wealthy man of cultivated tastes, she settled down in the position of cherished wife.

The fainting female had gone out of style. Mrs. Wheaton had grown into womanhood at a time which appreciated health even for young ladies, and instead of extolling the fragile female lectured her heavily on diet and exercise. Fathers were still sometimes shocked when their daughters, romping out of doors, acquired a suntan or freckles but they no longer extolled the pallor once thought irresistible in ladies. Ladies were still properly white of skin, but protected by broad hats and thick gloves they were encouraged to go out of doors. Botany was greeted as a science peculiarly adapted for feminine study since its pursuit required what was probably the exact amount of exercise in the open air needed for feminine health.

Dr. Graham, the father of vitamins yet unnamed, had already developed the cult of brown breads, a cult that was to continue to the present time, proclaiming its virtues in multitudinous and multicolored packages of bran and roughage.

Dio Lewis was still in the future with his advocacy of more strenuous exercises than were yet thought of in the eighteen-thirties. Schools of the thirties frequently advertised their equipment of swings, jumping ropes, battledore and shuttlecock, adding comfortingly that those who felt disinclined for this heavier exercise might substitute walking. Calisthenics, however, already existed. Beloved by the educational leaders, Emma Willard, Catharine Beecher, Zilpah Grant, it took its place in the curricula of the more serious schools. Zilpah Grant's enthusiasm survived her own discomfiture. In leading calisthenic exercises she injured a tendon in her heel so severely that for months she had to be carried in a chair by two strong men who deposited her (in the chair) on the schoolroom platform. From twining wreaths and decorous marches calisthenics was to become ever more strenuous until in the twentieth century summer camps make of our girls and boys Amazons and Samsons; and high schools make of them accomplished circus tumblers.

In the eighteen-thirties the health urged for young ladies was not the cultivation of muscle and brawn. Female delicacy no longer required languishing on a sofa, but the acquisition of a strong constitution was not to lead daughters out into the world. No one doubted that woman's place was the home; or if any one did dare to doubt, it was not for lack of masculine direction. From pulpit and press there was a constant barrage.

Ideas of woman's sphere had not changed fundamentally since the Garden of Eden, a place whose customs were intimately known to the early nineteenth century. Though opinions as to what constituted a wise woman varied somewhat from those of the remote past, woman's sphere as wife and mother was well charted. Libraries of books had been written in the past and were still pouring from the press comfortably convincing and persuasively encouraging. Since there was never a doubt as to the wisdom and necessity of the continuance of the human race, a woman was entitled to a place in the sun primarily as a mother.

It was in the thirteenth century that a worthy gentleman, Philippe de Novaire, stated the case of woman's education with convincing clarity: " Women have a great advantage in one thing; they can easily preserve their honor if they wish to be held virtuous,

by one thing only.   But for a man many are needful,
if he wish to be esteemed virtuous, for it behooves
him to be courteous and generous, brave and wise.
And for a woman, if she be worthy of her body, all
her other faults are covered and she can go with a high
head wheresoever she will; and therefore it is in no
way needful to teach as many things to girls as to
boys." [1]

Though various prominent writers of the eighteenth century spoke well of woman's intellectual
capacities, the eighteenth century closed with the cyn-
ical pronouncement that a woman needed to know
only " chemistry enough to keep the pot boiling, and
geography enough to know the location of the different rooms in her house."

In 1796 Thomas Gisborne published *An Enquiry
into the Duties of the Female Sex* which within a year
required a second edition, crossing the ocean to find
an appreciative audience in America for many decades.   Mr. Gisborne was a friend to the education
of women, but he distinctly asseverated that women
were intended by a wise Providence for different
spheres of activity from those of men, as their weaker
physical frame attested.   He was as sure as were all
men and most women of his generation and the generation whose education they guided, that woman's
sphere was unchanged and unchangeable.   Woman's
task was to contribute " daily and hourly to the comfort of husbands, of parents, of brothers and sisters,
and of other relations, connections, and friends in the

1 Power, Eileen. *Legacy of the Middle Ages.*

intercourse of domestic life, under every vicissitude of sickness and health, of joy and affliction." " By society and example " she should succeed in " forming and improving the general manners, dispositions, and conduct of the other sex." And finally, and most important of all, woman was properly concerned " in modelling the human mind during the early stages of its growth, and fixing, while it is yet ductile, its growing principles of action; children of each sex being, in general, under maternal tuition during their childhood, and girls until they become women."

An earlier volume of advice was equally popular in America in the eighteen-thirties, James Fordyce's *Sermons to Young Women,* already in a fourth edition in 1767. Fordyce warned women that they unsexed themselves in asking for a share in man's affairs. In the preface he quoted a woman who, as a single lady of talent, was full of understanding for the problems of marriage. " When a man of sense, says Mrs. Hannah More," wrote Fordyce approvingly, " comes to marry, it is a companion whom he wants; not merely a creature who can paint, and play, and dress, and dance; it is a being who can reason, and reflect, and feel, and judge, and act, and discourse, and discriminate; one who can assist him in his affairs, lighten his cares, soothe his sorrows, purify his joys, strengthen his principles, and educate his children."

In America no less than in England Hannah More was read constantly and constantly quoted. Her death in 1833 was lamented on both sides of the Atlantic. Hannah More's life was as blameless as her prose. The only approach to scandal in her life had been the breaking of her engagement, presumably by the gentleman who in recompense, all unknown to her, settled an annuity upon her in lieu of his affections. As a literary lady Hannah More achieved great fame and more than a competence as well as the friendship of Samuel Johnson, of Reynolds, and of Garrick.

Two of her books were especially cherished in America, *Strictures on Female Education,* originally published in 1799; and the best seller of 1809, *Coelebs in Search of a Wife,* a two volume tract. In vain the *Edinburgh Review* attacked its priggishness; the public found it both amusing and instructive. Purporting to be the tale of a bachelor in search of a suitable and desirable wife, it presented type characters of women, frivolous and frail, benevolent and blessed, with their happy and miserable households, nor were there forgotten models of childish propriety (drawn supposedly from Macaulay and his sister).

At the very outset Hannah More's Coelebs quotes Milton: woman's perfection is to

> "study household good,
> And good works in her husband to promote."

Carefully excluding drudgery and servility the bachelor adds that if a woman know not how to promote household good " she is ignorant of the most indispensable, the most appropriate branch of female knowledge."

Though the American women who advised their sex were less explicit than men like Fordyce or women like Hannah More, they were still sure of woman's duties in guiding a household. They did not say to young ladies as Fordyce did, " Your business is to read Men, in order to make yourselves agreeable and useful." They did not advocate education, as he did, that wives might be more interesting to their husbands.

Women did, however, see that an educated woman might gain a more interesting husband than her less intelligent sister. It was in 1814 that Abigail Adams wrote, " It is very certain, that a well-informed woman, conscious of her nature and dignity, is more capable of performing the relative duties of life, and of engaging and retaining the affections of a man of understanding, than one whose intellectual endowments rise not above the common level." Such a woman should never forget that the household tasks devolved upon her or upon servants under her direction; she should remember Napoleon's rebuff to Madame de Staël: " Madame, who educates your children? " But it was in private letters that Abigail Adams uttered her views; she was not one to agitate publicly and violently for feminine liberties though she did remind her president husband that the constitution declared all men, meaning all mankind, born free and equal. Even political equality would not remove the necessity of educating daughters for " the useful and domestic duties of life." Mrs. Adams believed definitely that " every American wife should herself know how to order and regulate her family; how to govern her domestics, and train up her children.   For this purpose, the all-wise Creator made woman an help-meet for man, and she who fails in these duties does not answer the end of her creation." [2]

Seminaries occasionally felt it necessary to state in their catalogues that they did not undertake to prepare students specifically for this part of woman's duty.   " This feature of the Institution [the performance of the cooking and housework by the students themselves] will not relieve mothers from the responsibility of giving their daughters a thorough domestic education; but it will throw before those who are seeking for them the privileges of this Seminary, additional motives to be faithful in this important duty " [3] — so read the Mount Holyoke catalogue for many a year.

Women educators were careful to divorce themselves from any association with those who urged that women be trained for leadership, for life in the world of man.   Mary Wollstonecraft's *A Vindication of the Rights of Woman* which had voiced such views was thought to be a bold, bad book by most men and their docile wives.   The book had no wide circulation in America, but it was known.   Though there was a general acceptance in America of the true views of Mary Wollstonecraft, that wives should be the companions not the toys of their husbands, few troubled to seek

2 *Letters of Mrs. Adams, the Wife of John Adams.* Vol. II. Boston. 1840.

3 From Mount Holyoke catalogues of 1852 and 1854.

out the true views of a woman thought to have been shameless. The man whose common-law wife she had been was an American, well known and respected. Mary Wollstonecraft's opinions were not respected in America. She was unquoted for the most part because unread. Her name was a symbol for the unwomanly woman.

No educator of the eighteen-thirties failed to state a strongly rooted belief in the essentially domestic character of woman's true interests. Careers for women were not advocated even by the women who achieved them most satisfactorily. Catharine Beecher modestly carried a brother on lecture tours sending him to deliver the speech she had composed. Emma Willard, happy in her marriage, successful in her school, deferred constantly to her husband — who by law was entitled to all her earnings and who, to secure to her her own enterprise, had to will it to her.

Catharine Beecher would have married, deterred only by the death of the man to whom she was engaged. Zilpah Grant married. Eunice Caldwell, the first principal of Wheaton, married. The public needed from time to time to be reminded that woman's education did not unfit her for the domestic duties.

When Mrs. Hale, the enterprising editor of the *Ladies' Magazine* of Boston, which the even more enterprising Mr. Godey later absorbed into his Philadelphia magazine, called attention in issue after issue to the need of education for women and inserted " puffs " for various schools already in existence, she

was besieged with warning letters which she oblig-
ingly published. Mrs. Hale was herself an educated
woman, though her learning had not been gained in
the schoolroom. Step by step she had followed her
brother in his course at Dartmouth. It was this
masculine education which had stored her mind,
which had taught her how and where to obtain material for a magazine, which had made it possible for
her when widowed to make a living for herself and
her children. She was forever bolstering the cause
of female education with articles as well as with
notices of existing schools and prospectuses of those
about to be established.

Men wrote, warning her lest she unsex women.
Any good woman, any true woman, wrote an indignant male signing himself " Bachelor," would rather
be the mother of Washington than any one of these
so-called distinguished women, than Hannah More
herself. A later critic of Mrs. Mill's *Enfranchisement
of Women* was to echo this in his indignant hope that
the mother of John Stuart Mill would regard it as
her chief honor to have reared her distinguished son.
That friend of women, Thomas Wentworth Higginson, voiced his scorn at such arguments in 1853: " In
the name of common sense, why so? Is it not as much
to *be* an useful woman as to rear an useful man? "

Higginson was far more radical than any one in
America, man or woman, in the eighteen-thirties.
Higginson pointed out — in the eighteen-seventies —
that the father of John Quincy Adams trained his son
at the same time taking his own place in public life.

No man, however much he might devote himself to his children — consider the father of John Stuart Mill — limited himself to fatherhood or was educated with fatherhood in view as the end of his education. Higginson felt that if there were queens there might just as logically be women presidents.

The eighteen-thirties would have argued that the mother of Henry the Eighth was more fortunate than Queen Elizabeth. They had no high regard for Elizabeth. In 1840 A. B. Muzzey in an appropriately titled book, *The Young Maiden,* voiced the common animadversions on Elizabeth: she had no love of home; she was lionlike, not womanlike. " She passed through life, it is said, without a single bosom friend."

Since Victoria did not come to the throne until 1837, the thirties could know little of her prosperous reign combined with the performance of domestic duties including the rearing of a very large family. Ignoring Victoria, 1934 Commencement speakers and magazine writers still argue that women are happier as wives and mothers and as daughters than as individuals with careers; oblivious of modern statistics which give husbands to only a portion, albeit the larger portion, of the female race, and children to even fewer — and not many children to each — these moderns take their stand with the Bachelor of the eighteen-thirties. Yet there are women, even after this century of education, who would prefer to be Rosa Bonheur, rather than the mother of Whistler; Miss Perkins, the first woman member of the Cabinet, rather than the mother of any of the Roosevelts.

The eighteen-thirties were alive to this danger. There were many fears expressed lest this higher education unfit women for their sphere. Educated women might not care to marry, or men might not care to marry them. Hannah Adams, Hannah More, Catharine Beecher, Mary Lyon were all single women. On the other hand, the most prominent of all the women advocating higher education for their sex was undoubtedly Emma Willard, who had, as long as Dr. Willard lived, been a model wife. So great was her prestige, so firm the belief in her essential womanliness that she survived the publicity of her disastrous second marriage which ended in divorce in 1843.

It was well that there were prominent examples of learned women who did their duty in the home, for there was a fear that educated women would not be content to become mothers, or that they would neglect their children. They might cease to be feminine and become loud-voiced, rough-mannered, and indelicate. They might forget their place, the place to which God had assigned them. Science, which was soon to challenge a large body of fixed ideas, had not yet disturbed the literal belief in the Bible. It was only to his diary that Bronson Alcott ventured to confide his belief that religion would be forced to change. Religion he felt to be the most important science of all; surely it would develop as all other sciences were now developing. Not yet could an advanced thinker like Alcott voice such views. Genesis stood unquestioned. God had *created* Adam; He had *fashioned* Eve from Adam's rib. Not a creation she, but a sort of manufactured by-product.

Biblical arguments abounded for both sides of the female education argument. Eve [4] was made from Adam's rib, not from his foot; made as a companion to Adam, not as a servant. Adam could have had an ape, a coney, a squirrel, a bird of paradise for a toy; he could have had all creation for slave. Eve was the answer to his wish for a rational companion whom he could respect, a dearer self who could counsel and instruct him, be counselled and instructed by him. If Eve had been designed as a companion to Adam, then woman should be regarded as man's companion, not his inferior.

Turning to *Paradise Lost* for Milton's interpretation of Genesis, the friend of female education found comfort and support in spite of Milton's views on the naturally subordinate position of woman: he for God only, she for God in him. For when Eve stood confessed of disobedience in eating of the fruit, Adam considered the possibility of his remaining sinless, but he could not refuse to share the fate of one without whom life would lose its savor. Even, he reflected, if God created another Eve by his sparing another rib, loss of this Eve would never be absent from his heart. They were one, and her fate must be his; he chose banishment with her, rather than Paradise alone or with her successor.[5] However much he might declare his superiority, by his deliberate eating of the apple, aware of the consequences, he proved the equality of their relationship. Milton's Adam proclaimed woman as man's companion.

---

4 Emerson, Joseph. *Address*. Saugus. 1822.
5 *Paradise Lost*. Book ninth.

Even more respected in America was the judgment of the clergymen who again and again preached on woman and her place, woman and her education. In 1820 the Reverend Daniel Clark preached a sermon directed to " the females of the first parish in Amherst." Fervently he urged his audience to show the men who slandered their abilities that they were capable of intellectual dignity. The mind, he pointed out, is capable of vast improvement and enlargement, growing by exercise. Imploring his congregation not to be ciphers in their families he bade them explore the world of the mind.[6]

Down in Virginia a year earlier a sermon had been preached and then published in the *Virginia Evangelical and Literary Magazine,*[6] which added to other arguments for the education of women that the personal appearance of a young woman with a cultivated mind was more pleasing than that of her less tutored sisters. Home, the sphere of a woman, was of too great importance to be trusted to the ignorant. A wife should be a companion, a counsellor; how could a woman be these if her mind be not improved? " The importance of this subject justifies the expression of deep regret on account of the miserable state of female education in our country." This was in 1819.

In 1825 Gardiner Spring, a noted theologian who had once been a lawyer, preached in the Presbyterian Church in New York a sermon, *The Excellence and*

[6] Pamphlets and magazines in the Library of Congregational House, Boston.

Influence of the Female Character,[6] which was important enough for publication.

" The influence of the female character has a predominant sway over human society. Public taste and manners, public virtues and vices, are under the control of woman." This was a large order. Once more woman's sphere was emphatically declared to be the home, but in the home there was need of a well cultivated mind. The minds of the sexes were pronounced equal without reservation. " I know of nothing which a woman may not study and acquire to advantage. . . . I would delight to see her plodding her *steady* course through the departments of classical knowledge." Science, history, philosophy, mathematics, logic — all these women had shown themselves able to master, and all these should be open to them as to their brothers.

In Portsmouth, New Hampshire, the Reverend Charles Burroughs gave an address on female education in 1827[7] in which woman's mind was emphatically declared the equal of man's and woman's education was pronounced essential to the moral improvement of society. As the equal and companion of man an educated woman would gain dignity, would influence the infant mind, and would benefit society.

In America the companionship of man and wife was much more of a reality than in England or on the

6 Pamphlets and magazines in the Library of Congregational House, Boston.

7 Burroughs, Charles, Rector of St. John's Church. *An Address on Female Education.* Portsmouth, N. H. 1827.

Continent. Since the American man was too busy to make an art of lovemaking — a busyness and an omission which all travellers from France deplored — he did not cultivate the arts of gallantry. Frenchmen pitied the wives and daughters whom they saw walking alone of an afternoon in Philadelphia. No lovers at their side, no soft nothings whispered in their ear, no pressing of soft hands, no fervent notes pressed into their clinging fingers. The lot of the American woman was undoubtedly hard. Even Englishmen pitied her, regarding her as a sort of upper servant in the home, since almost never did she have what seemed to the European the most necessary service. When she did have her husband at her side he was as like as not to discuss with her his business affairs — fine conversation between a man and a woman!

North or South, the American man did not strive for a life of leisure; the European might have understood his devotion to business, had his aim been to accumulate capital, and then live on his income, filling his time with hunting, shooting, travel, and lovemaking. The Southern gentleman, though he had overseers, rode over his plantations and personally supervised his vast holdings of land and slaves; his wife was burdened worse than he, for hers was the task of dispensing clothes and pills, comfort and religion to the irresponsible blacks.

The Northerner was still more objectionably occupied, even when by inheritance or by hard work or by shrewd dealing he had risen above the working class. Still he put in long days at law or medicine or

business. Men in America lived near their mills,
their wharves, their fields. If the ten hour day seemed
to them too short for their hired help, it was because
they themselves put in a ten or twelve or fourteen
hour day. Business was the breath of life to them
whether or not they had already accumulated ample
fortunes. No man was content with the fortune or
social estate of his father; young men were ever striving to raise themselves in the world. In a new
country without an aristocracy, this was natural
enough. And business, which was a means of getting
ahead in the world, soon came to be an end in itself.
Men who spent the day in such activities did not come
home ready to pay compliments or glide over the floor
of a ballroom. They were more likely to sit by the
fireplace — if it had not been closed up, giving way
to the newer stove, or the still newer furnace — and
talk things over with the companion who would understand. He might smoke, or he might chew.
America, founded by Godly men, was as serious about
its tobacco as about all its occupations. Visitors vied
with one another for vivid phrases of disgust at the
chewing American. He chewed his way through
journeys and business transactions; and at home, he
sat where he could dexterously spit into the eyes
of his andirons; andirons made to represent the
mercenaries of the Revolution, handsome Hessian
soldiers.

Busyness was in itself a virtue, since idleness gave
opportunities to Satan. The first law for compulsory
education was the " ould Deluder " law of Massachu-

setts. Children were to be taught that they might
read the Bible and thus outwit the Devil. The
busier a man, the safer he was; the busier his wife,
the safer she. He did not worry how to remove the
reproach of her being labelled an upper servant; he
was content to have her work hard, because he worked
hard himself, and because he believed in hard work.

The energy of the pioneer who could not rest at
his fireside until he had cleared the land of trees and
stumps as far as eye could reach, had fastened itself
upon the people with the strongest of tentacles.
Americans could never be satisfied with the farms they
had planted, the cities they had built, the industries
they had developed. There was laid upon them the
necessity of making everything bigger and better.
Their forefathers — either by blood or by spiritual inheritance they were all the descendants of the Puritans
— had come to a new land where civilization had to be
rough hewn out of wilderness. There had been no
time to stop; there was no time now though on the
Altantic seaboard the cities, save in age alone, were
the counterparts of European cities, differing outwardly in little save the physical aspect of their
buildings.

Seeing that the world was conquered here, young
men were looking ever Westward. Instead of settling
on their fathers' farms, or in the prepared niche of
their fathers' offices, they pushed their eager way
West; sometimes with the consent and blessing of
their parents, sometimes stubbornly setting out in
open rebellion. As soon as the frontier they reached

became a settlement, then a village, then a town, their restless spirits drove them onward. Not idleness and ease, but the effort of conquering difficulties, of turning waste acres into waving fields of grain — here lay the heart of the American.

If the American man was thus tireless, it follows that his wife, who was regarded as a companion, could not model herself on the European ladies of leisure. The American boarding house did flourish, perhaps to encourage " autocrats of the breakfast table," but in spite of its vogue, comparatively few American wives found refuge there from the cares of a home. Nor was it in American tradition that they should.

Many a Southern woman knew that she worked harder managing her hordes of servants, or suffered more from their insolence, if she were not firm, than her Northern sister who frequently had no servants at all. The men of Boston had early perceived the need of slaves to provide service, but the Indians whom they enslaved proved intractable at best, and at worst died of tuberculosis. Negro slaves were not more successful: they did not thrive in the harsh climate of the North. In the eighteen-thirties, too, there was much anti-slavery feeling, and slavery was no longer permitted in northern states.

Northern women, then, of necessity became active housekeepers. When they had help, it was frequently the daughter of some neighboring farmer who had more daughters than his own household required. Mothers' helpers these were counted rather than hired maids; they ate with the family, and were not thought of as menials. There were well-to-do families, like the Wheatons, who had cooks and maids; but the average middle-class American did not. When under the full tide of immigration a bountiful supply of kitchen help was assured, the maid did not share the family meals, but the old nomenclature held on into the twentieth century: Americans, except for that group of the wealthy who had uniformed maids, kept a " girl." She was definitely help, not the housekeeper. The American wife was her own housekeeper — as Mrs. Wheaton was, though her financial status was such that in England she would have had a hired housekeeper to supervise the household for her.

Growing up in a home where the mother as well as the father had affairs to keep her busy, American children were naturally different from European children. In general they had no nursemaids just as their mothers had no housekeepers. Again European visitors pitied the American woman — an upper servant in the home, she added to these duties that of nursemaid to her own children. In England children, even of those in moderate circumstances, were cared for by a nurse — she might be a highly superior person, or she might be a fourteen year old foundling. In any case she kept the children in the nursery, out of their parents' way. As soon as the boys got too big to be controlled by this type of servant they were packed off to boarding school. Girls were then turned over to an ill-paid governess until such time as they were introduced to society — if they were high enough in the social scale — in any case until they were ready for marriage.

American children, on the contrary, lived with their parents. They were tended by their mothers; they as like as not learned their letters at her knee. When their father came home they were with her, waiting to greet him, to tease him to play with them, to listen to his conversation. Since there was no servant to corral them in a nursery, they ate their meals with their parents. Even the busiest American father saw infinitely more of his children than the English father — one might almost add than the English mother. Travellers commented upon the fact that the American child was spoiled. It was doubtless annoying to a foreign visitor to find the children present when he came to pay his respects to an American business or professional man.

To their criticism the American parents offered for excuse, " Poor things! they will soon have hardship enough! " [8] America had been wrested from the wilderness, and the wilderness was still to be conquered if the vast land was to come within one government. Many a successful American had worked his way up through hardships, and his greatest desire was to make the path of his children softer than his own had been.

There was not in America as in England a landowning class which passed its holdings on from father to son. Most Americans had no hope of inherited

[8] Abdy, E. S. *Journal of a Residence and Tour in the United States.* London. 1835.

wealth, and were therefore at pains to make what they could for themselves. Where there was wealth, it was not held together as in England. There was no custom of primogeniture in America; the eldest son shared his fathers' accumulations with his brothers and sisters. Parents who lived with their children cherished an equal affection for them or showed partiality for other reasons than that of sequence of birth. However partial an English father to a younger son, he was bound by entail or by custom to bequeath his fortune, be it big or little, to his eldest son. Americans had never adopted this system. Hence they did not strive to build their estates into parks, their businesses into enduring companies. They worked in the present, hoping to advance their children's interests, but aware that under the uncertain conditions of human life, their children would have to make their own way.

The self-made man was already proclaimed. In the president's office in Washington now sat the first of a long line of self-made men. Andrew Jackson, son of Scotch-Irish immigrants, had lifted himself by his own bootstraps in the fashion which was recognized as truly American. His success entrenched firmly the belief that any American boy, born in a sufficiently humble home, preferably a log cabin or a wooden farmhouse, if possible perched on the side of a hill remote from neighbors, had a running chance of the presidency.

Americans did not stress ancestry or inherited wealth. These might be convenient aids in one's progress through life, yet the lack of either or both need be no handicap to one willing to work hard and to make the most of both talent and opportunity.

Life had become steadily easier in the settled portions of the country, with an increase of wealth, with an increase of inventions which lightened labor. The growth of industrialism had done much to relieve both men and women, sons and daughters. No longer was it necessary for households to grow their own food, weave their own cloth, make their own clothes; or to chop their wood and make their candles. Gaslighting was not yet in most homes; it was, however, in many city streets in the eighteen-thirties.[9] The fireplace had yielded to the Franklin stove, itself a metal fireplace which stood out from the old fireplace, radiating a great deal more heat. The Franklin stove was in turn displaced by the furnace which rapidly became an American necessity but is only now in 1934 making its way in England. The installation of stoves was aided by the railroads which by their ease of transportation made coal available to all. Coal mines were discovered everywhere, and their operation, begun with more hope than findings, frequently justified. In the eighteen-thirties a mine was operated in Mansfield, a town only five miles from Norton.

Though the trains ran but short distances in 1834, they were pushing onward as fast as roadbeds and rails could be placed. It was soon discovered that

9 Baltimore 1816; New York 1823; Boston 1829; Philadelphia 1836.

they could carry food, so that it no longer became imperative for every one who had a bit of land to keep his sons home from school to help plant and harvest.

For the women there was greater relief even than for the men and boys. The household tasks were immensely lightened by the new utensils in the home, by the removal of the spinning wheels. Factories now made the cloth, and tailors cut it. No longer did men go about in homespun if they could possibly afford factory cloth; and no longer did their womenfolk work from dawn to dark to perform unending tasks. Kitchen work was lighter; the new tinware brought to the door by gay gossiping peddlers was easier to keep clean than iron or copper. If it lasted less long, it was the more easily and cheaply replaced. Rag rugs were discarded — to the emancipation of the woman — put in attics to be reinstated in public pride by twentieth century antique shops. The families of the eighteen-thirties took far more joy in the new carpets which covered the floor from corner to corner, hiding the wide boards and the gaping cracks. The new-fangled bells saved time, since they could be heard more easily; best of all they did not require polishing as the knockers did. In the eighteen-thirties it was more fashionable to ring than to knock; in the nineteen-thirties the knocker is the aristocrat.

Candles, dear to the twentieth century tearoom, yielded to oil lamps, though since the oil was expensive at first, many a young lady had to sigh by candle-light. The first crude matches had come in 1825, the first friction matches, really displacing the flint and tinder box, being produced in America in 1836.

The joy over the lightening of labor was tempered, at least in New England, by the thought that there might be more leisure than was advisable. It was argued in the eighteen-thirties that the factories which employed women and children incredibly long hours were really a blessing since, with the new inventions lessening the work of the home, women and children might get into mischief. Cotton factories posed as benevolent institutions, taking care of little children who, with their mothers working in the factories, were thus kept under supervision and out of temptation. It was not until 1843 that Massachusetts forbade the employment of children under twelve for more than ten hours a day. Whatever the fear of the Devil, there was in Massachusetts a respect for the Lord and his creatures.

Labor agitation had started before the close of the eighteen-twenties and by 1836 there were said to be fully three hundred thousand men in the labor unions. In 1835 a New York court declared strikes illegal; in 1837 there was a period of depression which made any efforts for better labor conditions futile; yet in 1840 President Van Buren declared ten hours the legal working day on government works and in Massachusetts in the same year Justice Shaw interpreted common law in such a way as to permit strikes.

All these various conditions of American life helped to promote education.

The conditions of the home tended to put daughters on a parity with sons. Daughters who would inherit an equal share of whatever property there might be were entitled to a share of the income while their parents lived, and hence had a fair chance of gaining equal privileges of education. Legally women were still pretty much nonexistent. Once a woman married she owned nothing — nor were her children hers. Over her, her children, and her property her husband had complete control. If she inherited money or property, it was his; if she earned money, it was his; he could — and indeed did — collect it; if she had money in the bank, he could withdraw it; if she wrote books or articles, the payment could be collected by him. In the letters of Catherine Sedgwick, a popular novelist of the time, one reads of a cultivated woman who, unable to endure the abuse of a drunken husband, left her home with her young daughter, concealing the child and herself in an obscure part of the city. She had no difficulty in earning support for them both by her pen, but her husband, unremitting in his search, found her out, removed the child, and immediately took steps to have her royalties and payments from magazines remitted to him. A husband had the legal right to collect dividends, to transfer to himself or to any one else he might choose, any property or money his wife might have. He might divorce her; she could not divorce him.

There are on record cases of women who did succeed in divorcing husbands — by an act of legislature in those few states which admitted a woman's right to divorce. By declaring that her husband was a notorious drunkard and gambler, a man unfit to bring up children, a Southern woman did gain a divorce and the custody of her children.[10] Few women, however, would risk either the publicity or the reproach of their children by such action.

The injustice of existing laws was made glaringly apparent by the case of Andrew Jackson's wife. Unhappy in her first marriage, she had been deserted before she met Jackson. Her husband let her know that he had sought divorce, leading her to believe that the divorce had been granted. She then married Jackson, only to have her husband create a scandal by suing for divorce, charging her with adultery. What he had done earlier was to file an intention of divorce, a proceeding perfectly legal. Having thus tricked her into what she believed was marriage with Jackson, he discredited both of them. Jackson, truly devoted, married her again immediately after the divorce, but the poor woman was crushed. She did not live to enter the White House with her husband.

Undoubtedly it was this injustice to his wife which

10 In the issue of March 14, 1835 the *Boston Courier* reported that the North Carolina legislature had given a divorce to Isabelle A. Porter from the " notorious Robert Porter " with the right to change her name and that of her children. Her husband had been expelled from the House of Commons and " is now, as far as she can learn, a wanderer and a vagabond, with whom no one but the most debased can associate. Branded as he is by the judgement of his fellow citizens, his name is a disgrace and to his children will be a reproach from which your worships can and I hope will save them. They are as yet young in life, and have not learned to blush for a parent's shame."

led Jackson to champion the cause of Peggy Eaton, fighting her battles with his Cabinet whose wives would not receive her. Mrs. Eaton had been married twice, too, and gossip associated Eaton's name with hers before her marriage. Judging her slandered, because he knew his wife to have been, Jackson frothed at the mouth, and insisted upon retaining Eaton and in placing Mrs. Eaton in the position to which she was entitled at all the social affairs in the White House.

These extreme cases do not alter the fact that in spite of political and financial disabilities most women were reasonably content with their lot. It is never the majority that is dissatisfied or revolutionary. It is the power of an ardent minority that brings reforms to birth. Woman's rights in the eighteen-thirties did not loom large on the horizon. Newspapers classed abolition, prohibition, and woman's rights as the unholy trinity.

When women organized, with or without the aid of their pastor, various charitable societies, such as societies for the care of destitute orphans, or penitent females, or societies for the promotion of education, or anti-slavery societies, it did not occur to the ladies themselves or to their menfolk that they were transgressing the bounds of propriety. And for a time the management of such societies contented them.

But the greater leisure which had come to women as more and more of the traditional household tasks were taken from the home, the greater confidence gained by excursions into organized charity quite naturally led to the feeling that more schooling was desirable. Daughters were on friendly enough terms with their fathers to impress them with their desires. Fathers often perceived that a daughter was fully as clever as the son. Elizabeth Cady in later life felt that she had been allowed to go to the boys' academy because her brother had died.[11] She resolved to take his place and was constantly grieved because her father, as she brought home her prizes for proficiency in Latin and Greek instead of saying, " I am as proud of you as of a son," would renew his laments for the lost son, exclaiming, " Why are you not a boy? " It was this attitude of her father's that made Elizabeth Cady a feminist, not her masculine education,

The average American father seems, however, to have been content with his daughters, and easily persuaded to grant them privileges similar to those allowed his sons. For one thing, when a daughter had no steady occupation in the home, when her hours were no longer filled with spinning or weaving or tending babies, she was as much of a problem about the house as a son. Indubitably one of the reasons for the prosperity of schools has always been and will always be the occupation of children. Having no nursemaids, Americans early established schools as a substitute. In the seventeenth century two year olds were immediately started on the path of learning. In the eighteen-thirties children were

11 Stanton, Elizabeth Cady. *Eighty Years and More 1815–1897.* New York. 1898.

ordinarily received in the primary schools at four. But Boston boasted of infant schools which, says an 1837 volume, Bowen's *Picture of Boston,* were " designed to supply completely all that was wanting to perfect our system of free education. . . . Infant schools take the child from its mother's arms, and fit it by natural gradations of task and play, for a place on the primary benches at four years of age." Not unlike the modern nursery school, then, were these schools of which there were already several in Boston.

The infant school was one more aid to the daughter in the home, since no longer did she have thrust upon her the whole care of her mother's or her stepmother's babies. Families were smaller than in pioneer days, too. And girls who did not go to school might fall into dangerous idleness.

Though marriage was the certain destiny of all girls, it could not be denied that marriageable young men were fewer, and that all daughters did not find husbands even if they sedulously avoided higher education and devoted themselves to the domestic arts — even if they devoted themselves to the art of charming prospective husbands. In the thickly settled portions of the country women now outnumbered men, the reverse of the early conditions of the colonies. Young men were going West, often forgetting to invite to join them the girls they left behind. There was plenty of West still to conquer — beyond the Mississippi it stretched its fertility, waiting for the coming of settlers. There was small chance that the marriage age would revert to the fifteen of Puritan days. Mrs. Wheaton had married at twenty, but many women married later, twenty-two or three being a common enough age for marriage. If, however, a girl was not to marry young, if she was not needed in the home, just what was she to do with the years of waiting? Schooling offered the best possible answer, not only because of the advance in learning which might make a daughter better appreciated by eligible men of intelligence, but also because with education a girl might occupy herself creditably and profitably in teaching others.

For it was immediately obvious that men teachers would not do for either infant or primary schools. In small towns where only one teacher was provided, children were often unhappy, and when once the experiment had been tried of using women teachers in the summer session, when the boys did not attend in any large numbers, the superior patience of the women was immediately apparent. Since American parents were averse to cruelty, they extolled feminine gentleness which cast aside the ferule and taught more as it punished less. American parents refused to permit in the schools the severe discipline of the English schools where birching and caning were supposed to develop manliness. American parents might not wholly spoil the child but, as they lived with their children, they frequently found that gentler methods obtained better results. So the female teacher grew in popularity.

Teaching then came to be regarded as genteel. It was not respectable for a girl to have to earn her own living, unless she could earn it in some way which did not injure her standing in the community, or her father's prestige. Teachers were respected; they ranked below the ministers, in general, but their worth was never measured by their pay. Here, then, was a profession which a girl might enter as a stop-gap before marriage; here was a profession in which she might remain if single. Miss Sarah Pierce was directed into teaching by her father, as was Catharine Beecher. Since the demand for teachers was likely to exceed the supply for many a long day, more and more women turned to this, almost the only genteel method of self-support.

It was in 1836 that the city of Providence, Rhode Island, decided to replace " ushers " by female teachers in the grammar schools, assigning two to each school at a salary of one hundred and seventy-five dollars a year. Only the year before one Asa Peckham had opened a private school for young ladies in Providence in a room in the rear of Grace Church. Mr. Peckham's advertisement [12] offering a bewildering list of studies from reading and writing up to *Evidences of Christianity,* with Latin and music extra, pointed out the dangers of the new leisure. Education such as he offered was the best corrective to the feminine tendency to indulge in vanities. Perhaps the willingness of cities to employ them as teachers was an even surer corrective.

Though women were employed in the primary schools of Boston, it was still customary to use men

[12] In current issues, *Providence Daily Journal.*

in the grammar and writing schools. By law it was required that " the master of the grammar or reading school shall have been ' educated at some college or university, and be a citizen of the United States by birth or naturalization.' " Such a master received twelve hundred dollars, his assistant one thousand. No such qualifications were stipulated for the writing school where nothing was taught except writing and arithmetic. Here in time women might hope to enter. A child remained in the primary school from four to seven — ages at which a child would be much happier under a female teacher. From seven to nine he might attend a grammar school, from nine to seventeen one of the upper schools, either the Latin or the English classical school, being taught, then, for the most part by men.

As, however, girls were admitted both to town schools and to private institutions, it became a matter of economy to use female teachers who often did more work for less money. With the increase of academies and seminaries, with the growth of new settlements in the West with a great need of teachers, there was opened a large field for women which could scarcely fail to affect the state of female education. Though the men who controlled the purse-strings were willing to half-pay women teachers, they began to have their doubts as to the wisdom of half-educating them. If a man sat at table with his son and that son quoted his teacher, as young children invariably do, and the quotation revealed not knowledge but ignorance, a father would take thought. When, in country districts, in the summer session, the teacher boarded around with the parents, it was easy to make comparisons from season to season. The better educated young woman seems to have convinced parents of her greater competence.

Thus was the task of persuasion made easier for an ambitious daughter. Determined girls did, indeed, occasionally defy their parents as did one young lady who packed her bag despite her father's flat refusal to give his permission, and took the stage to Norton, there to attend the seminary. Such action took extraordinary courage, since the fifth commandment was rarely forgotten; it also took extraordinary faith in one's father's payment of bills incurred without his consent and approval. Few girls had money of their own; and hence, unless the father approved or could be coaxed into approval, had to be content with self-education.

In spite of inadequate home and town libraries, many a girl did achieve an education, as did those popular sister poets, Alice and Phoebe Cary.[13]   Their studies were interrupted by their father's remarriage, for the second wife was by no means sympathetic to learning.   Sternly she held her step-daughters responsible for household tasks, inventing busy work for any moments she suspected of being idle.   The girls dutifully worked without complaint, gaining release at night when they could take their books out of hiding and snatch hours from slumber acquiring knowl-

13 Ames, M. C. *A Memorial of Alice and Phoebe Cary.* New York. 1873.

edge. It was not long before the stepmother discovered their fraud, immediately depriving them of
candles. Undaunted they fabricated a wick, dropping
it in a saucer of butter or lard. Courage like theirs
was duplicated here and there, though few had the
temerity to leave the family home as they did, to
seek refuge in the city of New York with only their
pens to support them. That they succeeded, moving
from their first tiny room to a comfortable home
where they finished their lives, carefully tended, and
much honored for poems the world has long since
forgotten, writes a pretty chapter in the book of
feminine achievement.

The attendance at the various private schools and
seminaries proves, however, that most parents were
friendly to their daughters' ambitions; probably even
to the point of encouraging and forcing those of
weaker inclination. The success of the many literary ladies led fathers to believe that their own daughters might write — no daughter would bring fame to
the family in the same way that her brothers might;
yet the seminaries did emphasize training in writing
— and one would not mind having a sweet singer like
Lydia Sigourney in one's home. Compositions were
many in the seminaries, on carefully assigned topics;
and the practice of composition was apparently considered its own reward, for the comments made by
the teachers were usually helpful queries such as,
" Could you make the commas a little more legible? "

Beside Mrs. Sigourney there were many women in
America who, if they did not rival Maria Edgeworth,

the popular Irish novelist, had a great vogue of their own. Maria Edgeworth wrote voluminously in her father's home, greeting sweetly each of his successive wives, loving indiscriminately the children of each marriage. She herself almost married — on a journey she was the recipient of a most flattering offer from a Swedish count. Her father, however, felt that he needed her in his home, and assured her that she would never be happy in Sweden.

Lydia Sigourney married — an elderly widower. As Lydia Huntley,[14] the daughter of a gardener, she had been befriended by her father's employer, a benevolent lady who thought the child bright and hence deserving of an education. She had Lydia schooled until she was ready to take charge herself, starting a small school of her own. When, however, Mr. Sigourney offered himself, her friends counselled acceptance; he was eligible, wealthy, and presumably kind. After marriage Lydia found that he did not approve of her writing. But she loved to write, and she loved the fame which came to her. Outwardly obedient, she published without signature until such time as financial reverses made her husband's restrictions less imperative. At first still anonymous, she came to print her name, using the funds which now flowed freely to indulge herself in travel, crossing the ocean in the fashion of celebrities.

Catherine Sedgwick,[15] a writer less deservedly forgotten than Lydia Sigourney, remained single and

[14] Haight, G. *Mrs. Sigourney, the Sweet Singer of Hartford.* New Haven. 1930.
[15] Dewey, M. E. *Life and Letters of Catherine G. Sedgwick.* New York. 1871.

happy through a long life. One of a large family, she lived with her mother, her brothers and sisters, in Stockbridge where the father left them insisting that Washington, where he was, would not be found suitable for the children. Coming to Stockbridge for his vacations he found his children ever dutiful and respectful, though they may have been aware of their mother's pitiful appeals to him either to return to her and her children, or to let them come to him. She begged him not to deprive her of his help in rearing the family, all in vain. Gentle and obedient, though sad, she remained where he bade her, eventually losing her mind, but not the love of her children. So strong was the father cult, the respect paid to the " author of my being," that no reproaches were ever made Mr. Sedgwick for his neglect and its disastrous consequences. When he introduced a new wife to the Stockbridge home, she was received in friendly fashion by her stepchildren.

Perhaps it was the warning of her mother's fate which kept Catherine Sedgwick single. She did not, however, occupy a small niche at the family fireside, but maintained an apartment for herself in New York. With a companion she lived an independent life, visiting her relatives frequently but keeping her separate household.

Her most popular novels were *A New England Tale* and *Hope Leslie,* tales placed in what was already deemed the remote past, and therefore involving a certain amount of historical study. *Hope Leslie* is a story of the early days of Massachusetts when the western part was scantily peopled. There are there-

fore plenty of savages, Indians in full warpaint, cruel
in revenge.   But there is also a tender-hearted Indian
maiden who accomplishes the white boy's escape at
great sacrifice to herself.   Here is one of the earliest
pictures of the Noble Red Man — in this case
Maiden.[16]   In this novel, too, is the romantic conversion of a white girl to Indian ways: Hope Leslie's
little sister, captured by Indians, grows up in the
tribe and marries an Indian.   When as a young
woman she is recaptured she pines and frets and finally escapes.   She has forgotten English words and
English ways, and can be happy only by rejoining
her husband in his more primitive community and
his Catholic faith.   In describing customs and backgrounds with some accuracy here as she did also in
A New England Tale wherein the quiet life of a village untouched by industrialism is pictured, Miss
Sedgwick won recognition as a scholar.

A later novel, *Married or Single,* came in 1857,
thirty years after *Hope Leslie.*   Here Miss Sedgwick
defended her own way of life as against " the miserable cant that matrimony is essential to the feebler
sex, — that a woman's life must be useless or undigni-
fied — that she is but an adjunct of man — in her
best estate a helm merely to guide the nobler vessel." [17]
Woman's rights were more articulate in the eighteen-
fifties than ever they had been in the eighteen-thirties.
Men, Miss Sedgwick conceded, were best fitted for
the " great tasks of humanity " yet woman was well

[16] Cooper's Leatherstocking tales began in 1840.
[17] Preface. *Married or Single.* New York. 1822.

able to steer her own course through lesser tasks, among which was charity. There was a place in the home and in the community for a single woman. *Married or Single* was, as the Preface declares, designed expressly to lessen the contempt felt for the " old maid " and to raise single women to their rightful place of respect and dignity. Such a place was always Miss Sedgwick's, either in her own home, or in the homes of her brothers.

Yet in the novel after showing how highly regarded a single woman could be through her services to the community, through her love for her family, Miss Sedgwick neatly marries off her heroine to a highly eligible suitor. Miss Sedgwick was no more of a radical or a propagandist than Mrs. Wheaton herself. That woman's place was the home, that the true sphere for woman's honor and happiness was that of wife and mother was not questioned by the most prominent of single women.

Miss Sedgwick partly by inheritance and partly through her literary efforts, which were extremely popular, achieved a financial independence almost impossible for most women. Then as now the women-folk of the poor worked — in factories, piecework in the home, house-cleaning by the day, needlework. The women of the rich lived in great houses tended by slaves or servants. Neither class was stable, as in England; the rich sometimes dissipated their wealth or lost it through misfortune; the poor sometimes lifted themselves to prosperity. Every day one was aware of the fluid state of a democratic society.

The bulk of the population was the middle class. The Mayflower had brought over no group of aristocrats and no organized group had yet established the social worth of descent. The middle class consisted of those able men and women who worked hard, reverenced success, and believed confidently that America was the golden land of opportunity. Travellers from abroad over and over asserted Jonathan's (Uncle Sam was scarcely heard of) worship of the almighty dollar. Jonathan was a shrewd trader, who counted his pennies and boasted of their rapid accumulation into dollars, yet his true allegiance was not to money; it was to success. Success in a new country often registered itself in dollars; that is, a man was likely to reap large monetary reward from any kind of success. Andrew Jackson was a successful man; it was a matter of course that he was wealthy; yet it was his success not his money that was respected.

The women of the middle class might work hard over home and children, but they were assured of support as long as their husbands lived. Very few American fathers could guarantee their daughters a respectable annuity after their deaths; very few husbands could offer their wives security in widowhood, though life insurance was now established. Brothers might be expected to have families of their own. However much Miss Sedgwick might praise the lot of the single woman, it was noted that she placed her heroine in comfortable circumstances. For most women in the eighteen-thirties, as it is in only a slightly less degree in the nineteen-thirties, marriage

was the chief means of livelihood. Almost any marriage seemed better than being the poor relation helping in the homes of married brothers or sisters.

Benjamin Franklin, with his shrewd common
sense, had reflected on the lot of women as he reflected
upon most of the practical things of life. He noted
that women were not trained to make their own living, yet were often required to do so. Neither single
nor married were they secure from this necessity
which chance might thrust upon them through the
illness or death or misfortune of the men upon whom
they depended for support. Widowed, a woman
more often than not had a brood of children to provide for. Not always were there relatives rich enough
or willing enough to help. Where a widow was left
with funds, she was hardly more fortunate, since her
ignorance of affairs made her easy prey for the un-
scrupulous. Franklin suggested that girls be trained
in accounts, so that if occasion arose they might be
able to handle an income, and manage property. One
of the subjects taught in the first high schools was
bookkeeping.

Because a girl might as maid or widow have to
earn her living, because marriage was less certain
than it had been with the present surplus of females
in the population, because training as a teacher
helped a woman bring up her children — all these
reasons paved the way for the seminaries.

If the seminaries were to succeed they had to emphasize the fact that education did not unfit girls
for matrimony. Sermons, magazine articles, books

poured forth the superior qualities of the educated wife, whose well stored mind kept both herself and her husband from boredom. Even if women had not immortal souls, they needed education for this life's passing and for their sons' training. But it was believed that they did have souls. Then, though they might pass three score years and ten without education, what of eternity? The thought of the æons of eternity with an uncultivated mind, an eternity of boredom, spurred many a young woman to study from dawn to breakfast, from supper to midnight. Hours of severe intellectual toil were self-imposed by these girls to whom education was a privilege. The rapid growth of the seminaries is sufficient proof that women's education was established in the public respect. Fewer and fewer girls from the eighteen-thirties on were to struggle with their books alone, or with the guidance of their brothers at college; more and more they were to attend schools, there gradually to lose that first fine rapture.

The value of education had been definitely proved; most communities used women as teachers at least part of the year, in part of the school system. Some communities boasted of schools like Miss Pierce's, Catharine Beecher's, or Emma Willard's, schools which were considered a credit to the town. When Lafayette visited America in 1824 he naturally went to Albany, the state capital, and quite as naturally from there to Troy to visit the famous Mrs. Willard and her famous school. Lafayette also visited the Adams Female Academy in Londonderry, New

Hampshire. America in the eighteen-twenties was already proud of her advanced schools for young ladies. Here again is proof that the founding of a female seminary was far from rash or radical or new in the eighteen-thirties.

Men may have held up as examples to their wives and daughters these women more or less in the public eye: educators like Mrs. Willard and Miss Beecher, writers like Miss Sedgwick, Mrs. Sigourney, and Mrs. Child. Though Mrs. Child hurt her standing with many of her wide public by her open espousal of the anti-slavery cause, hers was always a name to conjure with. The admiration which men expressed for these women, the manner in which they thronged about them whenever they had the opportunity had more effect upon their womenfolk than multitudinous sermons. If men admired learned women — and all the writing ladies were indisputably admired — then women would endeavor to be learned. However much the shrinking violet may have been extolled, it was the scribbling ladies who were received with adulation on both sides of the Atlantic. It might not be polite for a lady to earn money, but neither educators nor writers lost prestige from their quite obvious financial success. When profit is mixed with fame, it is easily glorified into gentility and pleasantly freed from taint. Men had ceased to admire the fainting female; the intelligent woman appeared.

Public sentiment had developed rapidly since the Revolution. It was in 1803 that Nancy Eaton wrote

from Framingham to the man to whom she was engaged, "Some men desire a slave, some a toy, some
indeed are more rational in their choice, but who but
my lover wishes for a rational companion?" [18]   Joseph
Emerson, to whom this was written, was among the
first earnest partisans of education for women. Falling in love with one of his pupils, he set himself the
task of educating her beyond the bounds usually set,
wishing her to be his intellectual companion, living
with her after their marriage in a boarding house that
she might have the more time to study.

"Euclid is a book not often recommended to females by their lovers," wrote the young minister
when, a new-made widower, he looked back upon his
happy courtship and brief married life.

It was in 1803 that Joseph Emerson began, in his
letters, to set forth those ideas on education, especially education for women, which were to be of permanent influence. Like all very young teachers he
was overcome with the deficiencies of the existing
system. Looking back at his own education he was
appalled at its errors. His teachers had rarely interested him, yet surely it was proper to interest one's
pupils in the subjects presented to them. At Framingham he found that his lessons were truly interesting to the young ladies. He inspired his
pupils to master the material; this was what teaching
should be.

There were in 1803 no journals of education in
whose columns he could publish his reflections upon

[18] Manuscript in Wheaton archives.

schools and methods of teaching; had there been he would still have hesitated. His was the modesty of an age that believed that knowledge preceded method, that one should acquire wisdom before instructing the public. He therefore set to work upon a treatise on education which he hoped to complete " in twenty-five or thirty years."

Though he never himself succeeded in establishing a permanent seminary Joseph Emerson, dying in 1833, left the cause of woman's education much better than he found it, having prepared his pupils to reap the benefits of his thirty years of devoted labor. His greatest work was the training of great teachers, sending them out to fulfil his dreams of endowed seminaries.

" My dear Teacher," Mary Lyon would always say, attributing to him rightly the most progressive ideas of the seminaries, of which he was the true inspiration. In 1803 when he began to voice his views Catharine Beecher was two years old, Mary Lyon five, Emma Willard sixteen. Miss Pierce's school was already in its second decade, but Bradford was not yet open.

His pupils, Mary Lyon and Zilpah Grant, did much to focus attention upon woman's education in Massachusetts. Following his exhortations they pleaded for permanent endowments, adequate equipment, and regular courses of study.

Zilpah Grant became, indeed, an educational oracle. To see her — and Niagara Falls — travellers came to America. It was to her that men, planning

to open new schools, would address their prospectuses [19] asking for advice. When in the eighteen-
sixties Vassar College opened it was one of her Ipswich pupils who was chosen as first lady principal.
To the home of Zilpah Grant (now Mrs. Banister)
came Vassar's president to consult with her about the
choice of a lady principal and to secure her advice on
the plans for the new institution.[20] Within a month
of Vassar's opening Mrs. Banister by special invita-
tion had spent two weeks there, though at this time
visitors were not generally received. An English
traveller, Sophia Jex-Blake, expressed keen disap-
pointment at not being allowed to visit the classes at
Vassar in these early days when it was felt that the
experiment was too new to offer itself for criticism —
save from so competent and trusted an adviser as
Mrs. Banister.

By 1830 Zilpah Grant was already very well known
as a prominent educator. In 1830 there came to her
a most flattering offer from Catharine Beecher, en-
dorsed and strengthened by a plea from her father,
Lyman Beecher, to become the chaplain of the Hartford Female Seminary. Miss Grant refused because
she wished to place Ipswich on a footing equal to that
of Hartford, and because she did not wish to part
with Mary Lyon. There was a further reason: the
Hartford school was an expensive one, attracting girls
who were inclined to be extravagant. Miss Grant

[19] Rich, E. A. *A System of General Education, Designed but not
Exclusively for Females of the Middle and Less Opulent Classes.*
Keene, N. H. April 1835.
[20] Guildford, L. T. *The Use of a Life.* New York. [1885].

reported in a letter to Miss Lyon that "one young
lady there one term last summer" used more than
three hundred dollars "and she was well clothed at
the commencement" of the summer. If this extrava-
gance was characteristic of the school, she alone
could not set what she considered a healthier tone.

Then came an offer from Greenfield. Here was a
town in the western part of Massachusetts dear to
Mary Lyon's heart. She thought Miss Grant might
well consider this offer. Miss Grant investigated, rejecting the offer at once when she learned that French,
music, and oil painting would have to be kept in the
curriculum. "Our past success," she wrote to her
"very dear sister" Mary Lyon, "calls upon us to show
the world what can be done on our plan, and we must
not sacrifice it for a handsome house or for conven-
iences." Both Miss Grant and Miss Lyon felt that
a school which taught the "ornamental branches"
would permit pupils to hide behind them and escape
the solid work which constituted true education.
Also they felt that the charges at these other schools
were too high. The usual price of tuition was ten
dollars a term, two terms in the year, with extra fees
for French, Latin, music, drawing. Sometimes a
school mapped out a simple course which was included in the term fee, all other subjects — of which
there were always legion — being extra. Board varied from one dollar and sixty-seven and a half cents
a week, to two dollars and a half. Sometimes washing
and fuel were included, sometimes charged as an
extra.

What Miss Grant and Miss Lyon were trying to do
at Ipswich, where Miss Grant in 1830 definitely decided to remain, was to have a boarding house large
enough to accommodate all the pupils. At first the
pupils had boarded around; then Miss Grant had
gathered a group in a house with her. The house was
neither large enough, nor near enough to the recitation building to be satisfactory. Nor was there a
settled endowment for either building so that their
permanence could be assured. Miss Grant believed
that Mary Lyon agreed with her in placing this first;
and in planning upon a mixed group of girls, those
from the middle class, and those from the richer
group. Though the expenses should be less than at
Hartford, perhaps less than those at any other good
school then in existence, this matter of low cost was
not " a very prominent object."

It was in 1831 that the two women presented a joint
letter to the trustees of Ipswich Female Academy,
asking for a new building, with a hall large enough
to accommodate one hundred and seventy-five pupils,
with recitation rooms, laboratory, and library, as well
as a boarding-home for one hundred and fifty young
ladies, surrounded by acres of playground. Their
request stated that they desired quarters that would
compare favorably with those of young men at college.

Finding the trustees slow to yield to persuasion,
they in 1832 interested themselves in writing out a
prospectus for a new institution, location unknown,
though it should be " central for New England," " a
liberal proportion of the funds " to be raised by the

town and its vicinity.   It should be in the country.
Ignoring Albany and Troy, Bradford, Abbot, Adams,
and Hartford, the prospectus declared that there were
no permanent female seminaries.   It is true that these
schools did not have all the equipment now demanded, nor so large an endowment.

It was doubtless because of this agitation that the
Wheatons turned to Miss Lyon to help them launch
their project.   Miss Lyon by 1834 had announced to
the saddened Zilpah Grant her intention of severing
their companionship to launch the new project herself.   To the plan as drawn up under Miss Grant's
leadership, Mary Lyon had added her scheme of truly
low tuition, one dollar and sixty cents a week which
would include not only board, room, fuel, but also
tuition; that is, for a fee lower than the lowest charge
for board alone, she was offering everything.   To
make this low cost possible, she relied upon the hope
of securing a large endowment — sixty thousand dollars — upon the payment of very small salaries to
teachers, and upon the performance of all the household tasks by the students themselves.

In this she differed sharply from other women
leaders, as she did also in the aims of her school.   All
advanced schools maintained a class for those who
either had taught already or were planning to teach.
This, however, was less a main project with them
than it was to be with Mary Lyon.   And whereas in
the beginnings of missionary zeal, all schools were
proud if they counted among their alumnae one who
went out into pagan lands as a missionary — or even

among the Indians in America — few emphasized
the calling of missionary as the very highest.

Bradford Academy was proud of the two young
women who had gone to India as missionaries in 1812,
one to die within the year, the other to return for a
visit in ten years, waking in youthful hearts a strong
desire for similar self-sacrifice. Parents of daughters,
however, were less anxious than romantic young
girls to have the missionary calling emphasized.

Girls might properly be prepared for teaching,
since this was a training that would not be wasted.
Teachers constantly married — and the most important teaching a woman could do was within the
family. Always the final argument for woman's education was the obvious fact that a mother had the control of children during their first formative years.
With its love for children America wished to provide
them with the best of schools, the best of mothers.
Remembering how he learned his lessons at his
mother's knee, many a man waxed sentimental though
none in the eighteen-thirties could have foreseen a
Mother's Day stamp.

No one yet crooned "A man's best friend is his
mother," but many a man in public life asseverated
that history could show no example of a great man
who did not have a wise mother. So ministers
preached. So Bronson Alcott, never suspecting that
his final fame would be that of father to a famous
daughter, confided to his diary: "Wrote to my
mother. Kind and benignant spirit! how much I owe
thee for all thy influence during the years of infancy

and childhood! How mildly didst thou guide the young current of my feelings, and fill my heart with the sympathies of thy own bosom, pure and generous amid the forms of selfishness and apathy around thee! " [21] Benignant and mild, these mothers of the early nineteenth century were the true pioneers of woman's education. Through their forbearance and sympathy, their patience and their understanding, they won the love of their children, so that their sons, sentimentalizing in middle age, were wont to attribute to the feminine influence all that they valued in life.

The American mother lived close to her children. The American mother needed education if she was to guide their first steps in learning, if she was to give them the aid and encouragement they needed as they climbed the steep steps of knowledge. All women were teachers, so it was declared, first by their very natures, and second by their noblest occupation, that of motherhood.

So when Wheaton opened its doors in 1835 it found the world ready to receive its existence as calmly as Mrs. Wheaton with her reticence could have wished. Advertisement had been made quietly. This was a school already provided for by an initial gift which was to be swiftly augmented. Judge Wheaton planned on an income from endowment of four thousand dollars a year. The 1837 act of incorporation names ten thousand in real estate, ten thousand in

[21] Sanborn, F. S. and Harris, W. T. *A. Bronson Alcott, His Life and Philosophy.* Boston. 1893.

personal estate; by an act of 1839 the real estate is valued at twenty thousand and the personal at another twenty thousand, in addition to the initial gifts. Adams Academy had been founded with four thousand dollars, Abbot with an original thousand followed by ten thousand at Mrs. Abbot's death.

It was in 1819 that Emma Willard had vocalized the demand for endowments for girls' schools. Her *Plan for Improving Female Education* was addressed to the New York Legislature, asking for an appropriation. Such appropriations were made to boys' educational institutions. To public men, to the Governor of the state, to legislative bodies, state and national, to the President of the United States she made her plea. Governor Clinton voiced his approval, but though the matter came up for consideration, no grant was made.[22] Instead of a state grant she received an offer from the city of Troy. Troy in 1821 was a city on the make. With five thousand inhabitants and numerous thriving manufacturing establishments, it felt that it could afford this advertisement — any woman who could thus gain the public attention for a project to educate girls was worth having, along with her latest modern improvement in education. By a special tax Troy raised four thousand dollars to buy and remodel a building — though it was necessary to add to this sum by private subscription. These sums contributed by a grateful

[22] The Legislature did put Mrs. Willard's Waterford Academy on the list of schools, otherwise all boys' schools, benefited by the State's "literary fund." In 1837 Troy Female Seminary received a portion of this fund.

city were nothing like so large as those contributed by Judge Wheaton, or raised by Mary Lyon's house to house campaign. Yet it was an endowment. And Mrs. Willard, a woman in the early thirties, had made the first effective appeal to the public, an appeal which was fortified eight years later in 1827 by that of Catharine Beecher, herself already a prominent educator who had for four years run a school in Hartford, Connecticut, " for those who wish to pursue the higher branches." Miss Beecher at the start emphasized regular attendance, entry at the beginning of a term, a regular course of study. The *American Journal of Education* not only published her pleas to the public but praised her school in 1827 as " one of the most liberal arrangements for the education of females " ever attempted.

Mrs. Willard's life [23] reads not unlike a modern success story. At seventeen she was teaching primary school; at eighteen she studied winters, and in summer conducted her own school for older boys and girls in her father's home. By the time she was twenty she was flattered by being given the unusual responsibility of a winter term — she had charge of the female department of a co-educational school. At twenty-two she retired to become the wife of a teacher; John Willard was connected with Middlebury College, a man much older than this second wife, and a man of wealth. The following year a son was born. Three years after the marriage Mr. Willard

[23] Lord, J. *Life of Emma Willard.* New York. 1873. And Lutz, A. *Emma Willard.* Boston. 1929.

suffered severe financial reverses. Mrs. Willard, eager to help, turned to teaching. She opened a school in her own home, calling it Middlebury Female Seminary. This was in 1814, the year in which an academy was started in Albany, New York, an academy which was perhaps the inspiration for the generosity of the citizens of Troy a few years later. Troy, near enough to Albany to be aware of the academy's success, sought to rival its fame with Troy Female Academy under Emma Willard.

Mrs. Willard was no longer teaching, as she had before marriage, with a feeling of impermanence. With a husband much older than she, she had every reason to believe that both must look to the school for their main source of income. Since the school would be permanent, she set about making plans to improve it. Her *Plan* came as the fruit of five years' experience. Though the legislature would not pass an appropriation, the *Plan* brought favorable publicity with the result that Waterford, New York, asked her to move her school there. This she did in 1819, confident that the state would soon make her an appropriation, since there was much public sentiment in her favor. There was of course much opposition to this education of females, and all the stock arguments of its unfeminine tendencies were dragged out of the mental ragbags, culminating in a disgusted farmer's, " They'll be educating the cows next! "

The opinions of farmers were, however, less influential than the opinions of ministers, who were for the most part enthusiastic supporters of woman's education, of governors like De Witt Clinton, of distinguished visitors like Lafayette.

Mrs. Willard was a woman of the world. Men liked her; they liked to talk with her; they appreciated the vigor of her mind, the clarity and intelligence of her speech, the reasonableness and logic of her demands. She was an " elegant female," presenting a distinguished figure. Her interests were wide, confining themselves not at all to the advancement of her academy or the cause of female education. She went through the world in a large way, not absorbed in any one interest, but intelligently concerned in world affairs. It was fitting that Lafayette should entertain her at a *soirée* in 1830, that she should be received at the French court in 1831. Such honors came naturally to her. Zilpah Grant, Mary Lyon, Catharine Beecher were inspired school-teachers. They were not concerned as was Mrs. Willard, as early as 1820, in the cause of universal peace. Mrs. Willard published a plan, to be enlarged and republished forty-four years later, suggesting a league of nations.

It is interesting that the woman who has followed most closely in Emma Willard's footsteps should be the successor of Mary Lyon, President Mary E. Woolley of Mount Holyoke College. Mary Lyon holds a place in the public mind to-day partly because the college which grew out of her seminary found a leader in Miss Woolley who, though deeply interested in the missionary field, has far wider and broader sympathies.

Yet Mary Lyon deserves to be remembered because, though she was not early in the field, opening her seminary in 1837, one year before Emma Willard retired from her well-established and famous seminary, two years after the opening of Wheaton, she belonged to the unforgettable race of reformers who, not by sweet reasonableness, not by patient waiting, but by force of personality, by monotonous insistence, by passionate exaggeration, always have made and always will make the world listen.   Mary Lyon made people believe, as reformers must, that she was an innovator; that her seminary must be founded in order to save women from ignorance.   She was not afraid of risking her personal dignity; she was not inhibited by having been brought up a " lady " who must escape notice or lose caste.   Metaphorically at least she plastered the landscape with billboards; she made every place into which she set foot " education conscious."   She was a missionary, working with the zeal which knows only one path.   Single-track minds arrive because they never see by-paths.

It is right that the world should remember Mary Lyon, then, rather than Mrs. Wheaton.   Mrs. Wheaton was disinterested; she was moving quietly in an already established orbit.   Even though Mary Lyon's direction was mainly the same, she believed that she was charting the unknown.

Yet of the female schools established before Mount Holyoke many remain, among them preparatory schools and junior colleges such as Abbot and Bradford in Massachusetts; Albany and Emma Willard in New York; and Wheaton College.

The young ladies of the eighteen-thirties had a joy which their nineteen-thirty descendants can presumably never know; they had the supreme joy of knowing what education was for; they knew exactly what preparation for life meant.   Here was the map of knowledge, with the lanes of travel carefully charted.   Along these lanes leading to the professions went some of their brothers; it might be that occasionally one of themselves might go along as companion, not with the intention of actually guiding the vessel into port, but as a sustaining complementary spirit, one ready and willing to take the helm, under sympathetic direction, in order that the master hand might rest. For most of their brothers this was not the way. There were other lanes of travel which led not to the ministry, law, or medicine, but to other arts and skills, which were not for feminine hands.   Yet there were broad lanes leading to secure ports which both brothers and sisters might travel side by side.

The aim of education was to discipline the mind. The most sternly disciplined mind must be that of the professional man, especially the minister who must guide not only his own family but his parishioners.   For him, then, large measures of Greek and Latin and Hebrew along with mathematics; for his professional fellow citizens, the lawyers and doctors, the same rigorous training, minus the Hebrew.

For other citizens, the routine might be more varied, but there must be rigid training, a course of study that would discipline the mind never so well as with Greek and after Greek, Latin; but as well as mathematics, modern languages, philosophy (science) and theology for the layman could.

If any one needed a well disciplined mind it was a mother. She more than teacher, male or female, needed a mind trained to deal with problems of morals and of wisdom. If her children were to respect her she must be able to answer their why's with intelligent instruction. It was she who would guide their infant steps toward knowledge, who would influence throughout their lives the daughters who would be the mothers of the future — a never-ending cycle while the world should last — and the son who might well be the future president of the United States.

CHAPTER III

THE RELIGIOUS BASIS OF AMERICAN LIFE

IN this age of the world, distinguished by what
some men, in ridicule, and others in seriousness,
term the 'march of mind'" — so reads the *Journal
of the Proceedings of a Convention of Literary and
Scientific Gentlemen, Held in the Common Council
Chamber of the City of New York, October, 1830.*

The march of mind — a true description of the
widespread interest in education. With pride born
of the Revolution and of the war of 1812, the American eagle opened its mouth for a heartening scream.
No longer would the country look to gentlemen of
the English stamp to lead the country; Washing-
tonian republicanism yielded to Jacksonian democracy. Not British customs, but American customs;
not British education, but American education. New
occasions taught new duties; a new people needed a
new education.

In England a tinsmith's son as like as not became
a tinsmith, his daughter married a tinsmith or a
laborer no higher in the social scale than her father.
In America classes were not hard and fast; any man's
son might become a gentleman; it was the duty of his
father, of his town, or of his state to see that he was
given the opportunity to rise in the world. That
opportunity, it was stoutly believed, came through

education. And because education was the firmest rung on the ladder of success, or at least of public honor, education came to have a cachet of its own. Education for leadership had been established early in the days of the colonies, when Boston men founded Harvard as a training school for ministers, the rulers of the time. Learning and authority were one.

Whereas the country elected Andrew Jackson president, it was something of a shock to have Harvard, the aristocrat of the colleges, bestow an LL.D. upon Jackson in 1834. College degrees were held in such reverence that the newspapers frothed with scorn at the " Cambridge nursery " for its " puerile proceedings." The *Boston Post* knew, if the President and Fellows of Harvard did not, that Andrew Jackson was not a learned man. Yet he ought, by right of authority, to be learned.

This reverence for learning, this belief in the learned man as the proper guide for the country, was responsible for the "march of mind." It was responsible, too, for the extension of educational privileges to women.

" My fingers," says Elizabeth Bennet in *Pride and Prejudice,* " do not move over this instrument in the masterly manner which I see so many women's do. They have not the same force or rapidity, and do not produce the same expression. But then I have always supposed it to be my own fault — because I would not take the trouble of practising. It is not that I do not believe *my* fingers as capable as any other woman's of superior execution." Thousands of music

teachers have been saved from the lists of the unemployed by just such faith on the part of daughters
and parents. Thousands of students knock at the
gates of the colleges to-day with the same conviction.
" Not college material " is a phrase which all parents
believe to be dictated by prejudice.

The eighteen-thirties were confident that all boys
and girls were capable of absorbing education, and
were concerned only with the best means of giving
it to them. The faith in education was second only
to the faith in religion. To understand the wave of
expanding intellectualism, the rising tide of school
attendance, it is necessary to understand the religious
temper of the people of the United States, their historical and emotional backgrounds.

The men of Marblehead, in the seventeenth century, may have insisted that they came to America to
catch fish, not to glorify God, but the men of Marblehead were of small importance beside the men of
Boston and Plymouth. The men of Boston and
Plymouth, however much they may have been influenced by economic motives, were sure of their purpose, to establish a Godly country wherefrom the
Devil, hoof, tail, and claws, especially as represented
by his children, the Indians, should be effectively
repulsed.

By the eighteen-thirties the Devil's children were
sufficiently checked, corralled on Reservations; but
though bereft of his human allies, the Devil was not
yet without power. He lurked unseen tempting the
children of men to disbelief and sin. The temper of

the times was still profoundly religious, and to religious men belief in the Devil was as essential as
belief in God.   No longer, however, was suffrage
dependent upon church membership nor church
membership upon a public declaration of faith, as
had been the case in the early days of Massachusetts.
By 1834 the citizens of Massachusetts were further
relieved of the obligation to contribute support to
some sect or church.

Yet man's relationship to God remained his funda-
mental problem.   Humanitarianism was only just
beginning to gather force, humanitarianism which,
by turning man's attention to his relationships with
his fellow man, came to obscure his relationship to
God.   In becoming his brother's keeper under nineteenth century humanitarianism man tended to forget that this brotherhood had originally depended
upon their common Father.

The sermons of the eighteen-thirties still offered
religion as man's relationship to God.   The pictures
of the corruption of man were somewhat less vivid
than those of the seventeenth century, but they did
not yet look forward to the twentieth century sermons
on the New Deal, or Harvard's refusal of a Nazi gift.
If they dealt with the topics of the day they were sure
to search for support in the testimony of the Bible.
Man was the son of God, not of the latest psychologi-
cal theory or the most recent sociological data.

And evil was very real.   In the twelfth book of
Paradise Lost Milton had the angel present to Adam
the foreshadowing of the future in concrete scenes of

evil. The good he left to Adam's imagination. Horace Mann, just beginning his career as an educator in the eighteen-thirties, was soon to question this emphasis upon evil. He voiced a strong protest against a popular book, John Abbot's *Child at Home,* because it stressed sin and punishment and hell. Brought up a Calvinist, Horace Mann fought long for tolerance, against the Calvinistic willingness " to be damned for the glory of God."

New England, at least, had not yet turned away from Puritanism. Children were still treated to concrete pictures of the Devil and of evil, though they were not constantly reminded, as they had been in the early days of Massachusetts, that at every moment they were on the threshold of death, and must be therefore prepared to meet judgment.

Even Bronson Alcott, that gentlest of educators, whom his wife pictured as " blushing into obscurity " stressed evil for his young pupils in Boston. Elizabeth Peabody, his assistant teacher, protested, urging that good, not evil, be made concrete. Such a book as he had recently bought and taken into the schoolroom she considered " a direful abortion of the imagination." This was a work translated from the German version of a French original under the somewhat forbidding title: *The Spiritual Mirror or Looking-Glass; Exhibiting the Human Heart as Being Either the Temple of God, or Habitation of Devils.*[1]

Such meretricious books gained ground because daily life was still woven on the thread of religion.

[1] Newburyport, published by Chas. Whipple, 1830.

Family prayers, grace at table, church attendance were a matter of course. Visitors from England were at first somewhat taken back by the custom of grace, even at a public dining room. At the inns at which travellers stopped either for the night or for a transient meal, all travellers sat at a common board at which grace was said; the procedure was so universal that no one but a foreigner remarked upon it. The Bible, as well as daily prayers, was as necessary a part of the routine of living as food. Chapel at least once a day — at Harvard it was at dawn and again at five o'clock in the afternoon — praying closets and quiet half-hours for religious meditation, were a commonplace at schools and colleges for many decades to come.

It was as natural in the eighteen-thirties to think and talk about one's soul as it is to-day to think and talk about one's automobile or golf game. It is a modern mistake to regard the men and women of the eighteen-thirties as religious fanatics. Religious exercises were part of the daily routine, pious expressions the current vocabulary. Letters to husbands, to wives, to parents, to friends, closed normally with the earnest wish that God would guard the absent one. Religion, travellers from abroad concluded after a period of bewilderment, was a habit of mind with Americans; it was, some felt, a diversion, the caviare, Marryat declared, to whet the American appetite for living. Where the Englishman would discuss his hunting, the American would prefer to discuss his soul.

The soul was, indeed, a respectable subject for conversation — not that the American did not have his frivolous moments. Theaters prospered in Boston as well as in New York; lecturers drew large crowds in any city when they announced their subject as " Love and Marriage ";[2] the Siamese twins were viewed by all the curious;[2] and Barnum was about to start his long and prosperous career built upon the idle curiosity of gullible Americans. Newspapers were filled with jokes — frequently lifted bodily from English papers, but often home-made. A poor negro arrested in Boston would be referred to as " an oak colored nigger," a poor bedraggled woman of the streets as a follower of " night errantry." [2] The English papers had for some time reported police court news facetiously; American papers, now in the eighteen-thirties often of the penny variety, copied first the actual items, and later merely the English manner. With the growth of cheap journals came the purveying of sensational news, including murder cases in which public sentiment sometimes tended to make a hero of the criminal.

Schoolbooks preferred to make heroes of little boys who gave up their hours of play to instruct other less fortunate boys in reading and writing. Such tales had a double morality: they taught the child who could read them to value his school privileges, besides awakening his benevolent impulses; and impressed upon his parents to whom he might communicate the tale if they did not listen to his reading of it, the de-

[2] Current newspapers.

plorable fact that there were still children for whom free education was not provided.

Schoolbooks also reminded children that they possessed souls. *The Child's Book on the Soul*[3] went into seven editions its first decade. *A Third Class Reader*[4] first published in 1834 informed young children: "Every person has a body and a soul. . . . The soul cannot be seen, because it is a spirit. To die is to have the soul leave the body. . . . When the soul leaves the body, the body loses its life, it is a dead corpse; it is buried, its flesh turns to corruption, and its bones moulder away, till there is none of the body to be seen, but the soul still lives; so that there is not an end of us when we die; the better part remains alive."

Even the nonsensational newspapers kept sin before their public, mindful of its effect upon the circulation. More than half a respectable newspaper's four sheets were devoted to advertisements, nearly a quarter to the doings of Congress, but there was still space to be filled in with police court news. The American readers, no less than their English cousins, liked to read of the doings of sinful folk.

No sympathy was expressed for these vagrants; their scanty attire, their sleeping in barrels, their homeless and foodless days offered the pen of the reporter subject for mirth. Occasionally a judge seems

[3] Gallaudet, Thomas. *The Child's Book on the Soul.* 7th edition. 1847.

[4] Emerson, B. D., Late Principal of the Adams Grammar School, Boston. *The Third-Class Reader Designed for the Use of the Younger Classes in the Schools of the United States.* Claremont, N. H. 1847.

to have had humane impulses. There was the case
of the ten year old boy brought in to court by his
mother as a "stubborn and disobedient" child.
Pressed for detail she could only reiterate that he
played truant from school. Perhaps in memory of
his own schoolboy fishing and nutting expeditions,
the judge reproved the mother and remanded the boy
in her care. In self-justification the mother stated
that she had acted under the advice of a deacon of her
church in bringing the boy to court. The judge gave
vent to scorn of a church member, a deacon, a man
of religion, who could thus forget the best interests
of a fatherless boy and wish him sent to a place where
he would consort with thieves and criminals.[5]

Such a reproof, with the emphasis upon the social
responsibility of a deacon, was more characteristic
than the ribald mirth over wrongdoing, the sentimentalizing over murders, murders which were not
reported in anything but the less reputable newspapers. The modern idea of newsgathering was in
its infancy; newspapers purveyed for the most part
political news and advertisements, with odd spaces
occupied with mild jokes and insipid anecdotes, with
death notices, and accounts of misfortunes: a skater
fallen through the ice, a rider thrown from his horse,
a child burned. There was a lamentable occurrence:
a young lady driving alone with a young man was
thrown out when the sleigh overturned, being killed
by her fall upon the ice. "It is understood, however,
that she was engaged to the young man." No other

[5] *Boston Post.* January 13, 1834, and following issues.

comment, beyond the implications of the " however," was made upon the absence of the chaperone whose presence was assumed by fashion.

Sober reporting was to lose ground steadily. It was in the very spring that Wheaton opened that James Gordon Bennett launched the *New York Herald.*[6] His aim was not merely to amuse, but to instruct by giving " a true picture of the world." That the picture was not always rosy testified to its truth; vice existed in the world and his was the task to present it morally. The way to virtue lies through vice. Bennett declared that he had seen " human depravity to the core "; that " Born in the midst of the strictest morality — educated in the principles of the highest integrity, naturally inclined from the first impulses of existence to be a believer in human virtue, I have grown up in the world holding fast, with a death grasp, on the original elements of my soul." [7]

In performing his " sacred and solemn duty " [8] to society Bennett resisted the attempt of his compositors to force him into paying higher wages by a strike instigated by his " enemies." Calling upon " every honest man and every pretty woman " [9] to help him he announced his " great movement of social reform. . . . I shall be ready with my moral and intellectual machines to reanimate the public mind — purify the public heart — and reform the corruptions of the age. Religion, politics, trade, fashion, manners, morals, — all want a renovation."

This was but a reiteration of a pronouncement two

6 Vol. I. no. 1. Wednesday, May 5, 1835.
7 July 27, 1836.   8 July 28, 1836.   9 July 22, 1836.

days earlier: "Neither man or devil — thousands of them — [10] can intimidate the editor of the Herald. I feel that the God of Jacob is with me. I can be assassinated but I cannot be frightened. . . . I go for a general reformation of morals — of manners. I mean to begin a new movement in the progress of civilization and human intellect. I know and feel I shall succeed. Nothing can prevent its success but God Almighty, and he happens to be entirely on my side. . . . I am the Voice of ONE crying in the wilderness, prepare ye the way of the Lord, and make his path straight."

Bennett was astute enough not to waste his thunder in daily tirades. Carefully spacing his pious editorials, spicing them with humorous appeals to the ladies ever "lovely and adorable," reminding them that "every great reform has been first patronized by the ladies," he led his readers through the heats and storms of midsummer to the climax of an August editorial: [11] "I am determined to make the Herald the greatest paper that ever appeared in the world . . . the greatest organ of social life. Books have had their day — the theatres have had their day — the temple of religion has had its day. A newspaper can be made to take the lead of all these in the great movement of human thought and of human civilization. A newspaper can send more souls to Heaven, and save more from Hell, than all the churches or chapels in New York — besides making money at the same time." Lest the fervor of this be lost, he re-

[10] Probably also a pun on printers' devils.
[11] August 17, 1836.

inserted the whole next day, along with the announcement of the increased price of his paper, now two
cents instead of a single penny.   Proud of himself he
boasted a week later: " I am the only philosopher
from the time of Socrates to the present day that ever
knew how to take care of himself," a skill for which
he believed himself indebted to the " rogueries of
Vice President Van Buren and the Kitchen Cabinet.
He who can come through the Kitchen and Regency
with morals untouched can beat the Devil."

When all the bombast is sifted there remains the
conviction that Bennett knew his public, knew that
his audience of the eighteen-thirties believed in their
souls, were willing to talk about them, and wanted to
believe them saved.   He knew — none better — that
the public was genuinely pious; that by training and
inheritance they believed themselves Godly in New
York as well as in New England; that pious words
were the most generally accepted idiom of speech;
and that however much people enjoyed scandal, they
liked to think that in reading of sin they were being
not debased but elevated.

The discussion of evil came legitimately from the
Puritans who had ever contemplated sin as a warning.
Their earliest textbook, the *New England Primer*
started little children of two on the alphabet with

> In Adam's fall
> We sinnèd all.

The modern discussion of the moral or immoral influence of the films is not at all unlike the earlier
emphasis upon textbooks as moral influences.   The

Puritan ideal that the child should grow in goodness as he grew in knowledge was still considered
sound in the eighteen-thirties. Knowledge was not an
end in itself; unless it made children better as it made
them wiser it was of no avail in a life which was but
the stepping-stone to the life of eternity. No one in
the eighteen-thirties was repeating seventeenth century Massachusetts' belief that the chief reason for
learning to read was to read the Bible, though it is
safe to assert that no one of the people who achieved
prominence or whose influence was of any lasting
quality was without a thorough knowledge of the
Bible, a knowledge that included the ability to quote
freely, and a faith that made evidence from the Bible
the final argument in dispute.

President Andrew Jackson was a pious man, as his
own words testify. Toward the close of his second
term, he said to a New York minister, " Yes, my wife
was a pious Christian woman. She gave me the best
advice, and I have not been unmindful of it. When
the people in their sovereign pleasure elected me as
President of the United States, she said to me, ' Don't
let your opportunity turn your head away from the
duty you owe to God. Before Him we are all alike
sinners, and to Him we must all alike give account.
All these things will pass away, and you and I, and all
of us must stand before God.' " [12]

Jackson's last dying words to his adopted son and
to the servants gathered about his bed were: " Oh, do
not cry. Be good children and we will all meet in
heaven."

[12] Brady, C. T. *The True Andrew Jackson.* Philadelphia. 1906.

Jackson thus showed himself not to be unusually pious, but a man whose thoughts ran as did those of the men of his times; it was current speech to refer to one's relationship to God. Jackson was no more sanctimonious than Sir Walter Scott who died in Scotland in 1832 saying to his devoted son-in-law: " My dear, be a good man — be virtuous — be religious — be a good man. Nothing else will give you any comfort when you come to lie here." [13]

Knowledge of the Bible was quite naturally the background of all education in America, a country whose influential founders had sought a haven for their church. In the eighteen-thirties the Bible, interpreted in the traditional manner, remained the final arbiter of all conduct, the basis of all thinking. The study of science which had grown with rapidity had only increased man's reverence. Scientific textbooks ended on a religious note: " But remember that, in order that the study of nature may be productive of happiness, it must lead to an entire confidence in the wisdom and goodness of its bounteous Author." [14]

And the *Library of Useful Knowledge,* an enormously popular set of books though a highly technical five foot shelf, closes the introductory chapter of Volume I, which is devoted to physics, " The highest of all our gratifications in the contemplations of science remains: we are raised by them to an un-

[13] Lockhart, J. G. *Life of Sir Walter Scott.*
[14] Blake, Rev. J. L., Rector of St. Matthew's Church and Principal of a Literary Seminary, Boston, Mass. *Conversations on Natural Philosophy . . . Adapted to the Comprehension of Young Pupils.* 8th edition 1827 (first edition 1824).

derstanding of the infinite wisdom and goodness which the Creator has displayed in his works . . . we can feel no hesitation in concluding that, if we knew the whole scheme of Providence, every part would be found in harmony with a plan of absolute benevolence." [15]

It was not at all incongruous for the instructors of Oberlin to begin each recitation with prayer, invoking God before the production of sulphuric acid or the demonstration of parallel lines to infinity. " Divine Providence " and " the great Author of Nature," the " Great Architect of Nature " were never more close to man than when he embarked on a voyage of discovery in any of the newly developed sciences. The very workings of man's mind were marvelous proof of the power and the presence of God.

Quite naturally, then, the backbone of scientific education in the colleges, in the academies and seminaries, was in such books as Butler's *Analogy* and the various *Evidences of Christianity* of which Paley's was the most popular, Alexander's running a close second with Blake's for less ambitious schools. One does not look in vain for Butler in the curriculum of any of the reputable schools or colleges of the eighteen-thirties. Girls at Wheaton and Troy and Hartford, boys at Yale and Harvard and Dartmouth bent over the thick pages of Butler, learning that doubt ought to be non-existent since the truths of Christianity were manifestly proved in Nature.

In the eighteen-thirties the study of *Evidences of*

[15] *Library of Useful Knowledge.* London. 1829.

Christianity was a necessity, to support a firm faith that was facing challenges on all sides. In New England Congregationalism had not held undisputed sway for any very long period of time. As the colonies prospered England became increasingly aware that they had been founded with British money. Massachusetts, regarding itself as an independent adjunct, ruled itself to its own satisfaction without regard to the mother country. England remedied this state of affairs by sending over a royal governor. Naturally she chose no dissenter, but a good Church of England lord; and naturally enough, he wished to attend the services of his own faith. A Congregational church had to lend itself to Episcopalian services, and soon a new church was built for his lordship. The defection of Congregationalists was never dangerously large, yet there was a desire on the part of many a good colonist — and his lady — to be on the governor's visiting list. The colonies were not then looking forward to independence, and " my lord " and " my lady " went trippingly on some tongues.

So Episcopalianism was established. And before long a liberal party developed in the Congregational church, and set up for itself. By the eighteen-thirties there were numerous sects in America, with Unitarianism capturing the very stronghold of Congregationalism. Both Congregationalists and Presbyterians were horrified at the doctrines of the newer sects, Unitarianism and Universalism. These heresies were rejecting the sure truth of the doctrine of original sin, the Universalists shouting aloud their erroneous belief by their very name. Surely they were damned who proclaimed universal salvation, that young and old, sinner and saint, even the unbaptised infant would all ultimately be saved, receiving grace and standing on the right hand of God in eternal life.

Very nearly all the Congregational churches of Boston had turned Unitarian; Harvard, founded to educate for the Congregational ministry, had long since deserted to the Unitarian standard. Love to God and love to man summed up the new definition of practical religion, one which could not be acceptable to those of the older faith.

For the very reason that they were themselves tortured with fears of their damnation, the Congregationalists and the Presbyterians were devastatingly afraid of a doctrine of universal salvation. The record of tortured souls is too constant to be ignored, especially in the case of young women.

Nancy Eaton,[16] writing in 1803, in the happiest months of her life when she was looking forward to marriage with a man she respected highly and loved deeply, recorded her trembling fears lest she be damned; how can she, sinner that she is, hope for grace? Yet by her own hand there exists the record of her busy days, filled with household tasks, with the teaching of the younger children of the family, with church going and pious reading, beside the studying of geography and geometry undertaken to improve her mind, please her " dearest friend," and

[16] Wheaton archives.

make her a more worthy companion for him. She refrained from dancing, feeling no envy for her sisters who might indulge in frivolities, not being engaged to ministers. She went to church, to funerals, to ordinations; she read sermons by the most eminent clergymen of England and America; she prayed fervently. Yet was she overcome by fear, that had the quality of nightmare. Her sleep interfered with, her appetite vanished, her health injured, she longed for relief but could not seek it through the local clergyman who did not encourage serious conversation from young ladies. Frivolous, Nancy labelled him, and altogether uninterested in the state of her soul. A man well on in years, held in the highest respect by his congregation and the community,[17] he may well have been one of those advanced thinkers who questioned the value of introspection of this sort. He may have felt that it was much better for a young woman of twenty-three to discuss with her pastor the coming Sunday School picnic, or the rapid growth of her young brothers and sisters, or the flowers in her garden, or the plans for her approaching marriage, all healthier subjects than worry over her soul's salvation.

Yet this worry was very real, and there were then no psychiatrists. Fortunately young ladies grew up and married and had their attention diverted to child-raising. Or else they took to school-teaching, or charity, or missionary work, and morbidity vanished in thin air. Sometimes, however, they lost their

17 Barry, W. *A History of Framingham.* Boston. 1847.

minds, though rarely.   More often when relief did
not come a girl would lose her health, sinking into
the fashionable disease called a decline.

Nor were young men exempt.   They, too, suffered
deeply, especially after rousing revivals, of which
there was an outburst in the eighteen-thirties.   At all
the colleges, Unitarian Harvard excepted, revivals
were encouraged, and many a student recorded in
letters and diary his fears for the next life, which is
forever.   The Unitarians were not friendly to revivals but unfortunately the Unitarians did not establish the girls' schools.

Eager, earnest, hard-striving, conscientious young
women like Zilpah Grant and Mary Lyon in their
youth went through the deepest despondency, utterly
overcome by their own worthlessness, their inability
to acquire grace and rise to eternal life.   Elizabeth
Cady [18] (later Mrs. Stanton) having been balked of
her desire to go to Union College with her brothers,
entered Emma Willard's school in Troy at a time
when revivals were at their height.   So melancholy
did she become, so fearful for her soul, that she seemed
to be sinking fast into the dreaded incurable decline.
Waking her father in the middle of the night, she
implored him to pray for her.   Mr. Cady's common
sense was as ample as his purse.   He sent his daughter
packing to Niagara Falls on a pleasure trip, counter-
acting the agonies of doubt with the wonders of
Nature.

Toward the close of her life Angelina Grimke

[18] Stanton, E. C. *Eighty Years and More.* New York. 1898.

Weld looked back upon her youth earlier in the century, remembering vividly the terror of mind fostered in her by religion. When she left her southern home, she followed her older sister into the fold of the Friends, but the Quaker faith was no gentler than that in which she had been brought up. Life had offered her few gifts more valuable, she felt, than the lightening of the stern old beliefs, the relief from the fear of damnation.[19]

So editors of magazines sometimes spoke out in favor of the milder forms of religion, though they published strong articles pointing out the dangers of the spread of atheism. But life was steadily growing easier, under the new inventions, the new industrialism, the new means of transport, the new prosperity. It is harder for a people living in material comfort to believe in damnation than for a group of pioneers threatened with dangers. The revivalists attempted to keep alive these fears, lest worse befall; they were particularly anxious about young people in schools, lest in their zeal for learning they forget to allot a portion of time for God. There was a genuine fear that teachers in developing the minds of their pupils might forget their immortal souls. It was for the good of the pupil that the teacher's piety was an essential qualification.

To read in a schoolgirl's diary [20] that she went to a funeral on Sunday afternoon, there being no church service, has an odd sound to twentieth century ears.

19 Newspaper interview, lent by Mrs. Weld.
20 Wheaton archives.

Yet for these young people who felt acutely that the fate of their souls hung in the balance, every moment of Sunday was precious.[21] The Sabbaths which we are inclined to look back upon as blank, dreary stretches of sermonizing, were to them blessed days retrieved from weekday labor for the employment of the soul. To secure salvation, to gain a hope of eternal bliss, the Sabbaths were all too few. The word of God could not be heard often enough. Daily chapel needed to be supplemented by quiet hours in the praying closet.

Religious instruction was not, however, forced at most of the schools. Catharine Beecher gave religious instruction out of school hours, attendance being voluntary. Of the one hundred and thirty pupils in her Hartford Seminary in 1832, thirty remained for this class.[22] It was at Adams Academy in Londonderry, New Hampshire, that religion was heavily emphasized.[23] Under Zilpah Grant as principal and Mary Lyon as assistant, the school gave about one-seventh of its time to religious studies, a proportion only equalled, as the unsympathetic trustees pointed out, by theological schools — which Adams could not be since it was a female seminary. Miss Grant compiled an estimate of the number of hours devoted to these studies, obtaining a similar statement from Miss Lyon. The trustees were not appeased. Such a

[21] In the *Providence Journal* of March 17, 1835, a milkman's advertisement headed " Remember the Sabbath Day " promises daily deliveries " Sundays excepted."

[22] Manuscript description of a visit to Hartford Seminary by Angelina Grimke.

[23] [Guildford, L. T.] *The Use of a Life.* New York. [1885.]

strong religious bias was contrary to their intent, and to the intent of the seminary's founder.

Though the American Tract Society was publishing booklets approximating the early Puritan tales of pious children, there is no evidence that these were placed in school libraries. Rather were they in the private home and in the Sunday School. There was the *Memoir of Nathan W. Dickerman, Who Died At Boston, (Mass.) January 2, 1830. In the Eighth Year of His Age*. Little Nathan, dying, lingered for a period of some months, during which as the disease gained ground he grew weaker physically but stronger spiritually, strong enough to accomplish the conversion of his parents, not hitherto churchgoers. He went to his heavenly reward happy in the esteem of large numbers of worthy men and women, prominent clergymen and citizens, who crowded into his sickroom to question him about his dying thoughts, and to compliment him on his firm faith. It was Nathan and his like who produced Elsie Dinsmore.

Children who guided their parents' feet to the right path, straight and narrow, were rare even in America where children were indulged in many whims. More numerous were the children whose own feet needed guidance from parents, guardians, teachers. At a children's party in Philadelphia in the eighteen-thirties the usual candy lozenges with mottoes were served, but the mottoes of foolishness were replaced with sober warnings:

> " 'Tis not expedient the slave to free?
> Do what is right! — that is expediency."

" If slavery come by color, which God gave,
Fashion may change, and you become the slave." [24]

Less savory, though equally moral in intent than
this abolitionist propaganda, or the accounts of mor-
bidly pious or Christianly punished children, accounts which at best could have had only a very
limited circulation, were the anti-Catholic books
which Harriet Martineau found in western homes of
wealth — in a young girl's room, alongside of her
Bible and prayerbook.[25]

Fear of the Catholics was very strong. " Five hundred priests came to the United States last year,"
wrote a New England schoolgirl in her notebook in
1835, [26] adding that the Leopold Society in Austria
was sending more money to promote Catholicism in
the United States than " all our religious societies
send to the heathen." Harriet Martineau, a traveller
who left no cranny of American life uncovered, found
in the South and in the West a fairly general belief
that the Pope himself was in league with the Emperor
of Austria (hence the Leopold Society), and with
the Irish who were beginning to flood the shores of
America with their emigrants, the common goal being to " explode the Union."

Boston preached many an anti-Catholic sermon
until the mob, so easily raised at any time in Boston,
whether to dump tea, threaten abolitionists, or put
the fear of Protestants into Catholics, rushed to

[24] Hallowell, A. D. *James and Lucretia Mott*. Boston. 1884.
[25] Martineau, Harriet. *Society in America*. New York and
London. 1837.
[26] Wheaton archives.

Charlestown there to burn a convent which had been serving the community excellently with a school.

It was not Boston alone which read and discussed a libellous book called *Six Months in a Convent* written by an ex-nun. Newspapers carried advertisements day by day.[27] Though they were financially impartial in their acceptance of advertisements of the Mother Superior's answer, they were more ready to credit the attack than the defence. Newspapers and magazines, even the most staid of them, reviewed the book, giving it large space, though sparing little for the answer. From the *Liberator*[28] to the *North American Review* no publication overlooked it. That the Bishop played the flute and talked French to the Mother Superior was quoted as if this implied the very presence of the Devil. Not one of the indignities the ex-nun asserted was overlooked, from being compelled to approach a priest on her knees, to making the sign of the cross on the floor with her tongue.

In the eighteen-forties anti-Catholic feeling manifested itself in the destruction of a stone sent for the Washington monument by the Pope.[29]

For religious reasons P. T. Barnum went to jail in Danbury, Connecticut, before he began his career of gulling the American public.[30] In his newspaper *The Herald of Freedom* he had accused a deacon of the

27 *Providence Journal*, March and April 1835; Boston *Courier, Post, Transcript* 1835.

28 Current issues.

29 Current letter of Angelina Grimke Weld.

30 Werner, M. R. *Barnum*. New York. 1923.

church of taking " usury of an orphan boy." Had he used the term extortion he could not have been prosecuted; but usury was ungodly; it was expressly forbidden in the Bible; therefore no deacon could be an usurer. To accuse him of something Biblically forbidden was a serious offence.

With every facet of human thought and human endeavor thus based upon the Bible, religious fanaticism was rampant. Millerism [31] and Mormonism were both outgrowths of the times. Both were presented to a credulous community by uneducated men; the Mormons soon to move West, the Millerites to disband when their prophet's date for the ending of the world proved inaccurate. It was not difficult for Miller to find followers to prepare with him for the final day of the world, to come in the early part of the next decade (1843) a date arrived at by scientific deciphering of Bible prophecies. In the recent years science had offered so many all but incredible facts for people to believe that credulity was the proper frame of mind. The sudden appearance of a comet in 1843 confirmed — for a time — the belief. The eighteen-thirties needed no such confirmation. There was nothing they would not believe if it were given a scientific explanation.

Such credulity called aloud for practical jokes. The *New York Sun* increased its circulation and kept the world agog by its famous moon hoax in August 1835.[32] Here was a reliable, though astounding story

[31] Sears, C. E. *Days of Delusion*. Boston. 1924.
[32] Locke, R. A. *The Moon Hoax*. New York. 1859.

of the true character of the moon and its strange inhabitants. The famous scientist Herschel, of whom
everyone knew because of his important astronomical
discoveries, was purported to have made a telescope
so powerful that through it the moon had been
closely and accurately observed. Its mountains, lakes,
and valleys, its vegetation, its bisonlike animals, its
oddities of sheep, and its winged men were the subject
of excited speculation. People watched the issues of
the *Sun* as to-day they would watch the bulletin board
for the report of a Harvard-Yale football game, or the
Cup races off Newport.

Though the *Sun's* rival newspapers were for the
most part extremely wary in either rejecting or accepting these astounding discoveries, the general public
was entirely gullible. At St. Louis a traveller [33] saw
an alligator with a stuffed negro in its mouth; and
recorded that there had been five alligators in the
museum originally, but that four fought and killed
one another, while the fifth committed suicide by
jumping out of a third story window. However
gullible, the American had his limits, and his tempta-
tions.

The study of the sciences had, however, tended to
make men feel that nothing was impossible in a
marvellous world, every nook and corner of which
was crammed with scientific fact. In astronomy, in
physics, in chemistry, in geology, in zoology new
truths were constantly being made public.

Meanwhile practical science was revolutionizing

[33] Marryat, Capt. F. *A Diary in America.* Philadelphia. 1839.

the everyday world. Morse was already getting the telegraph into shape, though it was still in the experimental stage. Morse had returned from Europe in 1832, disappointed in his ambitions as an artist and haunted by the idea of the telegraph to which he was now to devote himself.

Of more immediate influence was the cotton gin which had already made of cotton farming a vast industry, and the development of machinery which had not only taken many tasks out of the home but had increased manufacture by the thousandfold. In a comparatively new country that was constantly creating new communities, with a population increasing rapidly by both births and immigration, there was no fear but that production would continue to lag behind consumption.

The new trains cut the time of travel and gave promise of vast changes through new means of transportation. In 1833 Boston to Providence in fast coaches took six hours — with four shifts of horses.[34] Rival coach companies advertised in the interests of safety that no racing was allowed; one company strengthened its guarantee by the statement that its coaches were in the hands of owner-drivers. Two years later the train cut the six hours to two, the most modern 1934 train taking forty-four minutes. But in 1834 the train ran only as far as Canton; and in 1836 trains were still so unfamiliar that students at Wheaton would take a walk to see the train go by, writing home that the "cars" did not go "as fast as I thought

[34] Advertisements in current Boston and Providence newspapers.

they would." The early trains were merely stage coaches drawn by spark-throwing engines threatening to ladies' clothes. Even the smudging of faces did not deter travellers. Their utility in cutting the time of travel and in transporting goods in quantities undreamed of by coach made them veritable marvels.

Already companies were organized and steamboats building to cross the Atlantic with a speed that would for some time seem fairly dizzy. Automobiles and airplanes were confidently predicted, automobiles visualized as modified steam engines. A current print [35] presents a street full of these self-propelling cars, each with its steaming chimney but otherwise the counterpart of the modern roadster, phaeton, coach, sedan, and omnibus. Save for the excessive amount of steam the street represented looks not unlike a modern city street, though not yet in 1934 do the airplanes circle so thickly overhead.

The interest in astronomy was manifested by such diversions as the diorama, which existed in Boston as in other cities, showing (to those who paid the entrance fee) the stars in the heavens, beautifully lighted. Lyceum lectures were heavily attended everywhere. People were eager to become acquainted with the new truths.

In a world where scientific wonders were constantly becoming manifest, it was natural for a religious people to be deeply concerned with all manner of reforms. The humanitarian impulse had its rise in

[35] Reprinted from the original of 1828 in *Printer's Pie*. London. 1906.

deep religious feeling. Orestes Brownson, deploring the number of infidels in the eighteen-thirties, said, " In the view of the infidel, man is nothing more than an animal, born to propagate his species and die. It is religion that discloses man's true dignity, reveals the soul, unveils the immortality within us, and presents in every man the incarnate God, before whom he may stand in awe, whom he may love and adore. Infidelity . . . cannot make us love mankind, and not being able to make us love them, it is not able to make us labour for their amelioration." [36]

Laboring for the amelioration of mankind — a religiously based humanitarianism, a zeal which brought forth good and bad: broader education; anti-Catholicism; anti-slavery; the anti-Masonic political party; prohibition; and last of all, woman's rights.

The anti-Masonic feeling ran high. It arose after the disappearance in 1829 of one William Morgan who had published a book purporting to reveal the secret rites of Masonry. Morgan was abducted, all trace of him disappearing at Niagara Falls. He was believed to have been murdered by a group of Masons. For some time any man who admitted to membership in the Masonic order was under suspicion; ministers and men in public office had to explain their continuance in an organization which protected its secrets by murder. A Mansfield man (Mansfield was but five miles from Norton) set up in Providence an anti-Masonic paper in which Masonic atrocities were re-

[36] Quoted in Appendix, Harriet Martineau. *Society in America.* Vol. II. New York and London. 1837.

corded much as the *Menace* has recorded alleged Catholic atrocities. Like the *Menace* it interpreted seemingly innocent occurrences as deep-laid plots, and found evidence of villainy wherever it turned its searching gaze. To the tune of Auld Lang Syne it recommended unctuous verses urging that Morgan's murder be not forgotten.[37]

Reform was not, however, always destructive. The Indians, those children of the Devil whose ownership of the land had been so bitterly contested, were drawn under the aura of sentimentality. Children of the Devil the Indians had remained to the early Puritans even after the savages embraced Christianity — more often than not it was to the French priest to whom they listened, and a Catholic Indian was no better than a pagan one to Godfearing men. With worthless gifts, with rusty guns as barter, the white men had driven the Indian from his fields of corn, from his favorite hunting grounds, from his camp-sites and riverways. With a lordly gesture the white man then granted him reservations — of land the white man did not want. Having long since gained possession of the fertile lands and desirable locations — though the Seminoles were still refusing to leave Florida — the white man tended to forget the very existence of the Indian save when he went pioneering in the West and found him still roaming the plains instead of accepting his square inches of allotted territory. By the eighteen-thirties the Indian in the popular mind was

[37] *Providence Free Press and Pawtucket Herald,* April 22, 1830. Published by Stearns & Wheaton. Lent by Mrs. Bertha S. Hopkins.

no longer a war-whooping bloodthirsty savage and was beginning to rise from his own ashes as the Noble Red Man, though not yet was he stalking through Cooper's pages.

In their humanitarian zeal the eighteen-thirties formed societies for the protection of the Indian. That he needed protection from the white man's cupidity just as much as the white man had once needed protection from his scalping knife was now entirely obvious. And he offered a fruitful field for home missionary work. America had not as yet given largely either of men or money to the field of foreign missions. Even with missionary fervor young ladies, or their parents for them, balked at the idea of crossing oceans to a remote country where they would be far from home and supplies. Missionary work among the Indians offered fewer terrors.

Reform need not stop with the heathen and the Indian. There were the insane, the deaf, the deaf and dumb, the blind, the prisoners. The insane were brutally treated, inhumanly confined. Dorothea Dix travelled about, visiting the forlorn creatures chained in unheated caves or cabins, inducing keepers to remove chains, provide proper food, clothing, and exercise. Personally she supervised the changes, watching and nursing, until the unkempt, neglected creature became a human being. Gradually the influence of her work spread, until finally the very name insane asylum vanished and we have instead hospitals for the maladjusted.

Thomas Gallaudet worked for the deaf, Samuel

Eliot Howe for the blind. That one of the objects
of teaching unfortunates was to give them correct
religious instruction is clearly shown in a group of
questions asked the pupils in an asylum: "What is
Despair? What is Hope? What is the Soul? What
is Eternity? What is the difference between Immortality and Eternity? What is Virtue? What is God? " [38]

With the Indians, the insane, the deaf and the
blind, all provided with assistance, there remained the
drunkards. Temperance societies began to spring up,
the first Total Abstinence convention occurring in
1836, one year later than the first temperance newspaper which William Lloyd Garrison published in
Boston in 1835. School girls in 1835 were given such
fascinating facts for their notebooks as that " alcohol
is a poison and enters the blood in pure state and has
been taken from the brain on dissection pure and
would burn as well and the same as ever." [39]

With brandy served at hotel and inn tables free,
with mint juleps quaffed by travellers at each stop of
the coach, it is not odd that the temperance societies
should have increased rapidly; the reform starting in
Boston in 1824 boasted of more than a thousand
societies in 1829. It became fashionable not to drink;
and what ceases to be fashionable easily becomes
immoral. Mrs. Wheaton as a young wife helped to
organize a great temperance meeting in Norton.
Each Sunday School child flourished a badge on the
shoulder, and with flags flying the procession marched

[38] *The Penny Magazine,* January 17, 1835.
[39] Notebook in Wheaton archives.

to a grove where a picnic supper was provided along with out-of-town speakers, whose words naturally bore more weight than those of local enthusiasts. The "Coldwater Army" of children met for years in the church vestry, frequently marching the short block to Mrs. Wheaton's house where she would address them with gentle insistence upon the temperate life.

The growing sentiment against alcohol had its rise from the increase of the dramdrinking of a tolerant population. In 1833 the *Litchfield Enquirer,* a weekly newspaper published in the town of Miss Pierce's School for young ladies and Judge Reeve's law school, offered in its pages a motley rhyme more or less in pentameter couplets, advertising the coach service. With rhymes of Goshen, Sharon; leaves, thieves; lines, untwined; him, time; A.M., P.M. it weaves its way through a schedule of stops and times and comes to the jolly conclusion:

"From Litchfield to Sharon our fare is very low
And money will be refunded if we don't carry you
   through.
One dollar twenty-five cents will be our regular sum,
It will hardly keep our horses well, and our drivers in
   good rum." [40]

To combat such good-natured acceptance of intemperate habits the water drinkers invoked religion. The *Boston Courier* of June 1835 reported a trial in which a witness, Dr. Edwards, was asked, "What is

[40] Vanderpoel, E. N. *Chronicles of a Pioneer School.* Cambridge. 1903.

your opinion as to the effect of ardent spirit on the soul? " to which he replied firmly, " Highly destructive."

The master or owner of the steamboat King Philip sailing from Providence, Rhode Island, was apparently of the same belief for in the *Providence Journal* of March 11, 1835 he advertised that the King Philip would not carry rum as freight " for any person whatever. None of that poison has ever been kept at the bar of the King Philip."

Many a man and many a woman looked back to a childhood where the home had been wrecked from the excessive use of drink. William Lloyd Garrison was a temperance advocate because his own father had been a drunkard. Garrison was only three years old, his sister new-born, when in 1808 the father deserted his family, never to return. It is small wonder that as he grew up to appreciate his mother's difficulties and her struggles, Garrison gave his sympathies to both temperance and woman's rights.

" Woman's rights " was slow of growth, partly because of the desire on the part of the women best qualified to direct such a movement, to subordinate the issues involved to more pressing reforms. Men asked that women mute their pleas until such time as abolition had been won; so strongly did they feel on the question of slavery that they would not have the issue clouded by association with woman's rights.

So women worked first for abolition, for the insane, for the prisoners — it was an Englishwoman, Elizabeth Fry, who had called public attention to the prisons in which women lived as wild beasts. What Mrs. Fry had done in England needed to be done in America where prisons did not exactly conserve the health of their inmates, though conditions seem never to have been so primitive as in older countries. Women in the eighteen-thirties were founding various societies for moral reform, being concerned primarily with women, though their charity was wide enough to extend to any creatures who were handicapped or wronged.

In 1836 the Ladies of the New York Female Reform Society published *An Appeal to the Wives, Mothers, and Daughters of Our Land in the City and the Country* urging that all women take an interest in this class of delinquents, begging women not to turn away from the need of this reform, from the fear of being thought indelicate. It was not indelicate to help fallen sisters; it was not indelicate to know of sin. God's word could be accepted by all as the standard of purity, and " how full and explicit is the language of the Bible with regard to the sin of licentiousness." Once more was the Bible turned to as the ultimate source, the ultimate arbiter, the guide even to right speech. The society, interesting itself in reclaiming fallen women, and in safeguarding young men, felt that its work belonged in women's hands.

No women — or men — went to the rescue or attempted the reformation of pirates of whom groups were hanged from time to time, the *Courier* (Boston) of June 12, 1835 reporting the execution of five Spanish pirates " yesterday." So huge was the crowd of spectators that the shed roofs upon which they crowded were broken by their weight, and many were injured. Spice was added by the pirates' unsuccessful attempt to commit suicide the night before; one had even succeeded in cutting his throat with a piece of tin, but the wound was dressed and he was carried alive to the gallows in a chair, and hanged to the glory of justice and the edification of the curious.

Perhaps it was because of the pirates of the present and the past that *Robinson Crusoe* was bowdlerized. The children of the eighteen-thirties received for their birthdays (Christmas was not celebrated by respectable people; it was still abjured as a heathen holiday) a *Robinson Crusoe* which would never tempt them to roam. In an 1830 edition " A Lady " (Eliza Farrar) addressed a preface to parents explaining why she re-issued a book already retold many times. She was anxious to preserve Defoe's style, which she considered superior to that of the later abridgments, but she also wished the book to be free from any deleterious matter. In the original narrative, parents might recall if they had read it, Robinson Crusoe went to sea in opposition to the wishes of his parents. This edition took care to make clear that though he failed to observe the wishes of his parents, he did not disobey their positive commands; had he done so he would have come to greater disaster. It was imprudent, unfilial to disregard the *wishes* of parents; it was positively wicked to disobey their *commands*. A neat distinction, all the more effective if the children, too, read the preface.

For his disregard of his parents' wishes Robinson Crusoe was punished by shipwreck, a moral lesson made more obvious by Eliza Farrar than by Daniel Defoe. Further improvements on the narrative were made by omitting the early voyages of Crusoe, voyages which were prosperous and which therefore had no moral lesson to teach; besides they were calculated to give to impressionable children a love of roaming which was not to be encouraged. Having thus made the story more " pure " Eliza Farrar made it more instructive by depriving Crusoe of the tools salvaged in Defoe's version from the wrecked ship. By this deprivation she increased difficulties — and the punishment of filial disregard — and also impressed upon childish readers " the great value of iron."

A much more needed reform for children than that of literature was a reduction in the hours of labor in the mills. As early as 1834 workers in Massachusetts protested the labor conditions of children whose plight was often pitiable The figures for 1831 showed that sixty per cent of all workers in cotton mills along the Atlantic coast from Virginia to Massachusetts were women, seven per cent children under twelve. Industrial cities like Lowell jumped from a few hundred inhabitants to many thousands in the space of twenty years, with a corresponding increase in the number of little children employed from dawn to dark.

However useful such prolonged toil may have been in preserving children from idleness and hence rescuing them from the wiles of Satan it was obvious to women, if not to men, that such a way of life did not offer much hope for boy or girl; a boy who started in the mills at the age of five, working all the daylight hours, would hardly have a chance to elevate himself to the White House; nor would a girl's chances of becoming the mother of a future president be enhanced. It was not until 1844 that a poetess [41] in England voiced the *Cry of the Children*:

" They are weary ere they run;
They have never seen the sunshine, nor the glory
Which is brighter than the sun."

but England was to lag behind America in such reforms though far ahead in the matter of abolition.

In England it was a woman [42] who had voiced the need of abolition, a woman whose pamphlet had been, so it was said, directly responsible for the act which abolished slavery. But England's problem was much less acute; her slaves were for the most part in colonies which few of her citizens visited. There was small chance that the slaves she freed would actually trouble her; they would remain in the West Indies, sufficiently remote from England's shores. In America by the eighteen-thirties slavery had been abolished in the Northern states, but slaves were considered by the Southern states the backbone of their economical existence.

In freeing the slaves the United States would have to face the problem of released slaves in the South, and the emigration of large numbers to the North. The North for all its " freedom " was none too kind to the

[41] Browning, Elizabeth Barrett.
[42] Heyrick, Elizabeth.

blacks. It accepted their freedom — if they belonged in the North or had been properly manumitted — but it did not love them. The North sometimes admitted them to white churches — if they sat on the benches provided for colored folk in the back. They might believe themselves saved — apparently for a colored heaven or the back benches of the white souls'. Even when the negro acquired the education forbidden by law in the South, he was not more welcome to a seat beside a white worshipper. Sarah Douglass, an educated colored woman, fought with her own pride, and continued attendance in the Philadelphia Friends' Meeting, but her brother writhed under the indignities, and removed to a church of colored brethren with whose faith he had much less sympathy, having been himself brought up as a Friend, and among whom he found no intellectual equals. It was better, he felt, to worship God among poor, ignorant blacks whose Presbyterian creed did not jibe with his own, than to listen to Quaker exhortation among those whose hearts held no friendship for him.

Going to a strange city Sarah Douglass attended Meeting regularly for a year before any white Friend spoke to her. At last a lady approached her.

" Are you a cleaning woman? "

" No."

" Then what do you do? "

" I teach."

The lady moved away.[43]

[43] Both incidents from manuscript letters of Sarah Douglass; lent by Mrs. Weld.

When it came to a question of blood, the Christian charity, the benevolent humanitarianism of the eighteen-thirties was wont to founder on the rock of blind prejudice. The North could not love the doctrine of states rights quite so well on any other subject.

Other reforms were on the whole a diversion of the eighteen-thirties; they liked reforming everything from sinners to rocking chairs. It was the day of Larger Interests with the brotherhood of man offering wider and wider fields for human endeavor. Woman's place was the home; but various reforms offered many earnest ladies an escape.

The anti-slavery reform, however, was a primed shell. Explode it and the Union would be disrupted. A meeting in Taunton, a speech in Philadelphia, a society formed in Boston or New York or some country village was enough to set the papers off on a tirade; that misguided people should put the freedom of the slave before the safety of the Union was cause for tears. In issue after issue the newspapers of the eighteen-thirties — save the mad sheets of men like Benjamin Lundy and William Lloyd Garrison — implored their readers to open their eyes and see to what precipice anti-slavery sentiment would lead them. Unless the enthusiasts moderated their tone, unless they silenced their persuasive speakers, the country would be plunged in civil war.

It is hard, after a century, to see political danger in the education of an occasional free negro child, but Boston was not alone in its immediate reaction against such latitude. Some Northern cities provided separate schools for the negroes; private schools were supposed to be exclusively white. Bronson Alcott's progressive school had already acquired a reputation that made it something of a distinction to have a child enrolled there; distinguished visitors from England watched a session or two with interest and inserted accounts in their published travels. But Bronson Alcott accepted a colored child as a pupil, and no Bostonian could pollute his child with a schoolmate in whose veins ran blood darker than his own.

Visitors from foreign shores were perturbed by American distinctions; they could recognize a negro only by his color. When in New York they visited colored schools they were troubled to find among the children many whose blue eyes and blond hair would have seemed to stamp them as of the ruling caste. They could have understood a prejudice which would have removed these children from the colored school; an agitation against a child, white in appearance, but with some dark heritage, among untainted white children was something to puzzle over.

Bronson Alcott's school crashed on the rock of prejudice, neither he, the gentle idealist, nor the patrons of his school, earnestly moral New Englanders, yielding to the obstinacy of the other. In his youth Alcott had been interested in education; though disappointed in his hopes for following an uncle to Yale, he had relied on that uncle's influence to obtain a school for him to teach. Unsuccessful, he travelled South believing that a New Englander would find less competition in Virginia than in the North which was flooded with college boys ready and eager to teach school for a term or two, or a year or two, before the serious business of life began. His desire for wandering was gratified rather than his desire for teaching, since he found Virginia with its own supply of would-be teachers. With a pack on his back Alcott had carried not knowledge to Virginia children, but pins and needles and the new tinware to their mothers, gay scarves to their fathers. But he cherished his ideas on education, and after seasons successful and unsuccessful in the South, after experimenting with the gayety of New York, Alcott had his longing for a school gratified. He could and did sacrifice this desire of his heart to his firm prejudice for what he believed to be right.

More dramatic was the experience of Prudence Crandall in Connecticut. Miss Crandall was peacefully conducting a private school for young ladies when she outraged convention by accepting as a day pupil a young lady whose fees were paid, whose dress and manners were modest, whose appearance was attractive; but it was known that she was not " pure white." Miss Crandall's feelings were aroused by the storm which burst upon her, no less than the feelings of the parents of her regular pupils. She became interested in the problem of the education of the free negro. There were at the time in many states — even in the slave states — free negroes who had inherited or acquired wealth, who had been given or who had obtained for themselves a sound education; who were indeed people of taste and cultivation. Yet where could their children receive the education to which their economic position and their inclinations entitled them?

Miss Crandall went to Providence, Rhode Island, where there seems to have been a group of comfortably situated colored people as well as an influential group of abolitionists. Canvassing here for pupils, she returned to her home, announcing that in future it was the white misses whom she would omit from her school.

The town was outraged. On all sides Miss Crandall met not only a lack of sympathy for her worthy venture, but the utmost in opposition, scorn, and vituperation. Had she committed a murder she would have been more welcome to her townsmen. She was promptly informed, when she took her " nigger girls " to church, that the House of God would not be polluted by their presence. It was an impious thing that she was doing, an insult to God who had ordained slavery. The North had not emancipated its slaves on religious grounds — it could not, since the Bible sanctioned slavery.

The men and women who believed that slavery was wrong, that in the divine sight all men, regardless of color, were created equal, were repudiated as menaces to the safety of the commonwealth. Slavery was the business of the South and the Northerner, however often Biblical phrases leapt to his tongue, was not in this instance inclined to consider himself the keeper of his Southern or his negro brother. There were times when the New Englander was eager to show God the path where He should tread; in this matter of slavery, the *laissez-faire* policy of most Northerners was the safest road for the Divine footsteps.

To the Northerner the slave auction was less of a shock than to the continental traveller. An Englishman, looking on in amazement at a Southern auction of a young man practically white, answered the auctioneer's request for a bid with a hearty, "No! Thank God, we do not do such things in my country." "And I wish we did not have to here, with all my heart," answered the auctioneer — with what the Englishman thought was sincerity, but what to the American smacks more than a little of blarney. The auction went on.

Miss Crandall's school did not go on. With childish vindictiveness the neighbors, finding her undaunted by the sermons preached against her in the village churches, began to assail her with bricks and mud, not waiting for her and her pupils to come out of the house for their greeting, but hurling their missives through windows and doors. When Miss Crandall gallantly persisted, she was arrested and carried to the town jail, there — so tradition has it — to be kept overnight in the same cell which had but just released a condemned murderer to his execution. Though it was found impossible to prosecute Miss Crandall legally, since the North, unlike the South, had no law forbidding any one to teach a negro so much as the alphabet, though the case fell for lack of weight, Miss Crandall was obliged to give up her brave attempt when her house was burned down.

However white in appearance some of her pupils, the good men and women of Connecticut saw beneath their skins into their blood. However black a pupil, however impossible her parading as a white person, she was not entitled to a school paralleling that of white folk. Even in the twentieth century, when faith in the powers bestowed by education is somewhat shaken, the South cannot believe that the schools it builds for the colored race should equal those built for the poorest white children. In Baltimore some years ago James Van Sickle as superintendent of schools endeavored to give to the colored children as fine schoolhouses as were being given to the white. To this day " Van Sickleism " is at times cited in newspapers as a danger to the city.

In the eighteen-thirties the educated black was feared in this world and the next. The South had to believe that their negroes were but so many head of cattle; they could be taught, yes, up to a certain point, just as a dog can be taught to sit up and beg. And just as a dog, taught too many clever tricks, becomes a nuisance, so a negro, whose learning would be acquired much as a dog's, would become a nuisance, if not a positive menace.

Knowledge was so definitely regarded as the way to power and the way to salvation that the South resisted every effort to teach an occasional slave to read, states passing laws with heavy penalties imposed upon the teacher. Negroes were not to enter Heaven.

Education, rooted in religion, was a serious matter, its whole fabric resting " on the sacred basis of

Christian love." [44]   Ignorance and vice were as closely linked as knowledge and purity. Knowledge was regarded as a divine requirement: " God has required *all* to take fast hold of instruction." [45]   Just as the body is sustained by material food, so the immortal soul is sustained by intellectual food. The neglect of knowledge became a crime, when it was remembered that those who hated knowledge fell under the divine displeasure.

Safety in both this and the future life seemed to depend upon a proper training of the mind. The great use of knowledge was to direct conduct; and the great aim of conduct was so to live that one would inherit the life to come. The other-worldliness of Christianity was not yet forgotten. " Knowledge seems a necessary ingredient to salvation." And as one of the best preservatives against temptation, knowledge became one of the strongest repellents of Satan.

If in the early days of America salvation may have seemed the exclusive right of a privileged class, by the eighteen-thirties few could have defined that class. In a democracy privileged classes incline always to extend themselves. Just as the vote, even in Massachusetts, had ceased to be the exclusive privilege of Congregational church members, so salvation had

[44] Preface to the translation of Victor M. Cousin's *Public Instruction in Prussia*. 1835. Preface by the translator, Mrs. Sarah Austin Taylor.

[45] Joseph Emerson's introductory lecture to his pupils in Byfield in 1821. Taken from Mary Lyon's manuscript transcript in the possession of Miss Clara Emerson of Beloit. Typed copy lent by Miss Frances Vose Emerson.

ceased to be the exclusive hope of a limited group. And since women, largely living in the home, came to be more deeply concerned with religion than men, it was women who sought knowledge to defeat the Devil, not only for themselves but for their dependents.

The morals of slavery crept into the mind of many a Southern woman when she found that the servants who were constantly about her and her children must not be given the key to knowledge. Women who taught their maids to read and write fell afoul of the law as well as of their husbands and fathers.

Most dramatic were the efforts of Sarah and Angelina Grimke, daughters of a wealthy South Carolina Judge. Sarah first, and then Angelina left the South, joining the Friends in Philadelphia. It was in 1835 that Angelina, the younger sister, made bold to write to William Lloyd Garrison her appreciation of his work for abolition.

At this time she was looking about for some occupation to add to her income which, for one brought up as she had been, was very inadequate. She had tried an infant school without much success; and she suspected that her failure was due to her own inexpertness of method. She learned that successful teachers had often had training such as she lacked, training which they received at some seminary. Hearing Hartford Seminary well spoken of, she wrote to Catharine Beecher asking if she might come there to learn how to teach. At this time Angelina was in the late twenties, but there were many precedents for

mature pupils. Miss Beecher made a journey to
Philadelphia, where she was much impressed by her
prospective pupil, but, reared under an eloquent
preacher, she found the Second Meeting very dull.
Perhaps she was incautious in expressing her opinion.
Angelina's hopes never got beyond a visit to the
Hartford School.

So she had no school to look forward to, either as
pupil or as teacher. When Garrison published her
letter to him in the *Liberator* the way suddenly was
made clear. She had written without her sister's
knowledge, and Sarah was only too ready with the
stock objections. The Friends had freed their own
slaves and were theoretically opposed to slavery but
they were not, as a group, active in the abolition
movement, since they objected to all heated discussion and agitation. Among them there were those
who boycotted slave labor products [46] but the general
sentiment was not sympathetic partly because there
was much dissension among the abolitionists themselves. The more powerful group of abolitionists at
this time advocated colonization: ship the negroes off,
and forget them.

Sarah Grimke, influenced by the Philadelphia
Friends, was convinced that her sister was merely riding a wave of emotionalism. The abolitionists were
persuasive and persistent speakers; had not young
men at Lane Theological Seminary debated for eight-

---

[46] James Mott gave up his prosperous business as a cotton broker
rather than rear his children on profits derived ultimately from
slave labor.

een evenings? [47]   Mad and dangerous doctrine went to the head like wine. She asked her sister to wait a year, and reconsider whether she ought to join a group of misguided enthusiasts. At the end of the year Angelina retired to the country to make her decision with God's help. It would have seemed to her contemporaries vain and foolish of any one to make an important decision without thus seeking guidance, without appealing for some sign. Both Sarah and Angelina Grimke now waited for some occurrence which could be interpreted as a command. To each it came. With Angelina it was the inspiration, which surely came from above, to write a stirring appeal to Southern women; whence otherwise the impulse? To strengthen her belief came the offer of the Anti-Slavery Society to make her their New York agent — a direct answer to her prayer for guidance. Why else should this have come at this time unless it were directed by divine influence?

To Sarah, too, came conviction that her sister was guided not by the Devil but by God. Sarah's keenly logical mind had not been idle during the year; she had examined the cause of slavery and, in the light of her own memories, condemned it. Yet, unwilling to be precipitate, she did not communicate her change of heart to her sister. When the Anti-Slavery Society's offer seemed to confirm her new stand, she still delayed. She wrote her mother, saying that she

[47] One of the young men was Theodore Weld who later married Angelina Grimke. When the trustees of Lane forbade any further abolitionist agitation, practically the entire student body withdrew, leaving Lyman Beecher in a difficult position.

would advise Angelina to accept.   In her mother's answer she read the will of God.   In obeying her mother's request that she should accompany Angelina to New York, she now knew that this was the right path for them both.   That her mother's sympathies were neither with the slaves nor with the fanatics who would free them, Sarah knew full well.   She realized that the mother's anxiety was wholly for this daughter who would enter New York, a city which schoolgirls of the time described in their notebooks as "a sink of iniquity and vice."   Yet filial duty now commanded her to go with Angelina to engage in anti-slavery activity.   Her doubts forever stilled, Sarah threw in her lot with the abolitionists.

It was not an easy fate.   Abolitionists were enormously helped in their cause by being made martyrs.   Their meetings were interrupted, their halls burned, their speakers put in jail or openly and flagrantly assaulted in the streets.   Women abolitionists were not physically molested; the munition used against them was by tongue and print.   They were verbally assaulted by many ministers, torn to shreds by the Congregational Association, standing firm on the Biblical bulwark of woman's place.

For the position of women was of clerical interest; it, too, had its roots in religion.   It was necessary for the church to take a firm stand when women outraged decency by speaking in public.   Had not Paul said that women should be silent in the churches?   Just how that pronouncement was to be interpreted was a matter of grave concern.   The Congregational Association sent out to all the Congregational churches in Massachusetts a *Pastoral Letter* denouncing the Grimke sisters and all women who followed their bold example. The Association warned clergymen of the dangers threatening "the Female Character with wide and permanent injury."

To-day the Congregational library in Boston has no copy of this diatribe which seemed in 1837 so vital to the interests of the world. It exists for us in a slim volume [48] containing Sarah Grimke's carefully planned answer in which she interpreted Paul's admonition as a reproof to the women who were too noisy in their questionings at church; in which she pointed out that if women kept silence in the churches there would be no Sunday Schools; in which she calmly proclaimed "the Scripture doctrine of the perfect equality of man and woman." According to "the immutable truths of the Bible" Sarah Grimke found the sexes equal in talent, equal in guilt for the Fall, equal in hope.

Yet the question of women's speaking in public was a very vexing one. Originally the Grimke's had spoken only to women; and for this purpose the vestry might often be lent. But one day the minister of a church, overcome by curiosity, hid behind a pillar, and listened; and, unable to hold his tongue, described the speakers and the speeches to his friends. This was the start of the violent controversy which found its most virulent expression in the *Pastoral*

[48] Grimke, Sarah. *Letters on the Equality of the Sexes.* Boston. 1838.

Letter. It happened that Sarah Grimke was a very forceful, logical speaker; but Angelina was very lovely. Bronson Alcott was moved to describe her in his diary, and there is small doubt but that her physical beauty, her habit of being well clothed, her personal charm all added to the force of her persuasive speech. After hearing her speak men were more than ready to say that the clergy had merely made themselves ridiculous with their protest. " I am informed," wrote a gentleman in July 1837 [49] " that the Genl. Association of Mass[s] are alarmed and are sounding it against 'woman Reformers.' Horrible!! — that woman should dare to reform the world — that there should be any Deborah, in this polished age of the world and in a country where man stealing is an honorable business in the church."

Whether in church or public hall the sisters now counted men among their audiences, surprised to find that their presence did not embarrass them. The men were as fascinated as their wives and daughters, and Garrison's belief in the power of his allies was justified. Though the country had been torn by the controversy, though feminine delicacy was thought to have vanished forever, the battle was no sooner fought than won — won by the serene persistence of the speakers, won far more early but less easily and quickly in America than in England. England had emancipated her slaves but it was not until 1840 that she could contemplate a female speaker without

[49] Manuscript letter written by Simeon Jocelyn to his " Esteemed Friends " Sarah and Angelina Grimke. Lent by Mrs. Weld.

horror — and then it was an American, Lucretia
Mott, who converted her.   Mrs. Mott and Mrs. Stanton, sent over from America to an international abolition conference in London, were neither recognized
as delegates nor allowed to speak at the meetings.
Herded in the gallery along with English women
abolitionists, among them Lady Byron, they were
comforted when William Lloyd Garrison voiced his
protest against the procedure by joining them as a
spectator.   It was at a public meeting not under the
control of the Conference that Mrs. Mott spoke.
London newspapers were immediately warm in their
praise.   Her dignity, her eloquence, her excellent
platform presence were all extolled.

But this was in 1840.   It was in the late eighteen-
twenties that America was first aware of the outrage
to masculine dignity and feminine modesty in the
public speaking of a woman.   The offending lectures
were free, their subject matter was reputed to be
scandalous, and the attendance in Cincinnati, St.
Louis, Baltimore, Philadelphia, and New York over-
whelming.

Frances Wright, born in Scotland in 1795, had in
1818 somewhat eccentrically chosen to visit America.
When her guardian urged the more conventional
trip to Italy and Greece, she had answered romanti-
cally, " The sight of Italy, my dear uncle, prostrated
under the leaden sceptre of Austria, would break my
heart."   Greece had not yet received the attention it
was soon to have through the death of Byron so that
in far-off American Troy Emma Willard would or-

ganize a society for the education of Greek maidens. And Fanny Wright turned to America for her sight of Freedom, and having seen, wrote a book.

Probably the only act of Fanny Wright's of which Americans approved was her shipping her negroes out of the country. For Fanny Wright had tried to establish an ideal community of negroes on a two hundred acre tract on the site where later Memphis was to rise. Illness forced her to leave for a time and the negroes, upon the complete failure of the community, were sent to Haiti.

Her own failure made Fanny Wright the more interested in the communistic enterprise of Robert Owen at New Harmony, Indiana. This was not an attempt to rehabilitate negroes, but to establish white citizens in a model community.

Earlier as part owner of the New Lanark Mills in Scotland Owen had attempted to alleviate the miserable condition of his two thousand workers, all from the lowest class of society. He had first improved living conditions and then turned his attention to the education of the children. Emma Willard came to visit his schools for which she could not find praise enough. She agreed with Owen that the state should be responsible for the education of all its children, and doubtless pointed out that in America much more was being done than in the British Isles.

The fame of Owen's mills spread. His people were decent and law-abiding; their children well-mannered, frank, and charming, as graceful as if they had been well born, and infinitely more polite. Owen's ideas on education received wide publicity and approbation and his suggestions for the handling of pauperism were well received by a committee of the House of Commons.

All was set for a career of public usefulness when Owen, addressing a large public meeting in London, instead of keeping to the subject on which he was now an acknowledged authority, began to discuss his religious views. He declared gratuitously that he did not believe in any of the existing forms of religion. Branded now as an infidel, he completely lost power and prestige, becoming the object of derision.

It was natural for England and even more for America, with its strong religious bias, to regard Owen's philanthropic enterprise at New Harmony with suspicion. Infidels were always immoral; their infidelity itself was sufficient proof of immorality, but in addition it was well known that infidels were entirely unprincipled. In denying the church, they seemed to their contemporaries to deny all accepted morality, since morality depended for its validity upon the Bible. That among the worthy people who accompanied Owen there should also have been a large intermixture of fanatics, adventurers, and downright rascals had apparently never occurred to Owen. The type of associates he had innocently gathered about him confirmed the prejudice already associated with his name. His ideal community endured scarcely two years — and by that time it had split into ten groups all at odds with one another. Owen returned to England, there to establish in 1835 the first society to use the term socialism. It is interesting that his four sons remained in America, all to have distinguished careers, one of them being instrumental in gaining for the women of Indiana control over their own property, and also in helping to establish in Indiana a system of free schools.

It is not odd that Fanny Wright, in speaking publicly in the eighteen-twenties in defence of the community at New Harmony, outraged the good people who thought that Owen and his colonists were the boon companions of Satan. Again and again worthy ministers denounced her from the pulpit; and in remote towns where the name of Fanny Wright had never permeated, pastors read lengthy sermons on Paul's warning to women to be silent. But Tammany Hall, the staunch defender of free discussion, found it amusing to shock the conservatives by rushing to the defence of a woman who though not handsome was graceful, pleasant, dignified, and earnest. An angel of light Tammany called her.

By the eighteen-thirties, when the storm rose again, finally to subside, Fanny Wright was all but forgotten, and the Grimke sisters seemed to have originated the sin themselves.

But as time went on and the women who spoke in public — Sarah and Angelina Grimke, Lucretia Mott, and many another woman interested first in abolition, and finally in woman's rights — remained feminine, altering neither their clothes[50] nor their manners, keeping their feminine voices, their feminine ways, the clamor ceased. Lucretia Coffin, marrying James Mott, whose assistant teacher she had been

[50] The Bloomer costume was tried and abandoned.

at the Nine Partners' School (founded in 1796 by the New York Yearly Meeting of Friends) became a helpful and companionable wife, a devoted and competent mother. Her children seemed not to suffer neglect or shame from her speaking; and her husband quite obviously took pride in her competence. Angelina Grimke married Theodore Weld, an ardent abolitionist whose efforts were aided by the sympathy and helpfulness of his wife.

The eighteen-thirties had become reconciled to the speaking of women in public; little more was asked. The Bible had been appealed to; and had been interpreted as favorable to the education of women. The belief which Americans had in education was surpassed only by their belief in the Bible, which was the foundation of all education. In the educational world the doctrine of Pestalozzi was spreading very slowly, but already disciples of his were founding schools in America, affirming a doctrine which with each repetition came to have less the ring of heresy, that men are born neither good nor bad; that "our *education is the only cause* of our becoming either good, useful, intelligent, rational, moral, and virtuous beings or wicked, noxious, ignorant, senseless, superstitious, criminal, and therefore, miserable creatures." [51]

Be good and you will be happy; to which the eighteen-thirties added with certain conviction: be educated and you will be good. For knowledge was God's gift to man.

[51] Neef, Joseph. *Sketch of a Plan and Method of Education.* Printed for the Author. 1808.

CHAPTER IV

THE CURRICULUM

IT was in 1837, two years after Wheaton had opened, that the Association of Mechanics and Manufacturers in the opulent city of Providence, Rhode Island, started a campaign for the enlargement of the school system which they declared entirely inadequate. Not only was there need of more elementary schools than had been so far provided, but of public high schools, both those that prepared for college, and those which gave instead " a sound English course." To the Association the City Council made reply that a high school was an " aristocratic and unconstitutional " establishment; that it " would educate children above working for their support "; and that " poor children would never be seen in it."

It was when mechanics became articulate, when an already literate group had children to educate, that education, in spite of a parsimonious city council, seemed suitable for ever wider groups of children and adolescents, and that education itself came to have a broader definition than in the days when education beyond the rudiments was for gentlemen only.

It was this broader definition of education which had really made possible the growth of female seminaries. Originally the scope of education was widened to provide for boys who were not destined for college. When Massachusetts embarked upon her educational policy, the prime need was to provide a steady stream of Congregational ministers without the need of either importing them from England or sending boys to England to be trained. Later came the need for lawyers and doctors. Still later came the need for an enlightened citizenry if the great experiment of democracy was to endure.

The Revolution in its demonstration of the power of the newer country, in its establishment of a government of the people, made the need of education self-evident in most states. Free schools, declared far-seeing Americans, were "one of the highest hopes of our land. Without them the breath of liberty would cease." [1] To guard against any possibility of failure of this great experiment of democracy the people must rise above the level of the European populace. America could not afford to keep within its boundaries an inert mass of ignorant people. Education for a free citizenry should be broad; it should develop man on all sides, physical, intellectual, moral, spiritual.

Idealists were ready with schemes and curricula long before there was felt generally any need for change, but dissatisfaction with the existing provisions grew rapidly with the turn of the century. Already in the eighteenth century, new courses of study had been introduced; by the eighteen-thirties the "sound English education" which had at first seemed an impertinence, had become almost as staid and

[1] Felt, Joseph. *History of Ipswich.* Cambridge. 1834.

quite as respectable as the routine program of college preparation.

There was little argument about the aim of education. Knowledge was power, education gave knowledge. Education consisted of the assimilation of knowledge in such a way as to secure that discipline of mind which fitted the pupil for the tasks of adult life. It was self-evident that the truest discipline came from the pursuit of the dead languages, the " classics " which offered difficulties; Latin and Greek were the backbone of a " liberal education." In the eighteen-thirties the study of modern languages was thought seductive; such studies led students away from the ancient languages which provided the true discipline of the mind. Mathematics was included as a necessary concomitant, a group of indomitable three to which, for the clergyman, Hebrew was added. Though President Quincy had to permit the modern languages at Harvard, he did his best to keep them under a cloud; and he tried to guard freshmen from their evil influence.

It was in the eighteen-seventies that President Eliot of Harvard was quoted as believing the discipline of speaking French and German equal to the discipline of reading Latin and Greek.[2] It is in the nineteen-thirties that Latin, having long survived Greek, begins to lose its hold upon entrance requirements.

In the eighteen-thirties Latin and Greek were sacrosanct; but there was felt a growing doubt as to

[2] Manuscript letter of Mrs. Cowles (Eunice Caldwell, first principal of Wheaton) to Mrs. Wheaton. Wheaton archives.

their absolute value. If only the professional men needed education, then Latin and Greek were the only branches of the tree of knowledge; if, however, schools were to consider the needs of non-professional aspirants, a broader curriculum was called for. The classics, holding their supreme position as disciplinary studies and as the proper equipment for minister and lawyer, were of doubtful use to the ordinary citizen. Since he would have no special interest in reading the Church Fathers; since he would have no call for interspersing his remarks or pleadings with learned or graceful quotations to impress a judge (who in America might even be without classical acquaintance) he might gain sufficient discipline of mind by studying mathematics.

A Boston weekly "literary" paper published in 1809–1810 aiming, as it stated in its first number, to be useful as well as entertaining, promised at the close of each issue "a few classical remarks." Its quotation from Virgil was accompanied immediately with outrageous punning. This paper, called, *Something*, edited by "Nemo Nobody," interspersed its serious essays on education and religion with the most airy fooling: it referred to weeklies that were not strong enough because they were weakly supported, to a defunct paper *The Emerald* which was not *read* because it was green, and finally quoted Latin to prove that Nobody knew Latin as well as English.

Such an attempt at humorous treatment shows that the study of the classics was already somewhat suspect. Yet no one questioned the disciplinary value, nor did any one question the prime use of all education as discipline. What was necessary to decide was what studies might properly be offered to the children of a democracy to accomplish the desired end.

European travellers who came to America at this time in considerable numbers never failed to remark upon the prevailing ideas of equality, the absence of class distinctions. These travellers, both men and women, came to gaze at new cities, queer ways, pioneer settlements, the city of Washington, a president, and slaves; and to record their findings in books which were avidly read on both sides of the Atlantic, the Europeans being eager to know what democracy was like, and the Americans thirsty for the good opinion of the older civilizations. " The Americans are the only people in the world blessed with leisure and equality," [3] was read with pride on the part of the pioneers, who were also pleased to find the American states compared most favorably with Canada. But less pleasing was the statement: " Though the Americans, in general, are civil and friendly, still an Englishman, himself a stranger among them, is annoyed and disgusted by their vaunts of prowess in the late puny war [that of 1812], and superiority over all nations, and they assume it as a self-evident fact, that the Americans surpass all others in virtue, wisdom, valour, liberty, government, and every other excellence."

Not all travellers were complimentary, but all were

[3] [Wakefield, E. G.] *England and America.* New York. 1834.

astonished at the prevailing customs. No laborer
pulled his forelock as he spoke to his master. He
spoke as man to man, as a free citizen of a democracy
and hence the equal of his employer in all but wealth.
In stage coach or train a laborer took his seat beside
a lady or gentleman without so much as " By your
leave." Laborers referred to themselves and their
womenfolk as ladies and gentlemen — to their superiors often as men and women. The coachman of a
stage coach would address his passengers familiarly,
asking them to help in difficult places, quite oblivious
of the fact that one of his passengers might be an
English gentleman who had never in his life served
himself or any one else. American men did not re-
sent being practically commanded to get out and walk
up a hill, or requested to help push the coach through
a bit of thick mud, or to lend a hand with a trunk,
any more than they resented a stonemason's being
addressed as " Colonel." Visitors found the absence
of servants annoying, the necessity of eating in the
public dining-room of an inn deplorable — though
such a custom permitted one to see more of the native
manners than would otherwise have been possible,
and also heightened one's appreciation of the servility and privacy to be had in one's home country.

Travellers found it odd that in America the poor
should have privileges which in Europe were reserved
for the rich. Indeed they had luxuries unavailable
to any in Europe, or to the very few. In Philadelphia,
thanks to the Schuylkill River and to American in-
genuity, every house apparently had water " laid on

from attic to basement." That the poor as well as the
rich should get water without labor seemed subver-
sive of proper social conditions. So in the nineteen-
thirties English visitors find it hard to reconcile their
ideas of propriety with the American workingman's
automobile.

In a country where at harvest time the farm help
ate with their employers, where cab drivers referred
to themselves as gentlemen, it was not even an incon-
gruity for one who would be recognized in England
as a gentleman to send his children to a free school,
one supported by the town. American fathers would
patiently explain that in a democracy it was fitting
for children to mingle regardless of their parents'
wealth or poverty. To an Englishman sending one's
child to a free school was equivalent to living off the
parish; to an American it was right and proper that
the taxpayers as a whole should educate his children
at least through the rudiments of the common school
curriculum. Private schools did exist, but many a
prosperous man preferred his children to associate
with the children of the neighborhood in both play
and school.

" Teach all men to respect themselves as men, and
then what man will be valet to another man, pull off
his clothes, and scratch his back when required? " [4]
In *Pride and Prejudice* Lady Catherine is shocked to
learn that the Bennets had kept no governess for their
children. In America it would have excited surprise
if a family in their circumstances had kept a gover-

[4] [Wakefield, E. G.] *England and America.* New York. 1834.

ness; only the ultra rich in America aped English customs. Education in America was advancing on a democratic platform. Poor boys had always gone to college — workingmen's sons had always attended Harvard along with Boston's Brahmins; not in large numbers, but always there had been the possibility of the highest education for the poorest boy.

Travellers found a widespread interest in book-learning, a reverence for schooling. In two of the fifty log houses of Sault Ste. Marie Marryatt, who believed that his fame as an author preceded him even to the backwoods, found complete sets of Byron, then a poet of great popularity and certainly one whose wit was too keen for clodhoppers. This unexpected appreciation of literature is, by a curious transfer, now found by Americans in England. In the nineteen-thirties American travellers marvel to find hotel porters in London reading Pater's *Marius the Epicurean*. In America, education is still sufficiently an open sesame (the depression of the nineteen-thirties has an excellent precedent in that of 1837) to make it unlikely that a man with the intellect to appreciate Pater would be restricted to a porter's job.

In the eighteen-thirties men of education were often pioneers in the western wilderness, carrying with them an interest in things of the mind which held over until the physical labor of settling a new community should yield to well-deserved moments of leisure. Yet leisure was little prized by the American, pioneer or urban. Whether or not it was the excess of sunny days creating an excess of nervous energy, the American valued the active rather than the contemplative life, the life of work rather than the life of gentlemanly elegance.

Naturally then the children of America would be trained differently from those of England. Just what their education should be was the subject of many a discussion, in the family, in the town, in the state; magazines were full of the matter, and public lecturers were forever bringing it to the foreground. Just what knowledge was necessary was never to be wholly settled, since education moves with the times, and the demands that are made upon citizens vary with the temper of each generation and the conditions under which it lives. The eighteen-thirties were feeling their way, sure of one thing, that boys in America were not to be flogged into Latinity, however much they might be feruled into pseudo-attention.

Education was thought of as education of the many. However much Rhode Islanders might protest the higher education of the children of workingmen,[5] America as a whole was not conscious of class divisions and the son of the blacksmith and the son of the minister might well learn side by side. It was to the credit of any town to produce a learned man, whether he were the son of a tinker or of a doctor. When towns published their histories, as they were fond of doing in the eighteen-thirties, they were wont to list the sons who had gone or were going to college.

[5] The chief point of the protest was against education at public cost.

If education was to be open to all, its method and content were of concern to all, method as yet being subordinated to matter. Americans were too shrewd to be long deceived by a confusion of memory and mind. Rote learning passed muster for a time; the acquisition of facts seemed to have magic, the magic which transmuted memory into wisdom. Parents at the annual exhibitions of schools thrilled with pride at the quick responses of their offspring to such questions as these: " Who was called, nineteen hundred and twenty-one years before the Christian era, to go forth alone from his people and his father's house? " " Who was Queen of Assyria, and who the Judge of Israel, when Troy was destroyed, eleven hundred and eighty-four years before Christ? " " In what year of the world did the ark rest upon Mount Ararat? " [6]

It was not that any one was really deceived into thinking such factual (?) knowledge valuable in itself, save as any fact that was linked with the Bible might have special significance. Training the memory was one step in disciplining the mind. Learn the symbols on a page, and you become educated. Against this there has always been a protest, equally exaggerated, which negates the value of positive, mind-mastered knowledge. " Potatoes," cries James Kenneth Stephens in the twentieth century, " are more productive than Latin roots, are twice as nourishing, and cannot be parsed." [7]

[6] Questions asked in Lydia Huntley's (Mrs. Sigourney) School.
[7] *Here Are Ladies.*

Fortunately or unfortunately the eighteen-thirties were less interested in potatoes than in Latin roots. Although they could not foresee overproduction of potatoes, they did foresee the urbanization of America. The East had been cleared, and though still predominatingly agricultural, was looking confidently forward to an era of industrialism; while in the West men were bringing under cultivation those vast tracts of land which under scientific methods proved capable of feeding a larger proportion of the world than they could serve. In time that land would be conquered and cities would rise.

The less demand life made upon a man's muscles, the greater the demand upon his intellect. If the country was to be neither monarchy nor oligarchy, men who were voters, legislators, presidents, needed minds able to grapple with problems that were growing constantly more complex in an expanding country. In the eighteen-thirties, every one of intelligence was aware of the struggle ahead; day by day the newspapers warned of the dangers of civil war, unless the abolitionists would moderate their speeches. Relationships abroad were, however, serene, now that England had learned through the war of eighteen-twelve the strength of her quondam colonies, and now that France, yielding to Jackson's threats, had paid reparations. Obscurity was not to be America's portion, though she meant to keep her hands off European tangles. Her own affairs offered scope enough for the talents of her citizens. Those talents must be properly developed; they must not be permitted to dissipate themselves in the misuse of the time gained from farm tasks under the new inventions.

The habits of the farm men carried with them to the cities. Days were never long enough for the manifold activities of an American day, even though one rose at dawn. At all schools, fashionable or not, the rising hour was five in the milder seasons and six in winter; four, four-thirty, quarter of five were not unusual rising hours. Men's colleges regulated the hour by placing chapel service, always compulsory, at dawn. And all schools and colleges regulated their students' time with a wary eye for Satan.

With the schools accepted as the proper place for boys, and then for girls, the question of the proper studies took on a new importance. The Massachusetts law of 1827 took account of the needs of the growing youth, settling upon " orthography, reading, writing, English grammar, geography, arithmetic, and good behavior " as primary essentials to which a superstructure of useful accomplishments might well be added: " the history of the United States, bookkeeping by single entry, geometry, surveying, and algebra."

Next to reading came writing — and it was a matter of pride to the eighteen-thirties that the new century had seen a sharp advance in literacy, practically all native Americans now signing their names whereas the larger number had made a cross at the time of the Revolution. Writing as an art was valued so much that the manuscript of the time is painful to modern eyes, meticulously careful in the formation of minute letters. But this had its practical side, as any thrifty American knew. The cost was defrayed by the recipient, who might not be good-tempered if the writer did not make the most of the space on his sheet, a sheet not wholly available since the outside had to be kept for the address. Envelopes had not yet been invented.

A nation of traders, as Europeans labelled the Americans, naturally valued arithmetic, and, indeed, all branches of mathematics, since geometry and surveying were invaluable accomplishments for pioneers. It was not forgotten that Washington had won his first success as a surveyor. Aside from its value as mental discipline, mathematics had practical applications that were obvious to even the backwoodsman. Travellers noted that every American boy çould calculate; he might not be able to read; he might never have been to school; but this one essential bit of Yankee knowledge a father would be sure to teach his son. Mental arithmetic was given an important place in the curriculum of all schools, girls as well as boys developing a nimbleness of wit, a quickness in handling figures that was highly valued. For the future grocer or housewife there were examples in tare and tret, suttle and cluff, examples which in the twentieth century are superseded by problems of the stock market.

The economics of war offered neat mental gymnastics in a series of questions: " If there were six hundred men in Pulaski's regiment and one sixth of them were killed, how many were left alive? And if two tenths of those alive were wounded, how many escaped unhurt? And if one in every twenty of those who escaped unhurt, lost a horse, how many horses were killed? And if each of those horses was worth fifty dollars, what were the whole of the horses killed worth?" [8]

English grammar gained a strong footing in American courses of study, based upon Latin grammar, with Milton and Pope to parse instead of Virgil. The aim was less that of the improvement of speech, than the discipline of the mind.

Geography was less disciplinary — though discipline was easily obtained in the memorizing of state boundaries — and much more romantic, too romantic to meet the approval of the colleges. Growth in prosperity had meant for America a tremendous increase in imports, all of which might well teach a lesson to the young. The far corners of the earth furnished things with which all, or nearly all, American children were familiar. They washed themselves with sponges, they had cut their teeth on coral; from far off Smyrna the sponges had come or from some place along the Mediterranean which had also sent tortoiseshell for the children's mothers' combs. Leghorn bonnets for the girls came from Marseilles, and so did the capers that were served with the lamb. Hairbrush bristles came from Germany, ivory for toothbrush handles from India or Africa, " hemp or flax to make you a good rough towel from up the Baltic," and castor oil from Sicily. So the readers listed the good

[8] Angell's *Union Series*. No. 5. By the principal of Franklin High School, Providence, Rhode Island. 1835.

things and their sources, not forgetting to mention with pride that " We need not bring away plates and cups and saucers from China now, for they make as good in Philadelphia." [9]   South America provided silver for tea and coffee pots, cream jugs and spoons, as well as cocoa and chocolate. Nor did the books omit the coffee from Arabia, and " choice wine from Madeira " — in the eighteen-thirties Madeira was the most valued and the most expensive of the wines.

The need of maps and globes became apparent, one of the arguments for permanent schools being this need of equipment. While rote learning was accepted as education, the mere memorizing of names passed as knowledge, but with a wider definition, wider comprehension was required. Since towns were not usually inclined to generous appropriations for equipment, the use of the private school was obvious. Since many private schools were mere money-making establishments, boarding houses run by shrewd proprietors who recognized the problem of unemployed daughters in the home, the desirability of endowed schools with trustees was widely recognized. Many private schools were, of course, beyond reproach, well equipped and carefully run. In April 1829 a Young Ladies High School advertised in the *North American Review* that it possessed globes, a solar Microscope, Ferguson's Compound Engine, a Tellurian, a Cometarium, and an Orrery.

History had worked itself into the curriculum, at first by a sort of side door of the classics. Enormously

9 *Third Class Reader.*

popular were the Reverend J. Goldsmith's histories of Greece and Rome, small one-volume accounts in clear, easily mastered style. History of England was the history of the homeland of America's dominant race. And now that the United States was full of pride over its own achievements it felt old enough to have a history of itself, a history that inculcated the patriotism never questioned as a cardinal virtue until Edith Cavell's, " Patriotism is not enough."

Proud as it was of its own history, the United States still stressed the histories of older civilizations. The United States had not sprung from Zeus's forehead; its history was linked with the history of the English, the French, the Dutch, the Spanish. Yet for many years the histories of Greece and Rome were to retain a greater importance. Boys destined for the professions, who devoted most of their time to the classics, might profit from the histories which gave the background for the literature which they parsed. Boys who were not to enter the professions might still derive profit from a study of those countries which had perished in their pride.

The other studies were regarded as practical: mathematics, surveying, bookkeeping. As for good behavior, that was the primary aim of all education; to conform to the rules of a society which conformed to the rules of religion.

Beyond these studies were those definitely intended as college preparatory: Latin and Greek, rhetoric and logic, all vocational training. Geography might be useful to a trader, but for the minister and lawyer rhetoric and logic in addition to the classics. The minister's need of confuting heretics and doubters was greater than the lawyer's need of outwitting an opponent, rescuing a client.

Once the need of other training than that for the professions was recognized, the development of a new curriculum began. Or rather, the need and the curriculum ran side by side. There seemed to be a definite field of knowledge, not yet boundless, in which paths could be laid out for the enquiring minds of young people. Their parents, brought up, for the most part, under the old limited education, were becoming acquainted with the newer wisdom in various ways: there were the many magazines, some of them frivolous in name [10] as in substance, some of them serious and solid. There were magazines which offered a digest of the material in foreign magazines, and with no international copyright all magazines borrowed freely from European sources, articles from English magazines being lifted bodily.

There were also the Lyceums. In many a town there still exists a hall with the name Lyceum over its door, standing in the civic center beside the church and the town hall. The Lowell Institute, still in operation in Boston, was established in the eighteen-thirties.[11] All over the East and South people in cities and in towns, even in small villages, were eager to extend their knowledge, eager to share in the new learning, especially in the field of science.

---

10 *Ladies' Cabinet, Mirror, Rosebud,* etc.
11 Established 1836. Opened to the public 1839.

All this material, offered by lecturers who made the information both interesting and important, seemed to parents worthy of study. There was obviously not room for it in the grammar or Latin school, but in the other schools, the department of the academy which was not preparing for college, and in the colleges themselves, there might be a place for science. And since these studies were not vocational training for the professions, there seemed no reason for excluding girls. So in the co-educational schools, and in the separate girls' schools, the " sound English education," the " English classical studies " gained a firm foothold.

It is interesting to note that in some seminaries [12] the sound studies are placed in the " first course " while the "second course" at the same time that it added Latin and Greek, included the ornamental branches earlier omitted: Fine Needlework, Perspective, Landscape, Figure, Flower, and Velvet Painting, and Music.

Even after educators had decided what constituted a sound program, and mapped out a course to cover the usual three years, there was no steady progress. It took many years to establish attendance for a settled period. Schools in the eighteen-thirties were still running in a series of practically independent quarters or terms. Many schools, far from being mere fashionable boarding houses, ran only in the summer, or only in the spring, summer, and fall, or only in the winter. A teacher would sometimes return from her labors

[12] New Haven Seminary, 1824.

to spend the winter in her home town, there to run a small school. Pupils — whether from restlessness or from a desire to come in contact with various teachers — often flitted from school to school. The great struggle of schools and colleges in the early nineteenth century was with this floating population. Even to-day in the nineteen-thirties the mortality is very high. Not as many graduate from grammar school or junior or senior high school as enter; not even all candidates for the Ph.D. finish their course.

In the eighteen-thirties the migratory population was fairly large. Leading educators were striving to overcome the careless method of entrance at any time of the year that the school was running. The attempt was being made to insist upon entrance at the beginning of a quarter or term, and upon continuance throughout the session. By making a diploma something of value as a certificate of accomplishment, or as the prerequisite to a position as teacher, the schools sought to retain pupils. Yet certainly in the girls' schools, the same names appear in the lists of two, three, or more schools. When Zilpah Grant and Mary Lyon left Adams Academy, they took with them to Ipswich a number of their pupils. When Mary Lyon opened Mount Holyoke Seminary in 1837 she gathered about her a large number of the best pupils from Ipswich and Wheaton, urging her necessity of having on hand pupils whose training had been such that they could form the nucleus of the new school. Mrs. Wheaton's somewhat pathetic letter [13] to Miss

---

[13] Shepard, Grace F. *History of Wheaton.*

Caldwell, the first principal of Wheaton Female Seminary, begging her to return to Norton, which suffered heavily from this withdrawal of students as well as from the loss of the principal, confirms the suspicion that there really were not enough pupils to go around.

Against the fitful attendance the leading schools offered a set program, and endeavored to refuse pupils who did not enter on the opening day. Yet as late as 1854 Mount Holyoke printed in its catalogue the early statement of its founder, that young ladies should plan on only one year at a time. To enter upon a three-years' course was still too solemn an undertaking.

Even where pupils did plan on completing the course and obtaining the diploma — whether from negligence in the picture-framing business or from lack of appreciation of symbols, diplomas were not always valued — they seem rarely to have steered a steady course. Whether young men at college or young ladies at seminaries, pupils were most likely to interrupt their course with periods of school-teaching, or periods helping out on the farm or in the home.

This dilatory or interrupted pursuit of a course of studies was to continue for many a long day. John Holmes, whose sly humor was never offered as freely to the public as the wit of his brother Oliver Wendell Holmes, was amused at the tendency even of Harvard to attract fewer and fewer persistent students. Himself a graduate of the class of 1832, he predicted a

Harvard of the future which would not be called upon to issue diplomas. Around the deathbed of a nonagenarian he pictured a group of Harvard faculty with their president, urging upon the dying man the advantages of living till the morrow, the annual Commencement day. " Rouse yourself! Make one more effort! Live until to-morrow, and die a Bachelor of Arts! " [14]

However much to be lamented by the schools, this dilatoriness had certain advantages; it meant that boys and girls did not leave home for a three or four year period with an occasional month at home — the twenty-two week term, making a forty-four week year was fairly well established. It meant rather a strong family interest in the school studies since the course was undertaken one term or one year at a time. Much depended upon the behavior in the home, the interest shown and the progress proved whether or not John or Betsy was sent back to school. Young people were still respectful in the home; they did not strut and parade their superior knowledge if the parents had had fewer advantages, mindful always of the fifth commandment.

Boys did frequently adopt a superior attitude toward their less favored sisters, thereby creating in the girls an inordinate thirst for learning. Many a girl who might otherwise have been content to pass her hours sewing and singing, was moved to a resentful demand for schooling. Many a girl with a more sym-

14 Higginson, Thomas Wentworth. *Contemporaries.* Boston. 1900.

pathetic brother proved by her application to his college books that her mind was more capable than his.

Though girls admittedly conquered the classics with ease, it was to the growth of scientific studies that they really owed their opportunities. There were plenty of arguments against women's entering public life, toward which the study of the classics led; but it was difficult to propound reasons why the scientific wonders of the universe should be masculine property. The stars could be observed by all; why should males alone know the marvels of their course? Divine Providence was illustrated by the insects, the flowers, the strata of the earth, the action of chemicals; to deny women the right to understand these things was to deprive them of part of their divine heritage.

To Amos Eaton,[15] an experimental scientist of note, American women owed a great deal. Educated at Williams, Eaton had gone to Yale to study with the distinguished scientist Benjamin Silliman who encouraged him in his desire to establish American studies in botany, geology, and mineralogy. Heretofore English textbooks had been used, which, though they listed what was known of American lore, naturally were not all-inclusive. In 1817 Eaton returned to Williamstown, there to deliver a series of lectures in botany, geology, and mineralogy, subjects not yet included in the curriculum of the college. As "voluntary studies" they were, however, permitted.

[15] Letters from President Ricketts of Rensselaer; also Baker, R. P. *A Chapter in American Education.* New York. 1925.

Williams students, under no compulsion beyond
their recognition of the work of a true man of science,
attended in a body, with the exception of four students, the unregenerates being freshmen and sophomores. At the close of the first series, the students
arranged for the publication of the lectures in book
form.

Stimulated by this response Eaton delivered lectures in many places, speedily becoming recognized
as the leader in natural history, the chief exponent of
field work. A wider understanding of the technique
and the function of laboratory experimentation was
one of the fruits of his lectures to the public. By
1824 there was a fairly general recognition of the
value of scientific studies, a fairly widespread feeling
that the schools and colleges should teach the sciences,
that colleges should contain definite departments of
science, and that students should be fitted for " scientific and mechanic employment and the active business of life." [16]

It was Stephen Van Rensselaer who seems first to
have grasped the immediate practical application of
the new sciences to what was still the prime interest
of America, farming. Not himself a scientist, not a
man of great originality, Van Rensselaer was quickly
aware that Eaton's study of the soil of America had
bearing upon progressive methods of farming. With
nine hundred farms on his own estate, in his position
of president of a Board of Agriculture, he took a utili-

[16] Report of a Harvard committee headed by George Ticknor.
1824.

tarian viewpoint. Though he had gone to Harvard, he was influenced more by his Dutch heritage than by his study of the classics. The practically minded Dutch settlers had small use for the colleges, not desiring to raise a race of ministers and missionaries. It was the man of business whom they respected.

Van Rensselaer provided funds for an agricultural survey, inviting Amos Eaton to undertake it. At a time when it was still believed that a man who could make two blades of wheat grow where one grew before was a public benefactor, the education of a farmer as a farmer seemed of importance. To Van Rensselaer's suggestion that he come to Troy, New York, there to help establish an Institute to train " the sons and daughters of farmers and mechanics " in " agriculture, domestic economy, the arts, and manufactures," Eaton responded with enthusiasm. With ninety per cent of the population still on the farms this education took on enormous importance — people had to be fed before the ministers could preach to them or the lawyers settle their disputes.

Though Rensselaer Polytechnic Institute was planned thus as a co-educational school emphasizing agriculture, its development followed Eaton's correlation of natural and social sciences. Eaton came soon to regard the Institute as a graduate school, a place to which college graduates might come to gain from the program knowledge elsewhere excluded, knowledge which was of interest to the scientist, but also to the minister, the doctor, the lawyer. For college graduates the course was half that required of other students. Rensselaer thus puts forward a claim to having been the first true graduate school in America.

For the sons and daughters of farmers, said the founder of Rensselaer. Though in 1824 opportunities for girls lagged behind those for their brothers, there were already enough educated women to disprove the idea that women had small brains, or that using the brain disqualified a woman for her duties as wife and mother. Van Rensselaer believed that intelligence was important for the wife of a farmer. Without telephones, radios, automobiles, the farmers of the nineteenth century were shut in upon their farms. The long winter evenings passed more pleasantly with a companion capable of reading the same books, of discussing the questions of farm or town or country, of literature or religion, than with a woman whose only interests were her troublesome hens, or her rag rugs.

That women were apt pupils in the sciences Eaton had already demonstrated. As early as 1819 a pupil of his in Northampton, Jane Welsh, had published a *Botanical Catechism*. Eaton had conducted a class for females in Northampton, probably the first course in science ever offered to women. He had taught women in various places, and had seen his pupils go out to teach others. In 1829 a pupil, Mrs. Lincoln, later Mrs. Phelps, published *Familiar Studies in Botany*. A sister of Emma Willard, associated with her in the school, she studied with Eaton that she might teach in the Troy Female Seminary, where the work in science was apparently directed by Eaton. It may have been Mrs. Lincoln who in 1828 was spoken of by the Institute as "a lady well qualified for the duty" who would give to young ladies experimental courses in natural philosophy and chemistry which should parallel those "proposed for the young gentlemen."

But the Institute, probably for financial reasons, never carried out the original plan for co-education. Sufficiently burdened with the department for young gentlemen, it was never ready to open the female department. To do so, consistently with the founder's plans, would have involved a provision for a boarding house. To be sure most schools of the day did arrange for their young ladies to board among the respectable families of the town, but Mrs. Willard, as well as most of the prominent educators of the time, was strongly in favor of a central boarding house under the direction of the school.

Amos Eaton, however, was unwilling to exclude girls; and therefore organized classes in his private capacity, serving as teacher himself, and utilizing his own pupils as they became qualified to teach. He was eager to train up a group of teachers in science who could establish courses in female schools. In 1835 he offered for public examination in mathematics a class of eight young ladies.

Emma Willard had been a pupil of Eaton's, and to him had come Mary Lyon, living for some weeks in his household at Troy, becoming ever more deeply interested in chemistry. In kindly fashion he re-

ceived a number of feminine pupils thus, sending
them out to teach others. It is perhaps fair to say
that the present emphasis upon science at Mount
Holyoke, its splendid laboratories themselves, are the
offspring of the laboratories of Amos Eaton.

By 1835 Rensselaer had ceased to offer a bachelor
of arts, substituting a degree in natural science. Sciences were the core of the studies, though many other
subjects were included in the curriculum. The very
"scholastic amusements" to which the afternoons
were given over, were scientific. Students might
amuse themselves with field work, if the weather were
favorable; otherwise they might take their recreation
in the laboratories. Even the languages were taught
scientifically, with emphasis upon etymology.

In most of the subjects there seemed no need of
sex discrimination. Young ladies could hardly be expected to be interested in courses in civil, electrical,
and mechanical engineering. Indeed, very few young
men were attracted to such courses, exactly four coming up for examination in 1835 when the degree of
civil engineer was first offered. But if a school like
Rensselaer, which considered itself in advance of the
colleges, believed that girls were qualified to take its
courses in mathematics and the sciences, it was obvious that the seminaries need not consider themselves inferior; and they might soon obtain qualified
teachers of the sciences among their own sex, trained
by Eaton.

With an eye to the colleges, with the example of
Rensselaer before them, with due attention to the

English course in the better academies for boys, the
female seminaries shaped their curricula.

At this time Harvard [17] had nine departments,
listed presumably in the order of dignity, and labelled
by the letters of the alphabet: A B C D E F G H I.
Theology led the list, with Intellectual and Moral
Philosophy, Civil Polity, and Political Economy,
second. Third came Mathematics and Natural
Philosophy (physics). The fourth place went to
Rhetoric and Oratory, both of prime importance to
future ministers, lawyers, and men in public life.
This department and the next two, those of Greek
and Latin, were most prominent on the day of the
annual Exhibition, when a large audience was gratified by the proficiency of the young gentlemen. Latin
orations, Greek and Latin dialogues, Greek and
Latin versions of famous speeches, especially those of
the American Webster, shared the platform with an
English oration on Reverence, and a conference between two students on the subject of public opinion.[18]

There was no public parade of the newer subjects,
the three last departments: Chemistry, Mineralogy,
and Geology; Botany and Zoology; and Modern
Languages. These had come into the curriculum in
response to popular demand, but the college was not
yet proud of their inclusion.

Though French, German, Spanish, Italian, and
Portuguese were all taught, they were not dignified
by recognition on Exhibition days. At the time that

17 Current catalogues and President's Reports to the Trustees.
18 Program of Harvard Commencement 1834.

Wheaton Seminary opened Henry Wadsworth Longfellow was resigning from Bowdoin to spend a year
abroad before going to Harvard as head of the department of Modern Languages. German was only
just beginning to come into prominence, its cause
pushed by men like George Ticknor at Harvard, who
constantly lamented the difficulty of procuring German books in Cambridge or Boston, no bookstore in
either city carrying them in stock in the early days of
the century. George Bancroft, not yet recognizing
his field as that of historian, had been sent to Germany
upon his graduation, very young, from Harvard,
there to study theology. It was understood that he
would repay his college's generosity by returning to
act as tutor, giving to students the advantages of his
superior learning. German universities were recognized as more advanced intellectual centers than the
American colleges, partly because of the greater
maturity of their students — in no country did boys
go to college as young as in America — and partly because of a deeper appreciation of learning for its own
sake, scholarship for the sake of scholarship. German
ideas were later to obtain almost a strangle hold on
American universities, but in the eighteen-thirties it
was still remembered that education had other aims.
Not that vocational training was narrowly interpreted. Vocational training meant a discipline of
the mind that would be useful in the chosen profession. A mind so trained would function properly in
any given situation — a different training from that
which concerns itself with training for specific situations.

The suspicion aroused by modern languages was that they did not sufficiently discipline the mind. To any one with a grounding of Latin, French was all too simple. German at least had the difficulty of a strange script. Yet no modern language offered much reward to a student save the discipline of conquering the grammar or the delight of conversing elegantly. Many prominent men in the educational world felt that modern languages were but ornamental branches; the presence of French in the curricula of the female schools, especially in those which specialized in the " elegant " accomplishments tended to add little luster to the study.

In 1834–1835 George Ticknor, as head of the department of Modern Languages at Harvard, had under him four " instructers," all on half pay, giving instruction only three days a week. Latin and Greek, though frequently studied in alternate weeks, were recited daily. " No student," says the president's report of the modern languages, " is compelled to study any one of them," but once a student had elected a course he could not " quit " until he had made progress. Presumably a student would be permitted to proceed at his own pace, no rigid classes being formed. The courses were not open to freshmen who did, however, attend as " voluntary " students. In the year preceding this report of 1834–1835 the voluntary students had equalled the number registered in the courses, the total number being half the student body or better. At this time the college numbered three hundred and sixty-six students.

Though of less repute than the classics, the modern

languages were dignified by the presence of the overseers at examinations. The overseers might themselves examine the students, which would seem to
point to a knowledge of the modern languages on the
part of the overseers. In 1834 twenty-five students
passed the examination in Italian, twenty-three in
German, forty-four in French, fifteen in Spanish, and
seven in Portuguese.

Methods in the colleges were often those of the
schoolroom, daily recitations being the rule, though,
probably under the influence of Amos Eaton, but also
in accordance with the taste of the times, lectures were
figuring large in the plan of instruction. Many subjects lent themselves easily to the lecture system. In
the sciences lectures were demonstrated by the teacher's performance of an experiment before the class, a
method which is being reinstated in some schools of
the twentieth century. Languages, however, were
less easily adapted to the lecture method. Students
in Greek had daily recitations, half the class reciting
each day. Such an arrangement would seem to indicate no overseriousness in the student's application
to his Herodotus or to the *Crown Oration* of Demosthenes. In the junior year Greek was studied daily
every other week, alternating with Latin.

This system of alternation was in great favor.
Schools, studying the catalogues of the colleges and of
rival schools, would prepare in their announcements
an astonishing list of languages, sciences, and philosophies, adding the comforting assurance that not every
pupil would be expected to take all the subjects

offered. A few weeks' steady application was rewarded with a complete change. Sometimes the
period alloted was very short, sometimes a full quarter
or even a term of twenty or twenty-two weeks was
given up to the pursuit of one study or a set of studies.
With mathematics and the classics " the chief labor
and crowning honor of scholarship " other subjects in
the male institutions had to take their chance.

In 1834 Harvard's announcement lists under each
department the number of weeks devoted to a course
or to an individual textbook. Thus Stewart's *Elements of the Philosophy of the Mind* and Paley's
Moral Philosophy take a term of the junior year for
mastery. The senior year included in the first term
Locke *On the Understanding,* in the second term Say's
Political Economy, the third term Story's *On the
Constitution of the United States.* The freshmen
gave twelve weeks to mastering Walker's *Geometry;*
the sophomores six weeks to Lowth's *Grammar,*
twelve pages a lesson; seventeen weeks to Whateley's
Rhetoric, twelve pages a lesson. In their first term
the seniors had seventeen lectures on rhetoric and
criticism, and wrote nineteen themes. The complete
list of a Harvard student's themes was fifty-five, nineteen in the junior, seventeen in the sophomore year.

In chemistry there were thirty-two lectures, three
a week, for juniors, with voluntary attendance permitted seniors. These lectures were intended primarily for those planning to enter medical school. In
mineralogy and geology there was a course of twenty-
four lectures, given over a period of four weeks, open

to seniors. The chair of botany and zoology was vacant. Dr. Gould came out from Boston to conduct nineteen recitations on Smellie's *Philosophy of Natural History,* each with a brief illustration of zoology.

At the botany lectures attendance was purely voluntary. So great was the interest, however, that practically the entire senior class, to whom the course was restricted, attended regularly.

In the junior year two hours a week of the first term were given over to Paley's *Evidences of Christianity,* ten pages a lesson completing the book by the end of November. This was followed by Butler's *Analogy,* the first part finished by the end of the fourth week of the second term.

This method of apportioning definite weeks to a given textbook was followed also in the seminaries, carried sometimes to excess when a preceptress would decide that the pupils all needed a thorough drill and would halt the regular program for two or three weeks. Such drastic measures were fortunately rare. At Wheaton in 1836 Mary Lyon imposed a week of " arithmetick," then another week of arithmetic with composition added, and then a third week. " Some of the young ladies liked it very much, others began to complain and say I wish we were not hurried so, . . . I wish we could have something else now, for I am tired to death with ciphering, and I don't see any use in it." [19] At the end of the period, students admitted that they at last knew one subject thor-

[19] Shepard, Grace F. *History of Wheaton.*

oughly, and were rewarded by Miss Lyon's promise, before her departure, that they need study no more arithmetic that year.

More general was the practice of rotating a group of studies. A section of a textbook would be completely mastered, and then put aside for a time. Schools finding their pupils deficient, or suspecting them of forgetting their early lessons, would often keep up a drill on fundamentals through the year. The Young Ladies High School of Providence, Rhode Island, which was opened in 1828 by a young man who had graduated from Brown only two years earlier, stressed elementary studies throughout its course. Believing in the importance of these rudiments, Mr. Kingsbury continued them unless his pupils were truly proficient, " so that spelling — old-fashioned spelling — and the higher ancient classics have sometimes been contemporaneous studies! " [20]

With the wide interest in education, textbooks were to change much as time went on, many women adapting old content to new method, or adding new content to bring old favorites up to date. Emma Willard and her sister both wrote textbooks, which received wide recognition, being used by boys' schools as well as girls' and crossing the ocean to be translated for European schools. Mrs. Phelps's *Botany* is listed among the textbooks used at Ipswich Seminary, and therefore to be used in the new Wheaton.

It was natural for the seminaries, considering themselves as the equivalent of colleges, to look to the

[20] Tolman, William Howe. *History of Higher Education in Rhode Island.* Washington. Government Printing Office. 1894.

colleges for their program. Similarly the academies, co-educational or male, kept their non-preparatory course close to that of the college. The "English Classical" course was designed as a thorough education for nonprofessional students. Omitting Latin and Greek, or including them as extras, it offered the sciences and the modern languages. The theology of the colleges was brought down, because of its importance: moral philosophy, evidences of Christianity, and Butler's *Analogy*. In the first published list of Wheaton's studies, the parallel with Harvard is easily seen. Instead of Paley there is Alexander's *Evidences of Christianity,* and Watts *On the Mind* instead of Stewart's *Elements of the Philosophy of the Mind*. Similarly Sullivan's *Political Class Book* takes the place in the seminary of Say's *Political Economy*.

Many of the texts used at Harvard were required of the earliest Wheaton students, as they were of those at Ipswich: Smellie's *Philosophy of Natural History,* Whateley's *Rhetoric,* Paley's *Natural Theology,* Butler's *Analogy*.

At Yale [21] in the senior year the hard drill in the classics yielded to this same mastering of logic, natural philosophy, and evidences of Christianity, while Columbia [22] in the eighteen-thirties, fighting for its life against the competition of the new University of New York, endeavored to attract students by offering a non-classical course. It was in 1830 when its rival was first seen as a menace that the trustees established

[21] Welch, L. S. and Camp, Walter. *Yale*. Boston. 1899.
[22] *A History of Columbia University*. New York. 1904.

a " scientific and literary course " which was supposed
to parallel the classical course, omitting only the study
of the Greek and Latin languages and adding other
subjects.   After thirteen years this course, which
during its entire existence attracted only forty-nine
students, was discontinued. Designed for " the education of young men intended for civil or military
engineers, architects, superintendents of manufacto-
ries, or for mercantile or nautical pursuits," it was
indeed an attempt to broaden the scope of education,
to attract to Columbia young men who might not
care to devote three hours a day to the classics. But
at this time competition was keen among the colleges,
as it was to be among the seminaries.

Whether at college or seminary, the study of Butler's *Analogy* was of the greatest importance. *The
Analogy of Religion to the Constitution and Course
of Nature,* originally published in 1756, was to gain
ascendency in American schools, for fifty years or
more, down to the final quarter of the nineteenth
century, held fast in the catalogue.

" Start me anywhere in Butler and I can go on in-
definitely," was the boast of many a college-trained
man, many a seminary-trained woman of the nineteenth century.

Not religious emotion, not mystical faith, but close
reasoning was Butler's spiritual food. " Probability
is the very guide of life," he declared in the introduction to his monumental proof of the truth of revealed religion. The deists were, in his day, casting
doubts about miracles, about the infallibility of the

Scriptures, even about the importance of man's world as the center of the universe. It was Butler's task to show that the deists were wrong, logically and completely wrong. Without mentioning either deism or the deists collectively or individually, he directed a barrage of argument against every opinion they had advanced or might advance.

Deeply interested in ethics, Butler declared that any weakening of the belief in religion would break down morality; either man was bound by the restraints of religious belief, or he could be led to conduct depraved, licentious, inimical to personal and social peace.

Butler's *Analogy,* though its viewpoint is that of destructive argument, builds up positive ideas of eternal truth and of right conduct. It shows carefully, steadily, that there is a direct, easily apparent analogy between the known course of nature and the Biblical revelation of divine government. There are three necessary premises: the existence of God, the known course of nature, and the limitations of human knowledge. Against atheism, though he recognized its existence, Butler did not waste ammunition. His book was directed to those who were willing to grant the existence of God, as his opponents, the deists, did. The *Analogy* was therefore well suited for America where atheism was in disrepute.

With probability as the guide Butler moved from the known in nature to the probable truth of religion, always postulating the existence of " an intelligent Author of nature, and natural Governor of the world."

A twentieth century scientist writes in 1934: The biologist " knows that physicochemical analysis will never give the final clue to life processes; yet he recognizes that 'vitalism' and 'neovitalism' are little more than a sort of amorphous theology born of a sense of helplessness of mere 'mechanism'"; to which he appends a footnote most interesting to the student of the eighteen-thirties, held firm in the grasp of Butler and Paley, " And indeed, ultimately they both [vitalism and neovitalism] encounter the same inevitable perplexity, since, as Paley rightly asserts, mechanism presupposes God as the mechanician. This is the difficulty faced by all the recent astronomical and physicist school of ponderers." [23]

For Butler the "intelligent Author of nature, and natural Governor of the world" was a moral God. " Our whole nature leads us to ascribe all moral perfection to God, and to deny all imperfection of him." If man were given the universe to direct, given free rein to rule, could he direct wisely? could he produce that happiness which all desire? In spite of isolated examples of the wicked flourishing like the green bay tree, Butler explained that careful observation would surely disclose that virtue meant happiness, vice meant misery. An easily comprehended example would be the drunkard. Drinking may often bring happiness; its first stage is conviviality. But this joyous state does not endure. Continued intemperance can lead only to physical decay and to utter misery. Could man with his limited powers of judgment have balanced better a system of rewards and punishments?

[23] Zinsser, Hans, in *The Atlantic Monthly*, November, 1934.

Could, then, an all-benevolent God be as credible as a just God?

Religion, said Butler, necessarily postulates a future state, where rewards and punishments are finally meted out — with justice. Even as no physician can repair the ravages of continued intemperance, so no just God can eradicate the consequences of human action.

The necessity for final rewards and punishments was, however, only one of the arguments for immortality. Butler asked his readers to consider the improbabilities of non-survival, as well as the various analogies in nature which argued for survival. The worm and the moth were the simplest of the illustrations. Another was human disease. The mind lives on unimpaired in case after case where the body is irreparably injured. A man who loses a leg or an arm or both is not thereby impaired in his mind; his conduct is not affected. Many portions of the body can be lost, many have been known to have been lost, without affecting the man's mind, his essential personality. How then could death and the dissolution of the body be taken as a sign of the death of the soul?

Belief in a future life is not even inconsistent with atheism. But religion without a belief in immortality is futile. A belief in immortality is " the foundation of all our hopes and all our fears." And therefore the *Analogy* attempts first to disprove all arguments against immortality.

The second part of the book is concerned with the

importance of Christianity and the Evidences of Christianity. This, in the colleges and schools, was fortified by the study of Alexander's or Paley's *Evidences*. Paley's clear logical mind arranged proofs with greater lucidity than Butler, perhaps because, while equally earnest, he was of a more cheerful disposition, less overcome with dread of the church's decline.

Now deism was not a threatening foe in nineteenth century America. Atheism was lifting its head, but only enough to make articles on its futility welcome in the more serious magazines. The growth of new sects, especially those of latitudinarian doctrine, and the growth of science, now widely studied and constantly applied to daily life, were the real challenges to traditional faith. It was the province of the schools to show that the new knowledge deepened rather than attacked the belief in a supreme ruler of the universe. The very laws of physics and of anatomy should prove that there was a guide; the construction of the eye of human or bird could be used as evidence of a guiding intelligence. The teleological argument put forth by Butler was echoed in text after text of *Evidences*.

In the nineteen-thirties the movies showing the marvelous construction of the eye of an insect, leave the audience, adult or juvenile, to make their own conclusions. The eighteen-thirties learned with one breath the construction of the lens of the eye and the all-wise Providence that directed its construction. The naïve wonder of the child at the " great round wonderful world, with the wonderful water round it curled," was supplemented and fortified in the nineteenth century by the wonder of the adult at the infinite provision for the finite world.

The curricula of school and college provided then for the correlation of science and religion. The facts of science were raised in importance at the same time that the ideas of religion were supported by glowing proof. When the conclusions of physics or the dissection of an anatomy could be linked to eternal truths which had their reverberations not only in this world but in the eternity to come, learning gained in dignity and became quite properly the major interest of man.

But the study of Butler — and of Paley — had other value for the eighteen-thirties than its application to the acceptance of religion. Any student who conscientiously applied himself or herself to the closely printed text, following argument after argument, examining the neatly balanced and carefully based statements, received a training in exactness and in logic that could scarcely be paralleled. The study of logic was part of the curriculum of all advanced schools. The best of logical training was gained through the mastery of Butler. If the well-trained mind gained its powers by discipline, then Butler deservedly held its place of first importance. Step by step the students followed his reasoning. The pages were ruled, the sections marked out. Each point in the argument was numbered and noted in the margin. Each sentence was digested, each paragraph summarized, each chapter burnt into the memory.[24]

24 Copy in the Wheaton Library.

Though Lydia Sigourney, in later years, believed that she studied Butler at fourteen, this is doubtful. The *Analogy* was usually reserved for the senior year of the colleges, the last year of the seminaries, with variations of time at different institutions. At Harvard Butler came in the second term of the junior year. It was not, however, to be undertaken before the mind had been trained by many other studies which required concentration and application. In importance the *Analogy* seems to have outranked all other studies.

In the program of the best schools of the eighteen-thirties all was integrated: history, science, and religion summed up in Butler's *Analogy*. Any student pursuing a full course, even if that course were interrupted, even if it were pursued at more than one school, moved forward steadily to Butler as to a climax which knit the fabric of many studies into an harmonious whole.

Only the more serious schools included it in the curriculum; and these might well claim to be of college grade. At Brown University [25] Butler was studied in the senior year along with Paley. President Francis Wayland had come to Brown in 1826, there to rule for thirty years. He found the college course in need of drastic revision. Before his coming juniors and seniors had fallen upon pleasant days, the juniors dropping to two recitations a day after the spring vacation, the seniors having two until April and thereafter until the August commencement only one

[25] Bronson, W. C. *History of Brown University.* 1914.

a day. Wayland decreed three a day for all students. Moreover, recitations were supposed to begin by the instructor's calling for a presumably brief analysis of the entire assignment for the day. Wayland himself lectured on intellectual and moral philosophy, and on political economy and also gave a course on the Evidences of Christianity.

It was Wayland who summed up the college in the changing world of the thirties as having three aims: [26] " 1. To increase the number of educated men in the whole community. 2. To raise the standard of professional learning. 3. To increase the number of ministers of the gospel."

It is this first aim which had vast importance in the world of education. The need of more ministers was easily seen; the raising of the standard of learning of professional men was obvious in an expanding intellectual world. To increase the number of the educated in every community seemed an educational aim worthy of a democracy. It was under the shelter of this idea that woman's education was born. Brown was not to admit women to degrees until the last decade of the century but far back in 1793 it had permitted a senior to give as his commencement address *A Dissertation in Favor of Female Education.* And in 1800 the newly formed Brown branch of the Philandrian Society at its first meeting debated the question: " Would it be good policy to allow females in the United States an Education equal to the males' ? "

[26] Tolman, W. H. *History of Higher Education in Rhode Island.* 1894.

Though this came before President Wayland's time, it was a corollary to his own belief in the necessity of increasing the number of the educated.

Certainly no girl at a seminary could complain much to her brother at Brown of her studies or her restrictions. In Latin she was probably behind him, since many girls had had no work in the classics when they arrived, but if she worked hard she could overtake him even there. In her other studies she paralleled his. Like him, she had to retire to her room to study, and like him she was supposed not to leave her room during study hours. President Wayland's system of sending proctors spying at odd times was less pleasant than the common custom of the seminaries, whereby each girl reported her own misdeeds. Like her brother at Brown, however, a seminary girl could, if it pleased her instructor, go to class without books, summarize the lesson, and take careful notes of a lecture. Seminary girls studied as hard as students at any of the colleges, under less compulsion. They were still eager to learn, still under the impression that learning was a privilege.

" All but three here are pious," wrote a Wheaton student in her letter home during the seminary's first year in 1835. College boys were pious, too. When in 1838 President Wayland of Brown learned that some of his students were planning to attend a theater in Providence, he warned the assembled students that he would take the strongest disciplinary measures against all who thus risked their souls.[27] He declared

[27] Condon, Charles T. *Reminiscences of a Journalist.* Boston. 1880.

his determination to report any such students to the pastor of their church; " those delinquents who were yet unconverted he threatened with suspension."

" Descartes supposes the small gland in the base of the brain to be the seat of the soul." [28] Physiology, astronomy, chemistry, botany, mineralogy — all the known sciences in renewing faith in divine guidance emphasized the importance of the soul. Indeed the discipline of the mind was of value only because such discipline strengthened the soul. Physical exercise was valued because the care of the body which God gave was conducive to care of the soul.

Yet not always were the needs of the other world pressing upon these earnest students of the eighteen-thirties. Knowledge in itself was a joy because it widened the horizons of an essentially stay-at-home people. Pioneers went West, to conquer wild lands, and to control the Indian. For them there was small contact with cultivated minds, with European civilizations.

For those who remained in the East, even those already in the cities, the opportunities for travel were not great. Well-to-do people did travel, but even though they crossed the ocean it was seldom more than once or twice in a lifetime. Emma Willard consorted with the aristocracy of France, with prominent people of England; Lucretia Mott, Elizabeth Cady Stanton, Julia Ward Howe were all to meet notables. But the ordinary American did not have this opportunity of mental expansion through direct contact

[28] Notebook, Wheaton archives.

with the leading minds of Europe. He got his learning from books and from lectures. And because he
was ambitious, he wanted his children to understand
more than he could himself. American parents were
in no small part influential in the widening of the
curricula of schools and colleges. It was with pride
that they watched their daughters learning from the
same books as their sons. For most girls Greek was
lacking — yet had they desired it ardently it would
have been included as Latin was. Often Latin did
not appear in the published list of studies, because,
like French and music, Italian and German — even,
indeed, like fancy embroidery — it was an extra. In
all places except Mount Holyoke it was charged for as
an extra; Mount Holyoke charged no extras except
for the use of a piano.

"Not more than one out of fifty ever receive anything more than a common school education among
the females of the United States," wrote a student in
her notebook in 1836.[29] A sobering thought this. It
emphasized the privilege of those at the seminaries,
making serious students of merry young girls. The
happy faces of the girls in the advanced schools and
seminaries were constantly remarked upon by visitors.
Rules might be strict, emphasis upon right conduct
strong, but life was full of the joy of human companionship, quickened with the growth of the intellect, made worthy by intellectual achievement. Pride
had its part, too, the pride of sharing studies so long
labeled masculine.

[29] Wheaton archives.

And many a weary hour with the *Analogy* was irradiated by the certainty that in becoming wise, one became good. For the right conduct of life was ever the aim and the test of education.

Latin and Greek, French and German, all the sciences from astronomy to zoology, what were they but the training of the mind to fit it for comprehension of the philosophies that brought man and God closer together! The pursuit of knowledge was a religious exercise, each step a rung in the ladder toward eternal life.

To fit in with this conception of knowledge the curriculum of the seminaries was shaped not greatly different from that of the colleges which trained men for the ministry. Though modern languages and sciences might be included more liberally and the classics restricted, the truly important studies which remembered that man's world was but a part of God's Universe were properly emphasized.

Education as preparation for life here and hereafter was the aim of college and seminary.

CHAPTER V

COLLEGES FOR WOMEN

IN May 1864 Frederick Barnard, Yale 1828, was inaugurated as the tenth president of Columbia. His inauguration address was "The Relation of Physical Science to Revealed Religion." [1] There was still at Columbia a Chair of the Evidences of Natural and Revealed Religion.

Strauss's *Leben Jesu* had startled Germany in 1835, but it was not until 1846 that it was available in England, and therefore America, through George Eliot's translation. Darwin's *Origin of Species* had focused the challenge in 1859.

The telegraph had become a thing of use, no longer a thing of wonder; gas lighting had ceased to be a municipal elegance and had entered the home; anæsthesia had risen from a medical, almost magical "stunt" into a surgical necessity. The discoveries and the practical applications of science were manifold. The scientific approach to the Bible was an obvious step, hailed by some scholars as a step forward in the enlightenment of the world, by others as a step downward into the yawning abyss of apostasy.

By 1869 parents were writing letters to the editor [2] protesting against their children's having to study the

[1] *History of Columbia University.* New York. The Columbia University Press. 1904.
[2] *New York Times,* December 25, 1869.

" wire-drawn, fine-spun ' Butler's Analogy ' " which, they asserted, was uselessly rubbed into the brain and forgotten " when we lay down to the hard work of life." Indeed these letter-writing fathers were inclined to disapprove of long school hours, visualizing their own youth as a time when winter school was sufficient for learning; when boys and girls spent their time out of doors " and never heard of Butler's Analogy."

These were the protests of the non-college bred against the education which they could afford to give their children. Successful business men, suspicious of fields of knowledge beyond their ken, looked upon the sciences as their fathers had looked upon Greek and Latin — as the frills of education intended for professional men. Their sons, destined for business, had no need of " botany, astronomy, physics, logic, and what not." Let them be prepared for life by a practical education. " The great business of the world is buying and selling." Trade supports itself; education is supported by trade. Then let the schools — at least the public schools — take heed, drop innovations, and realize their duty to a race of traders. This " mania for changing textbooks " would lead to no good.

At the same time the superintendent of the schools of New York presented his annual report to the Board of Education.[3] Evening schools were now flourishing with an average attendance of twelve thousand. Of the thirty-one evening schools, eleven were " female."

[3] *New York Times*, December 30, 1869.

The superintendent stated that he "augurs much good" from the establishment of high schools and especially of the normal schools which prepared female teachers. Massachusetts had established normal schools thirty years before this. To offset the complaints of parents — in letters to the editor — that children no longer liked to go to school, there comes the superintendent's statement that "no absolute necessity exists for a continuance of the practice of corporal punishment upon pupils." Its abolishment is therefore recommended. Thirty years before a superintendent had declared that it had "no sanction but usage."

However loudly occasional fathers objected, the good old days were passing. The body of knowledge was growing too large for any one person's assimilation. This, rather than the decline of strict discipline, led to the elective system deplored by the conservatives. While Latin, Greek, and theology were the sum of wisdom, education could move serenely within the appointed lines; when all the sciences crowded the curriculum, something had to yield; and as old-time requirements fell before the new knowledge, there were those who predicted sure disaster.

Schools had multiplied. More and more communities had been impressed with the need of public schools, of normal schools to provide teachers for the elementary schools — chiefly female teachers now — and of advanced schools for the preparation of teachers for high schools and academies. Unsatisfied with these, the Middle West began to establish state universities, a step in which New England was loath to follow. Massachusetts, in the twentieth century as in the nineteenth, declines to recognize the need of a state college of liberal arts. In the East college education is still provided by the parents' purse directly rather than through the state by taxation. Though the West takes justifiable pride in its great universities, prestige clings to the privately endowed institutions of the East. So in the nineteenth century, though high schools and normal schools filled rapidly, there was yet room for the seminaries, and demand for the colleges that were to be founded with private capital.

The seminaries had held their own, save for difficulties during depression and war years, because of their superior prestige, because of the greater ease with which they could adapt to a newer curriculum. Slowly as courses of study changed, they did change. English literature had crept in at first in the guise of rhetoric. The study of the history of English literature followed, perhaps stimulated by popular readings and discussions of Shakespeare. Richard Henry Dana had read Shakespeare in Providence to Margaret Fuller's pupils;[4] in New York as in Boston the public flocked to lectures on Falstaff.[5]

Progress in Latin had proved so satisfactory that young ladies had gone beyond Virgil into Livy and Horace. In mathematics they advanced through trigonometry to calculus. Science was ever more absorb-

---

4 Ossoli, Margaret Fuller. *Memoirs.* 2 vols. Boston. 1852.
5 Advertisements in current newspapers.

ing. The Lowell Institute in Boston conducted a series of evening classes for ladies, its laboratories offering fascinating opportunities for experiments. The Massachusetts Institute of Technology, opening in 1864, included a woman on its faculty in its second decade;[6] Ellen H. Swallow Richards, the wife of a professor, was an instructor from 1878 to 1911. She served as an assistant to Professor Nichols after her graduation from Vassar, and herself took a Bachelor of Science degree from M. I. T. in 1873.

Recognizing the importance of science, recognizing, too, the lack of adequate scholarly equipment in the regular staff of teachers, seminaries like Wheaton had come to adopt the custom of importing specialists who would give a series of lectures. Wheaton was fortunate in being close enough to Boston to obtain well known scientists without much effort, but even the more remote seminaries gave their students this advantage.

Meanwhile great changes had taken place in America. Travel by land and by water was steadily swifter and safer. The gold rush had made California definitely a part of the country, though still a far-flung borderland, a country of legend and dream. Ideas were adjusting to a vast territory, a country which could always remain absorbed in its own affairs. Americans were surer than ever that theirs was the greatest country on earth, even as Barnum continued to show them the greatest wonders. Travellers con-

[6] *A History of the Departments of Chemistry and Physics at M. I. T.* Cambridge. 1933.

tinued to visit American shores; continued to pour forth volumes of kindly or malicious criticism, but Americans were growing less sensitive. Dickens' observations in the forties created a storm of protest, though to a later day they seem mild enough. Anthony Trollope's *North America,* more kindly than his mother's earlier volumes of malice in 1832, created no great sensation in 1862. Americans continued to chew tobacco — even the rigidly moral President Wayland of Brown University was a chewer [7] — to assert their independence, to crowd European gentlemen in coaches and trains, to boast of their democracy and their wealth.

The growth of industrialism had led to waves of immigration which had made America somewhat class conscious. The newspapers poked fun at the awkward Irish servant girl who now replaced the negro in current jokes. The negro had become too important for jest. The cloud which had appeared dark upon the horizon in the eighteen-thirties had grown to a thunderhead by the eighteen-fifties, and in the sixties the storm had burst. During the war schools had their difficulties, but the cause of education was helped and advanced even as it had been by the Revolution. In the war years men teachers had been withdrawn into the armies, to be replaced by women, thereby accentuating the value of their services, the need of their training.

Moreover, during the long years of the war women had been drawn out of their sphere, left without the

7 *Memories of Brown.* Providence. 1909.

protection of a strong masculine arm, without the guide of a strong masculine intellect. They had successfully run farms, performing all the strenuous tasks of raising crops, tending cattle, even felling trees and sawing wood. It was not only in the pioneer settlements that women learned that they could do the work of men. In the cities there were men's tasks to do. And there were bandages to make, socks to knit, the wounded to care for. Women were not unaware of the part their sex had already played in precipitating the conflict. The number of ardent women abolitionists had grown to a mighty number, women directing their own organization, defending their own views on the public platform. Through the decades the abolitionists had pushed their cause, making their emotional plea sound reasonable. Impelled by an inner necessity, a moral conviction, an irresistible urge to right a wrong, they pressed their case. The logic of the institution of slavery was wrong, they knew; but men are rarely convinced by logic, or if convinced, are not moved to action. It was the triumph of emotionalism that precipitated the civil war — current newspapers referred to it as " the Revolution " — a war that was as definitely fought to save the Union as the World War of 1914–1918 was fought to save democracy. The United States might be a nation of traders, a race of men who knew the value of everything in dollars and cents, yet the economic motive was insufficient to free the slaves, to preserve the *United* States.

The eloquence of self-forgetful men and women

kept the subject in the foreground for a generation. And then in 1852 there appeared *Uncle Tom's Cabin,* the most potent of all anti-slavery arguments, since it presented both the good and the bad in the slavery system, and presented these in the guise of an easily comprehended and tear-compelling story. First run as a serial in 1851–1852 in an Abolitionist paper, it conquered the world when it appeared in book form.[8] Here was a book by a woman which at a time of modest sales became a best-seller in the twentieth century sense. The very day of publication saw three thousand copies sold; the first year three hundred thousand. It was on the advice of a man — a family friend and a Congressman — that Mrs. Stowe had chosen to accept from the publishers a straight ten per cent royalty rather than a fifty per cent share of the profits.

This success of *Uncle Tom's Cabin* merely confirmed the public impression of women writers. Maria Edgeworth had been imported along with Scott; and of native writers Lydia Sigourney, Lydia Maria Child, Catherine Sedgwick, and many a forgotten rhymester were placed beside Cooper, Emerson, Thoreau, Longfellow, Whittier, Poe, and Hawthorne. America had come to have a literature of her own. She even dared to prefer her native writers to those of Europe. Sophia Smith, whose fortune was to establish a woman's college, thought Thackeray's *Pendennis* frivolous.[9] America was to have its fri-

8 Stowe, Lyman Beecher. *Saints, Sinners and Beechers.* Indianapolis. 1934.

9 Hanscom, E. D. and Greene, H. F. *Sophia Smith and the Beginnings of Smith College.* Northampton. 1925.

volity in a different vein — Mark Twain's *Innocents Abroad* coming to delight in 1869, six years before *Tom Sawyer*. As travellers constantly remarked, America was a reading nation. Here Elizabeth Barrett Browning found as sympathetic an audience as in her own England; and here Robert Browning found his first attentive audience.

But in admiration of English authors there was no forgetfulness of native Americans, and poetesses like Lucy Larcom spoke directly to the hearts of the people.

Here was one more American woman who gained prominence on both sides of the Atlantic. Here was one more example of the fruits of democracy. Born in 1824 in a New England seaside town she puzzled as a child over the perplexing phrases in English poetry. Who were " servile minions " ? who were the rich? and who the poor? [10] The daughter of a shopkeeper, she was conscious of no social discriminations. When her father died the necessity of making a living for a large brood of children forced her mother to move to an industrial center, there to open a boarding house for the country girls who came to Lowell to work in the mills. Lucy Larcom was not yet twelve when she began to work in the mill, at first tending bobbins, a task which required attention only once every forty-five minutes, and then spinning. That these American working girls were bent on self improvement is proved by the factory rule forbidding operatives to bring books to the mill. Whereas there may have been frivolous souls who would have

[10] Larcom, Lucy. *A New England Girlhood*. Boston. 1889.

brought light tales to amuse themselves with, the main desire was for an education, an extension of the meager weeks allowed little girls for schooling. Lucy Larcom in her autobiography *A New England Girlhood* tells how easily she evaded the rule, pasting on the wall about her window-seat, beside her loom, newspaper clippings from the Poet's Corner. Most of the girls brought Bibles, refusing at first to believe that they could be deprived of these. But the overseer confiscated them all, though probably more than Lucy Larcom outwitted him, by carrying " some leaves from a torn Testament " in their pockets.

It was in 1840, when she was sixteen, that she joined with her companions in publishing the *Lowell Offering,* the fruits of the girls' creative talent. For these girls, working from dawn until seven o'clock at night, were keenly conscious of their intellectual needs. They attended lectures, they formed themselves in classes, they read, they discussed, and they wrote. The *Offering* in its five years gained wide recognition, its subscription list rising to four thousand. An anthology from its pages was published in London in 1849 under the sentimental title *Mind Among the Spindles,* and lecturers in Paris devoted a full period to " the significance and merit of the *Lowell Offering.*" [11]

Lucy Larcom was not to remain among the spindles. With democratic ease she transferred as teacher to a district school, soon to become a pupil herself again, this time at an already well known seminary in

11 Addison, D. D. *Lucy Larcom.* Boston. 1895.

Illinois: Monticello.   Here, teaching and studying, she passed pleasant years, graduating in 1852.   It was in 1854 that she came to Wheaton Seminary for four years, her chief task to teach composition, though her program called for classes in history and moral philosophy.

Her most popular poem " Hannah Binding Shoes " made her a veritable literary lady.   And her career emphasized alike the achievements of democracy and of the female sex.   Many of the mill girls worked but half the year, spending the other half in some academy or seminary.   In the cloth room to which Lucy Larcom was eventually promoted, the girls found time to read widely (here where there was no machinery to be watched, books were permitted) : Shakespeare, Milton, Coleridge, Wordsworth, along with Jeremy Taylor and Cotton Mather's *Magnalia*.

Though men might still argue the propriety of feminine learning, they no longer could dispute its possibility.   Too many men had attended the public exercises of co-educational or female schools, too many men had listened to women speakers, too many men had married educated wives for the old disparagements to sound anything but archaic.

Though there were by the middle of the century few subjects restricted to the masculine sex, there was not always an avid interest on the part of the feminine pupils.   In the classics, the young ladies in the seminaries were likely to accomplish only the tasks their brothers performed in preparatory school; often they did not take Latin at all, and practically always they sidestepped Greek. For the ambitious there were the fullest offerings of dead languages. Though only a fraction of the students at the seminaries chose to follow the classical course, yet the brilliance of their performance overshadowed the smallness of their numbers. In public examinations they gave ample evidence that the female mind was capable of reaching any heights set by men.

The resentment of a few young women at not being allowed to go to a regular college with their brothers stirred up a small group capable of vocalizing its desires. At Oberlin degrees had been granted to several women, a few women had already entered the professions, and as yet there were no disastrous consequences. Dio Lewis with his practical gymnastics, had persuaded young women to be healthy and vigorous, instead of prettily pale. Irish immigrants had begun to crowd the cities, only too eager to perform the menial tasks of farm and home and city, releasing both sons and daughters in greater number than ever before to swell the ranks of the schools.

In the South various institutions had long given degrees to women, inviting comparison of their programs with those of the men's colleges in their vicinity, but the North in general clung to the idea of degreeless seminaries until prejudice seemed to have receded, until benevolent people began to establish new institutions which followed the new trends in education. If the South could give degrees, if Oberlin and other co-educational colleges could honor women, it was natural to think of female colleges in the East. New York state led the way with Elmira.

Elmira Female College,[12] chartered in 1855, with an endowment including buildings and apparatus of some eighty thousand dollars proudly boasted its recognition as a college by the Board of Regents of the state of New York. It offered a six year course, the first two years preparatory for the true college course for which the degree of A.B. was granted. Greek was offered as an elective in the junior year, as an alternative with German, and Latin was continued only through the sophomore year. A man president, men professors, and women "preceptresses" made up its faculty, seven in all in 1861, with a student body of one hundred and four, of whom one quarter were in the preparatory department. Elmira permitted entrance at any time during the school year, requiring, however, that once entered, a student remain until the close of the year. The seminaries had long ago fought this custom of irregularity.

With Elmira establishing itself as a college, its curriculum measuring up with that of many men's colleges, though not wholly the same as that of the New England colleges, the way was open for another female college in the state of New York.

It was in the eighteen-fifties that the idea of Vassar College was born.[13] Milo P. Jewett, a Dartmouth graduate, had been forced by his anti-slavery sympathies to leave the South where he had headed the Judson Female Institute in Alabama. Coming to Poughkeepsie, he had bought a school formerly owned

[12] Catalogues of Elmira Female College.
[13] Taylor, James Monroe. *Before Vassar Opened.* Boston. 1914.

by the niece of a wealthy brewer, Martin Vassar. In his old age Vassar liked to think that this niece, who had died before Jewett came North, had inspired him to dedicate his fortune to women's education. His niece seems to have been as innocent of the idea of a woman's college as Sophia Smith who, a decade after Vassar, was to have the disposal of her fortune directed, much as was Martin Vassar's, by a man interested in education.

"A college foundation that was laid in beer, never will prosper," wrote a disgruntled graduate of the early years. "Well, it was good beer, wasn't it?" shouted Vassar from his office.[14]

It was a good college, but it was not the founder's original intention. With a large fortune and with no direct heirs, Martin Vassar had planned a hospital similar to Guy's in London. But Milo Jewett, hearing of these plans, thought differently; Poughkeepsie was not London; and Jewett was not a physician. The school which he had headed in the South was a "female institute"; the school which he owned in the North was hardly on a par with Troy Female Seminary or the now famous seminaries of New England. If colleges in the South could give degrees, if Elmira could, then Vassar might well serve the cause of education by establishing a female college, which with a large endowment, such as he would give it, would outstrip all competitors — and of which Jewett could be the president. Jewett seems to have been one of that shrewd group of men who saw in women's educa-

14 Wood, F. H. *Earliest Years at Vassar.* Poughkeepsie. 1909.

tion an opportunity to advance themselves. He had early found in female schools a wider opportunity than was afforded in the more heavily competitive field of masculine education.

Jewett met Vassar through the church of which they were both members. It was in the eighteen-fifties that he began to urge upon this worried financier the establishment of a college. Mrs. Vassar seems to have had no part in the discussion, and much did Vassar waver, being rescued from a plan to endow a boys' and a girls' high school only by Jewett's swift and decisive action. Jewett urged that these projects were hardly worthy of so large a fortune; that the current need was for institutions of higher learning for the sex which had proved its capacities so nobly in the seminaries and in the Southern colleges. The public, he urged, was ready for this next step, since the seminaries had always presented themselves as colleges. He drew up a plan,[15] much in advance of any existing system, which he felt would lift the new college out of the class of the seminaries, which would make it point the way even for the men's colleges.

Jewett finally pinned Vassar down to the founding of Vassar Female College, the name under which it was incorporated in 1861. It was Mrs. Hale, the editor of *Godey's* who insisted that the word " female " be expunged.

Jewett now gained Vassar's consent to a coveted European trip to study European universities, a foolish step some of his friends warned him, since in

[15] This plan seems to have originated with Charles P. Raymond.

Europe there were no women's colleges.[16] But education, not education feminized, was Jewett's aim and he therefore proposed to study various courses of study. Yet there was a definite understanding that Vassar Female College would consider the " peculiar needs of women " and would preserve the " feminine graces." [17]

Jewett, then, went to Europe; and in his absence Vassar was not without advisers. Another educator, Charles Raymond, stepped in with gratuitous advice, apparently seeing many chances for masculine service to the new venture. Outwardly approving the plans of his friend Jewett, he offered himself as vice president, after a time suavely suggesting that the vice president be entrusted with the actual work, the president retained as an honorary officer. Though Charles Raymond eventually became inextricably entangled in his own schemes, he did involve Jewett in his downfall, having insinuated too much for Jewett's extrication. Jewett lost his temper — in writing — and the way was open for a President Raymond — alas, not Charles. It was John Raymond who held the presidency when Vassar College finally opened.

It was during the war years that Martin Vassar prepared for his college which opened in 1865. Though there was criticism, the American world was too busy with the war and its consequences to be much

16 Girton in Cambridge, England, was opened in 1869, and did not give degrees. The Oxford colleges for women came a decade later.

17 *Vassar College Fiftieth Anniversary.* Vassar College. 1916.

wrought up. Women during the war had directed
all the activities which war thrusts upon the civilian,
and the coming of peace left women of abounding
vitality suddenly without pressing occupation. The
energy with which they had pursued their war respon-
sibilities was not easily laid aside; even their more
passive sisters missed their attendance at meetings.
Woman's rights which had started vigorously in the
late forties was in a position to inherit the speakers
and the audiences. The usual after the war reaction,
the usual difficulty of adjustment from a time of great
busyness to a time of " business as usual " opened new
opportunities for women. On moving day the children of a family have always been able to obtain for
themselves coveted articles previously refused.

It was early in the eighteen-fifties that The American Woman's Educational Association had been incorporated in New York by a group of " ladies and
gentlemen." Catharine Beecher and Harriet Beecher
Stowe signed the early circular [18] stating the aims
which were threefold: to train nurses, nurse-maids,
and " home physicians "; to train housekeepers, cooks,
sempstresses, mantuamakers, milliners; to train teachers. For some of these occupations college was obviously required, and the association was to interest
itself in the establishment of institutions of higher
learning. " Many wealthy ladies would as readily
endow institutions for their own sex as for men, were
they aware of the true state of the case," states the

[18] *Circular to Mothers and Female Teachers.* The American
Woman's Educational Association. New York. n.d. (1852.)

circular, adding that women have given from thirty to three hundred thousand dollars in one gift to men's colleges or theological schools.

In spite of Catharine Beecher, in spite of growth in the numbers of women's colleges and women students, twentieth century women of wealth tend to benefit the colleges of their husbands and fathers; and the women's colleges gratefully accept infrequent thousands while Yale and Harvard reap their millions, mainly, to be sure, from masculine pockets, but helped by gifts from women.

Vassar and Wellesley were given to women by men, and whereas it was the fortune of a woman which founded Smith, that fortune was diverted from other charitable purposes by the firm direction of a man.

Wellesley and Smith were a decade after Vassar, both opening in 1875. Wellesley [19] owed its inception to Henry Fowler Durant, a wealthy Boston lawyer, whose only direct heir, an eight year old son, had recently died. Profoundly religious, Mr. Durant was eager to benefit the world with his wealth. With the hearty co-operation of his wife, he replaced his original plan for an orphanage with a plan for Wellesley Female Seminary on the model of Mount Holyoke Female Seminary, of which he was a trustee. Like Mount Holyoke it was planned for the poor girl, with a similar plan of housework. Before the opening he wisely changed the name to Wellesley College. Though he appointed a woman president, Durant

[19] Converse, F. *The Story of Wellesley*. Boston. 1915.

held the reins very firmly; and long after his death his widow, as treasurer, held the purse strings. It was fitting that a woman should be treasurer, as well as president, for Wellesley's policy was to prefer a properly qualified woman to a man. Vassar had a man president, a woman for lady principal; Smith opened with a man as its head, but with lady heads of houses. Miss Howard, though dominated by Durant, was still president of Wellesley, and Alice Freeman was soon to become president in more than name.

The founding of Smith,[20] like that of Vassar and Wellesley, was dictated by the need of disposing a large fortune. This time the fortune was in the hands of a woman, Sophia Smith. Though legend presents a pretty picture of the young Sophia, pressing her ear to the closed door of her brother's classroom, eagerly imbibing Latin declensions, investigation, that wrecker of romance, shows that Miss Smith had in her youth all the education which she desired. She probably attended the village school, and she had a session at a seminary in Connecticut and at Hadley. Deaf at forty, she tended to travel less, and to occupy herself in her native town of Hatfield, Massachusetts, in her last years building herself a large and elaborate house. It was in the eighteen-sixties that she brought her perplexities to her young pastor, the Reverend John M. Greene. Her brother had died, leaving her his fortune, which, added to her own, seemed a heavy burden. She wished her minister to help her to devise

[20] Greene, H. F., ed. *Foreshadowings of Smith College,* 1928, and Hanscom, E. D. and Greene, H. F., *Sophia Smith and the Beginnings of Smith College.* Northampton. 1925.

a plan whereby her wealth might prove of benefit to the world. She had once heard her brother speak of leaving his money to his own college, Harvard. Would it, then, not be the right thing for her to follow his wishes? Mr. Greene was not a Harvard man. His own Alma Mater, Amherst, was close by, a deserving institution in need of funds. It seemed quite obvious that had Mr. Smith really wished to remember Harvard he would have done so in his will; he had, by giving the money unconditionally to his sister, expressed his wish that she should take full responsibility for its ultimate disposition. After a night of sleeplessness and prayer, Miss Smith agreed, asking that she be aided in making a decision.

She was a woman not without resolution, though her upbringing had made her naturally deferent to man's superior judgment. Converted at sixteen, she had so respected her father's Unitarianism, that she had waited to join the church of her choice until after his death — but eighteen years of waiting had not changed her belief. She was ready to listen to Greene's suggestions though not ready to adopt them unless she approved. She inclined to a school for the deaf and dumb. Much earlier Gallaudet's work in Hartford, Connecticut, and Howe's in Boston had attracted wide attention. That the deaf and dumb could be taught was clear; that there was need of a special institution for them was also clear. Or perhaps an asylum for the aged would be a wise benevolence.

In all earnestness John M. Greene sought for guidance, as did Sophia Smith herself. Reflecting that there is " no disease like ignorance, no curse like sin, and Christian education is the sovereign remedy for both," Greene was led to believe that Miss Smith's purpose would best be satisfied by the establishment of a school. When an asylum for the deaf and dumb was established in Northampton God seemed to have spoken; there was no need of duplication in the same neighborhood.

Greene's first thought had been for his Alma Mater, Amherst, which could well use an endowed scientific school. Miss Smith was not interested in Amherst. There was, then, Mount Holyoke, from which Mrs. Greene had graduated. Miss Smith was inalterably opposed to Mount Holyoke. The Sophia Smith Library at Holyoke would, persuaded Mr. Greene, perpetuate her name. " What's in a name," snorted Miss Smith. Neither Mount Holyoke nor Amherst would she visit; to the delegates of both institutions she remained courteously cold. She was never specially interested in education, masculine or feminine; she was decidedly not interested in either of these institutions. So far was she from yielding, that she took care to provide that her ultimate bequest — to found a woman's college in Northampton — should never by any chance benefit either. She had a fear that her college might be made an adjunct of Amherst or might turn out to be a scientific school for Amherst. She yielded to Greene's interest in female education, giving up her ideas of a public library for Hatfield though retaining the academy; she even consented to Northampton rather than Hatfield for a location, but she remained adamant in her prejudices.

Greene once said that he must have been born with an interest in education, and especially in women's education. When he became engaged to a young school teacher who had had one year at Mount Holyoke, one at Bradford, he urged her to return to complete the work for a diploma, feeling that a minister's wife ought to be as fully educated as possible.[21]   In 1857, at the age of twenty-seven, she graduated from Mount Holyoke which was nearer his parish than Bradford.

Feeling that the education of women was of the greatest civic importance, Greene developed the idea of Smith College, stimulated by the foundation of Vassar in the very years that Miss Smith had first turned to him for advice.   Although urged by her to secrecy, he divulged his scheme to men who, from their importance in the field of education, should be able to give him counsel.[22]   He turned to Professor Hitchcock of Amherst, whose interest in Mount Holyoke and in Mary Lyon had been friendly and helpful. Mr. Hitchcock definitely disapproved.   " No! " he advised, " the matter of the higher education of women is still an experiment."   From the presidents of Harvard, Yale, Williams, and Amherst Greene received scant encouragement; rather did the comments read:

[21] Greene, H. F., ed. *Foreshadowings of Smith College.* Privately printed. 1928.
[22] Hanscom, E. D. and Greene, H. F. *Sophia Smith and the Beginnings of Smith College.* Northampton. 1925.

"foolish," "hazardous," "dangerous," "wicked," "abnormal and perilous scheme."

But after the Civil War matters took on new light. In 1869 a committee reported to the Massachusetts Legislature that the state's greatest current educational need was a female college. Vassar was already flourishing and opposition to degree-giving schools for women seemed nearly conquered. The Southern colleges had suffered heavily, some of them having been annihilated, others continuing oppressed with difficulties. Meanwhile the West was talking in terms of state universities, open to both sexes. In the East there were persistent rumors that even Harvard would become co-educational. Boston University opened in 1873. In the West co-education had been easily established since the universities were supported by taxes paid by fathers who had daughters as well as sons. In the East colleges were not state supported; they were private institutions. Harvard had long forgotten that it had once been regarded as a state college.

President Eliot of Harvard was convinced that co-education would be a "demoralizing influence." He could not believe in the wisdom of herding young men and women in the same schools during the "electric" years. It was doubtless with a sense of relief that he saw Smith established, that he went as speaker to its first Commencement.

At Amherst [23] the matter of co-education caused a

[23] *Exercises at the Semi Centennial of Amherst College.* Springfield. 1871.

somewhat heated discussion at the semi-centennial celebration in July 1871, before Smith or Wellesley opened. So serious was the proposal to make Amherst include women that Governor Bullock made public offer of an endowed scholarship. In his address he brushed aside the question of curriculum readjustment, then in the air; the classical and the scientific ideals would not, he felt, remain in conflict since it was essential that both should prosper. A far more real question was in need of discussion, " something that cannot be turned aside, that may as well be confronted, whether it be a substance or a spectre. I would treat it as a substance. I allude to the question of the admission of the two sexes to an equality of privilege and benefit in the higher seminaries [24] of learning throughout New England." The presence of women in the classrooms of Amherst would have a refining influence and he therefore wished to endow a scholarship, open to a woman with the sole requirement that she pass the entrance examinations.

When Henry Ward Beecher came upon the platform, he referred — after the usual flowers of rhetoric expected of a prominent alumnus — to the governor's speech. He brought the matter to a head by telling what was probably not definitely known to his audience, that two young women had petitioned for admission to Amherst, and that their petition was now before the board of trustees. Stating his own belief in woman suffrage, Beecher admitted that he did not know whether or not that would be a workable

[24] Note use of term " Seminary."

scheme; but whether or not women should have the highest education possible in America was no longer a question; it had been answered. Academies, seminaries, women's colleges had already been established "unrebuked." If, then, women were to have the same education as their brothers, should they not have it at the same institutions? If churches for the two sexes were not separate, why separate schools? Sophia Smith's money was to establish a duplicating institution across the river; would not that sum have been more usefully expended in expanding a co-educational Amherst? That women could physically stand the strain of four years' study had been demonstrated. What, cried Beecher, was the strain of four years' study compared to that of bearing and bringing up a large family of children — and taking care of a husband at the same time?

" I was brought up in my sister's school at Hartford," Beecher continued. "That accounts for my womanish ways. But it is all outside, for I am inside, a man." Women, then, in a man's college would remain feminine, inside; they would make a " womanish use of education." Like Governor Bullock, Beecher urged his college to become a leader in this "march of progress," to follow its duty, which was manifestly to include both sexes.

To these ardent advocates of co-education Professor Park of Amherst replied that Amherst men had done their duty in helping to establish Mount Holyoke, as they would now help the new Smith. To lift the discussion from the serious he laughed it away with the anecdote of the student whose wits had gone woolgathering. The cause of his trouble, the president of his college had said, was that which might afflict all young men under co-education: shock from a gal-vanic battery.

It is noteworthy that the argument was against co-education, not woman's education. The West had definitely decided to favor co-education, in practice as well as in theory. The East was sometimes strong in theory, always reluctant in practice. The twentieth century still finds men's colleges fearful of feminine intrusion.

Amherst and Harvard breathed more freely when Smith finally opened, as did Wellesley, in 1875. Neither attracted any undue amount of attention — or even, their sponsors might have thought, the amount of attention legitimately due them. Some adverse comment there was, as there had been of Vassar, but as Smith's President Seelye remarked, the public was by now used to the idea of education for women. Vassar had graduated four students in 1867, two years after its opening; and in 1869 had given degrees to the first class to complete the full four year course.

The trend toward collegiate education is seen in the 1864 prospectus of a now forgotten college, Ripley Female College,[25] located in Poultney, Vermont, a town not far north of Troy, New York, the home of Emma Willard's Seminary and of Rensselaer Polytechnic Institute. The president of Ripley was a minister who for many years had been principal of

25 Prospectus for 1864.

an academy in Troy now turning into the college, and who for ten years had been professor of Latin at Union College — the college which Elizabeth Cady Stanton as a girl had longed to enter. With a group of men and women teachers — the women taught Latin and physics — he planned " the highest order of Instruction," adding that " the German method of *Lectures* will be combined with Recitations." So lectures in chemistry, philosophy of history, " architecture considered æsthetically and historically," astronomy, Biblical literature, history of Fine Arts, and English literature were to be given by professors of Union College. This system of lectures and recitations under instructors is not unlike the modern system wherein professors who are specialists in their fields lecture to a large group which is then split up in sections meeting with a tutor.

Though there would be a preparatory course, a course in art, a course similar to that of the best academies and seminaries, it was the fourth course, the Collegiate, which would be " the characteristic feature of Ripley Female College. This course will, with such modifications as are necessary the better to adapt it to the female mind and mission, be equivalent to that required for the Baccalaureate degree in our best American colleges." The degree of Baccalaurea Artium was bestowed on three students in 1866, which would indicate that these young ladies, like those who were to receive Vassar's first degrees the following year, had completed much work prior to entrance. Ripley definitely antedated Vassar, but it lasted at most for a decade, becoming once more Troy Conference Academy.[26]

Ripley Female College ambitiously published a *Quarterly Journal Devoted to Female Education.*[27] Though place was given to such articles as " Discipline the Chief Object and End of Study," and " Educate for Immortality," the *Quarterly* contained also a catalogue of the college giving the goodly list of students who came from near and far, and an explanation of the college program and policies. The report of the examining committee was included — a committee made up of prominent men with LL.D.'s, D.D.'s, Reverends, and Honorables among them. The committee extolled the grace and modesty of the students. "No longer the servant nor the pet of men," women might now consider themselves companions. To educate them for this new conception of their sphere institutions like Ripley were " now rising up in all parts of our country." Greek had no place in the curriculum, since women needed the " living vernacular " which would have to be neglected if Greek were included. Mathematics extended to trigonometry, Latin to Virgil; Butler's *Analogy* was nowhere to be found in the program, but *Evidences of Christianity* remained.

Save for their immensely larger endowments Vassar, Wellesley, and Smith must have seemed to the public little different from such colleges as Ripley. Their aims were similar, their faculties were simi-

26 *A History of the Town of Poultney, Vermont.* 1875.
27 *A Quarterly Journal.* Published by Ripley Female College. Poultney. Vol. II, July, 1866, No. 2.

larly selected, their curricula of the same general order — " based upon that of the best men's colleges." The richer institutions were equally strenuous in their assertions of the properly feminine atmosphere and training.

It was necessary, too, from time to time, to vindicate the healthfulness of study. A physician published an attack to which a group of feminists replied sharply with *Sex and Education*.[28] Under the able editorship of Julia Ward Howe, various prominent women, among them Mrs. Horace Mann, Caroline Dall, the literary lady who preferred always to sign herself " C," refuted the points made by Dr. Clarke. Thomas Wentworth Higginson, ever the friend of woman's rights, also contributed. Dr. Clarke's health objection was easily met, especially as he had incautiously used for an example a student who had presumably gone to Vassar at the age of fourteen. Vassar's records indicated that no student had been received under fifteen. The statement that women's health could not stand the strain of four years of college work was as absurd as Dr. Clarke's figures on the cost of co-education — two million would, he thought, be required to enable Harvard to become co-educational. Why it should be costlier to educate so many women than so many men was not easy to see. Perhaps Dr. Clarke foresaw a rush to the colleges which only the immediate post-war years of the twentieth century had the privilege to witness. And even

[28] Howe, Julia Ward, ed. *Sex and Education. A Reply to Dr. Clarke.* Boston. 1874.

in 1928, the year of blessed memory, the number of properly qualified men and women who were turned away from college doors was not sufficient to bring into being any new colleges. Though experimental colleges have appeared for women, there have been recently no new ones for students of regular college entrance requirements.

When the only careers open were teaching and motherhood, the curricula of the seminaries had seemed to many overbroad. Soon after the middle of the century the seminaries were adding a fourth year; and the colleges were starting with a four year course — often a six year course, with the two preparatory years. Whether or not women joined the woman's rights movement, they were taking a less limited view of their sphere, a less patient view of their legal disqualifications.

Education for marriage was no longer, in the sixties, a popular ideal. Not education against marriage, not a disinclination for marriage, but a refusal to accept for women this sphere and no other, when marriage, especially after the Civil War, was an arithmetical impossibility for all. The children of Civil War parents were not always impressed when speakers lauded the old loyalties, repeated the old platitudes of feminine duty. " Of course," wrote a Vassar student in 1870,[29] " any ' silly ' knows a girl would prefer a home and an adoring husband of her very own and would cling to him tighter than wax. But isn't

[29] *Letters from Old Time Vassar.* Written by a student in 1869–70. Vassar College. 1915.

this clinging business somewhat overworked? " This young feminist in the making wanted to be sure, before she developed the clinging technique, that there would be some one to cling to. Refusing to be deceived by " salvey talk " of the " home woman " she decided that she would rather prepare herself for wage-earning than for " the rocking-chair and tidy brigade — waiting."

At Commencement Vassar girls heard masculine speakers laud their own professor of astronomy, a woman receiving far more honor than a mere marrying maid, than their own mothers. Men told them that it was possible for a woman to find happiness in art or science as well as in marriage; and if they doubted they had only to talk with Maria Mitchell herself. When in June 1870 President Eliot of Harvard told them that in Latin, German, and French the classes he had heard at Vassar performed better than those at Harvard, and those in calculus equally well with Harvard, the young ladies rightly gained confidence in their ability to conquer the intellectual world. "There is talk of admitting women to Harvard if girls can keep up with boys."

College education was now a "working asset," an insurance against unwelcome dependence, if no eligible husband presented himself. Without it, a girl had to "over-burden" or "entirely swamp" some relative. This was the workaday aspect. Baccalaureate sermons endeavored to inspire students to noteworthy achievements. "But try as I would, I couldn't think of anything great to do."

Greatness was not to be the aim of the women's colleges to any larger extent than it was at the men's. In the early days of the colonies training a man for the ministry was training him for a career of greatness, but the colleges were ceasing to function exclusively as professional training schools. Vassar, Durant, and Sophia Smith did have wide views of the individual, civic, and spiritual betterment that would result from the education of women. Childless people, all of them, they recognized the importance of education for mothers. Yet the colleges founded by their generosity, with women professors and physicians, even with women presidents and treasurers, could hardly shut their eyes to the fact that there were other careers for women. The Civil War had increased the disparity between the numbers of the sexes, already existent in the days of the founding of the seminaries. It was becoming socially respectable — and economically necessary — for girls to earn their own living, even in fields other than teaching. And in spite of her predilection for marriage, the girl of the eighteen-sixties may have been aware that marriage and living happily ever afterward were not always synonymous.

It became increasingly obvious that for every woman there was not a husband waiting; and that marriage did not always mean a family of children. Catharine Beecher talked much of woman's need of training for woman's work. With her sister, Harriet Beecher Stowe, as collaborator she published in 1870 *The American Woman's Home or Principles of*

Domestic Science following her theory that just as men were trained for their professions, women should be for theirs. The dedication was to the women of America "in whose hands are the real destinies of the Republic." Yet thinking women knew that they would not all be called upon to direct these destinies since they would have no children to train.

The colleges, however, proceeded as the seminaries had before them, to emphasize the womanly woman, the future mother, at least in their prospectuses. "Discipline for fully developed womanhood," "a sound mind and pure heart in a healthy body," said Smith College,[30] offering all the arts and sciences "appropriate to her sex." Durant emphasized Wellesley's intention of developing every power and faculty, "reason, imagination, emotional nature, religious aspirations," all part of "feminine purity and delicacy and refinement." [31]

The trustees of Vassar College stated that, whereas there was no difference in education applied to either sex, they would not slavishly copy men's colleges, but adapt their plan to the wants of woman in order that womanly grace and refinement might be retained.[32] Bryn Mawr, founded two decades later when all discussion as to whether woman should be equally educated with man was "obsolete," stated as its aim the training of woman to earn a living "in any profession open to her sex" (emphasis was put upon teaching

[30] Hanscom, E. D. and Greene, H. F. *Sophia Smith and the Beginnings of Smith College.* Northampton. 1925.
[31] Converse, Florence. *The Story of Wellesley.* Boston. 1915.
[32] *Vassar College. Its Foundation.* 1873.

in the colleges) and to make her "accomplished, agreeable, and attractive." [33]

Earning her own living had long since been bravely declared to be not unfeminine. In 1851 [34] Catharine Beecher had urged women to look forward to " honorable employ " and not to marriage for support. She felt strongly that woman's education should neither limit itself to preparing her to be "somebody's wife," nor be a mere aping of that in the men's colleges, which itself needed revision. President Wayland of Brown had already opened the discussion as to whether the existing course of study was the right one for the young men at college, a course of study "too closely copied in our higher female seminaries."

In what ways, then, were the new colleges of the sixties and seventies to differ from the seminaries which had long contended, undisputed, that they were colleges? The name seminary confirmed their position since Harvard and Yale and Amherst publicly referred to themselves as seminaries. These schools for women did not take the " younger misses "; they had developed strict entrance requirements; they had recently either added a fourth year or had made preparations to do so; they had increased the amount of Latin in their course and had endeavored to remodel their curricula to fit the changing curricula of the men's colleges. In their own eyes they

[33] *Inauguration of Bryn Mawr College, 1885.*   Philadelphia. 1887.
[34] Beecher, Catharine E. *The True Remedy for the Wrongs of Woman.* Boston. 1851.

seemed to satisfy all needs. In spite, however, of the efforts of ardent women, in spite of the interest of prominent men, they lagged far behind the men's colleges in endowment, and hence in equipment. And they did not give degrees.

Was Vassar College in 1865 different from the existing seminaries? Alice Freeman [35] thought not, choosing instead the University of Michigan which opened its doors to women in the seventies. Alice Freeman had no method of judging other than hearsay.

The trustees of Vassar certainly believed that they were founding a school in advance of those already in existence. It was, however, a time of transition, when the physical sciences were pressing hard upon the classics, when students were feeling the need of a wider choice of electives, and when the whole value of the classics, and of disciplinary studies, and of the possibility or truth of transfer of training were constantly in dispute.

The founders of Vassar, Smith, and Wellesley had no educational theories or curricula ready-made; they desired only that the institutions founded by their philanthropy should be something more than " just another school." As the plans of study matured, one thing became certain: that since the classics had from the beginning been the backbone of the men's colleges and an extra in the female seminaries, in the colleges the classics would be required, or at least taught as far as at any men's colleges. At Vassar Greek

[35] Palmer, G. H. *Life of Alice Freeman Palmer*. Boston. 1908.

was optional, but Homer, Herodotus, Thucydides, Demosthenes, Plato, Sophocles were all offered. In Latin, which was required, Livy, Horace, Cicero and Quintillian occupied the Freshman and Sophomore years. Juvenal, Tacitus, and Cicero's *De Officiis* were elective.

Chemistry varied somewhat from the same science as taught at men's colleges, since the parents (who paid the bills) valued studies which had practical applications: just as French was useful for travelling, so chemistry could be useful for cooking. Mary Lyon had found it so in the early days of her seminary, when the students entrusted with bread-making reported that the bread did not rise. Using her chemical knowledge Mary Lyon herself made the yeast, made the dough, and produced an edible bread, truly the staff of life before the days of " slimming." So Alice Freeman Palmer, unskilled in cooking, called upon her scientific knowledge and her superior training, and made good bread after her cook had declared the flour impossible, the yeast impotent.

Vassar's " practical applications " went beyond bread making into " general culinary chemistry," " toxicology and its antidotes, dyeing and printing, coal tar and its products, curing, tanning, and dressing of leather, metals and electro-plating, photography, metallurgy and manufacture of steel." [36]

In the department of English language and literature courses in Anglo-Saxon might be elected. Here was a study not generally found in female seminaries.

[36] *Vassar College. Its Foundation.* 1873.

The languages, sciences, philosophy, intellectual and moral, were all spread before the young ladies, who might not, however, indulge themselves too deeply in the feasts made ready for them. Three subjects a year, twelve subjects in all were the portion leading to an A.B.

With an initial endowment of something like half a million and an additional bequest at his death in 1868, Vassar had given the college close to eight hundred thousand dollars. Beside this the endowments of the female seminaries shrank into insignificance. Yet with their smaller endowments the seminaries were still in the sixties charging much less than the new college. A Vassar girl who played neither the piano nor the organ, who did no "solo singing" (under instruction), who refrained from drawing, painting, or modelling cost her parents three hundred and fifty dollars for board and tuition against one hundred and twenty-five dollars at Mount Holyoke,[37] two hundred and forty-six dollars at Wheaton.

Costs were lower at Mount Holyoke because of the domestic service plan. Durant introduced the system to Wellesley where it continued for many years. Vassar stated at the outset that "servant's work" would not be performed by the students. It seemed wise, however, at Vassar to make provision for boarding the students, as was done at the better seminaries, though men's colleges did not always assume this responsibility. "Domestic arrangements have been

[37] Increased from $80 in 1866, and further increased to $150 in 1867, and to $175 in 1876.

of late regarded in this country as of doubtful utility in colleges for young men; but indispensable, for the present at least, in a college for young women." [38]

Of Vassar's first student body of three hundred and fifty students, from the ages of fifteen to twenty-four, coming from various places in the United States and Canada, not one was fully qualified for the freshman class; at most one-third had been well taught, and a few admirably. Its first year Vassar was an ungraded seminary. By the close of the second year, though nearly half the students were still in irregular courses, there were well-defined groups: the four college classes with the addition of two intermediate classes, one between the junior and sophomore years, one between the sophomore and freshman years; and a regulated preparatory course. By 1873 these were reduced to three groups: the collegiates; the specials or irregular collegiates; and the preparatories. Vassar was to continue a preparatory department until the eighteen-eighties; Wellesley starting a decade later, was to carry a preparatory department, too, for many years.[39] Smith refused from the start, with the result that a preparatory department distinct from the college but preparing for it was soon started in Northampton.

Smith accepted exactly fourteen students, and of these two did not continue to the first Commencement four years later. But Smith, besides requiring exactly the same amount of Latin as a New England

[38] *Vassar College, Its Foundation.* 1873.
[39] Until 1888. Domestic work was continued until 1896.

man's college, also required for entrance exactly the same amount of Greek. In entrance requirements as well as in requirements for the degree Smith challenged comparison with New England colleges for men, always more rigid than colleges in other parts of America.

The reasons for requiring Greek were not hard to understand. To escape any adverse criticism, to avoid any disparagement, Smith must measure up to the New England men's colleges in every particular possible. It must not be said, " Smith is just like a man's college, *except. . . .*" Not to know Greek was, for a man, not to be educated. Not to know Greek was, then, for a woman not to be college bred.

The reason, however, went deeper. Discipline, though under fire, was still believed to be the aim of education. Discipline of mind might be gained through application to other subjects, but again it might not; through Greek it did come beyond all doubt. Aside from its disciplinary value, the study of Greek provided the framework upon which the whole fabric of education was hung: contact with the best thought of the best minds. It was not an accident, said President Seelye of Smith, that Greek had been made the true basis of the true education; as subject matter even more than as disciplinary material it should be studied, content more valuable than grammar. And for it nothing could be substituted.

Ten years later Bryn Mawr, requiring Greek for the degree, but not for entrance, took the stand that

Greek was necessary for culture, being of especial interest "because in it the writings of the New Testament have been providentially enshrined." [40]

The colleges therefore required Greek for the B.A. degree. But there was the degree of B.S. for which modern languages could be substituted for Greek. The colleges also received students known as "specials," students who were not candidates for either degree, but who liked studying, and living, on a college campus without undergoing the strict discipline of a regular course.

Even at Smith, where there was the closest correspondence between the curriculum and that of the men's colleges there was divergence in that there was a freer choice of electives, and in that President Seelye advised less mathematics and more inclusion of those æsthetic studies neglected by men. In cultivating the feminine virtues, the students at Smith might study art and music — which at Smith were not extras. There were, indeed, three courses at Smith: the classical, the literary, and the scientific; and besides these three, the irregular courses taken by students working for no degree. Of the original fourteen in the first class, twelve survived the four years, eleven of whom were candidates for the degree, one taking a special course.

Smith started with a small faculty, and for its early years, though it did add steadily to its resident staff, was served by professors of Amherst, and also of Johns

[40] *Inauguration of Bryn Mawr College, 1855.* Address of President Rhoades. Philadelphia. 1887.

Hopkins.[41]   These visiting teachers were useful in comparing the work done at Smith with that done at the men's colleges where their regular teaching was done.   The comparisons were all in favor of the women.   Amherst professors — so the legends run — would pit their Smith and Amherst classes against each other: The young ladies are taking five pages a day — can you take seven?   The gentlemen are taking seven pages a day — can you take eight?

Thomas Wentworth Higginson constantly proclaimed that college faculties should include both men and women; he insisted that both masculine and feminine viewpoint were necessary for well-rounded education.   He saw no reason why women should not teach men at Harvard and Yale, nor men at Smith and Vassar.   The seminaries had long used men as well as women.   Vassar, headed by a man, immediately secured the services of such a well-known woman as Maria Mitchell, the noted astronomer; and made up the faculty from both sexes.   Wellesley, nominally headed by a woman, dominated by a man, tended toward a mixed faculty with women predominating; Smith, with men predominating.   In Smith's early group men were professors, women teachers.[42]   It was a man — and a minister — who taught elocution; a woman who taught chemistry; mathematics; French and German.

A chemistry teacher, Miss Bessie Capen, had already taught at Wellesley; an English teacher, Miss Heloise

[41] Bryn Mawr similarly made use of the faculty of Haverford College.
[42] Catalogue 1877.

Hersey, was later to teach at Wheaton Seminary.[43]
Graduates of Ipswich, Mount Holyoke, and Wheaton,
were naturally drawn upon in the early days of the
colleges until alumnae multiplied. Elmira Female
College printed in some of its early catalogues (1861–
1874) the schools from which its preceptresses graduated, notably Ipswich and Hartford; and already it
had on its faculty an alumna of its own.

Combined, then, with men who had taught in
men's colleges or were still teaching there, were
women who had gained their education at seminaries,
at the few early colleges admitting women, or who
had been privately taught. Vassar's first faculty of
ten included three women: the lady principal, Maria
Mitchell in astronomy, and a female physician.

The predicament of the colleges in finding women
to teach — and though Wellesley did not wish its
preference for women to be construed as a method of
economy, it was indeed true that women could be
hired for much less than men — is shown in the offers
made to Alice Freeman. After taking a degree from
the University of Michigan Miss Freeman had taught
in various schools, proving herself an excellent dis-
ciplinarian as well as a clever teacher. Wellesley
offered her an instructorship in Greek. She declined,
being unable to leave her family at this time. The
following year an instructorship in mathematics was
offered, and again declined. Another year and
another offer: the headship of the department of history, which was accepted. Now Miss Freeman was

[43] Catalogue 1878.

not a scholar in any of these fields; it is hardly possible
that she could be equally qualified in all three, even
had she been a thorough-going scholar. She had entered Michigan sadly handicapped; she had, indeed,
flunked the entrance examinations and had been admitted only by the intercession of the president who
believed he saw in her a promising pupil. During her
college course she was further handicapped by the
necessity of earning her way. She had had no leisure
for quiet, persistent pursuit of any one field of human
knowledge. She became, however, head of the history
department of Wellesley, stepping very quickly into
the president's office, an office which she resigned
after a few years to marry a Harvard professor.

Though offers were made most attractive for her
continuance in the presidency, with a special position
created for her husband, Alice Freeman Palmer followed the womanly ideals of her times, resigning
to become a householding wife. It was M. Carey
Thomas, herself a graduate of Cornell, the president
of a woman's college founded in the eighteen-eighties,
who publicly challenged the necessity of choice between marriage and a career.

But the earlier colleges, Vassar, Wellesley, and
Smith joined with the seminaries in their belief that
education was for life, not for a position in life; for
wifehood and motherhood, rather than for a wage-
earning "job." Speaking at the celebration of
Smith's first quarter century a graduate of the first
class, 1879, calling her address "Home and Family,"
restated the Tennysonian position: "The bearing

and rearing of children is the capstone of a liberal education." [44]   Tennyson's *Princess*, first published in 1846, said: " The bearing and rearing of children is woman's wisdom." Tennyson had depicted a woman's college within whose gates it was death for a man to set foot; a college on whose campus women flitted in gowns colored like emperor moths, or in dresses of maiden purity in the soft evenings when minds drifted from knowledge to thoughts of love; in whose classrooms learned ladies discoursed on the world's history, packing a four-year course into one stupendous lecture; a college which disintegrated the moment it was assailed from without by eligible suitors. Yet, though the Tennysonian maiden is securely pedestalled, her pretty curls turning to gentleness the masculine hand privileged to toy among them, Tennyson does at the close attempt a picture of man and woman working together for intellectual progress.

Very Tennysonian were the arguments for co-education at the very time the women's colleges were starting. The softening influence of woman; woman's natural tendencies toward the æsthetic; woman leading man to gentler manners, to an appreciation of music and art; woman by cultivating her intellect leading man away from the gross, from the physical to a society wherein the intellect as well as the graces should flourish — all a pretty picture, stressed by those who would have men's colleges

[44] *Celebration of the Quarter Centenary of Smith College.* Speech of Mrs. Kate Morris Cone, 1879. Cambridge. 1900.

opened freely to women. Women as mothers, women
as the gentle side of life, women as the ministering
angels, the calming influences.

In New England Bates College in Maine (becoming a college from an academy in 1863) , immediately
opened its doors to women — though few indeed took
advantage of its opportunities. With the cost of education thirty-seven dollars a term, one hundred and
eleven dollars for the year, the students were enabled
to reduce the sum by doing some of their own work:
the gentlemen might " fit their own wood," the ladies
" do their own washing." In some western co-educational colleges students divided the work, the gentlemen tending to the rougher occupations, the young
ladies sewing and washing dishes. And in the
curriculum Bates did not forget the "ornamental
branches." " Ladies are allowed to elect music, drawing, and painting for certain studies in this course." [45]

Bates was intended for poorer students, who would
interrupt their studies, if necessary, to earn their fees.
Teaching a term or two was still possible for both
sexes; and for the men there was work in the haying
fields.

Mr. Durant in founding Wellesley definitely had
the poor girl in mind; but though Vassar and Smith
felt the need of scholarships in order to permit all
qualified for college to have the opportunity, the poor
girl was not uppermost in their minds. And though
they were less inclined to speak of "ornamental
branches" the women's colleges definitely stressed

[45] Bates College Catalogue 1863.

" æsthetic culture," considering that for the female sex the studies of English literature, art, and music needed a true place in the curriculum. Smith fortified its belief by not charging extra fees for music and art, thereby incorporating both in the regular curriculum. Vassar's original catalogue listed only seven departments, with music, art, and riding extras.[46] In 1873 the departments of Design and Music were added as the eighth and ninth departments.[47] The fees, however, remained high, from sixty dollars for drawing to ninety dollars for " solo singing." Smith charged only for private lessons beyond those offered in course.

President Seelye of Smith felt that the arts were neglected at the men's colleges, overstressed at the female seminaries and academies. He wished to strike a balance, and therefore considered art and music part of the regular curriculum, to be substituted for some other subjects.

Yale,[48] however, had already added a department of Fine Arts, the gift in 1864 of Augustus and Caroline Street. Yale had had an art museum since 1831, originally erected to house the paintings of Colonel Trumbull. Mr. Street in 1864 explained his gift as something far more than an art museum: it was to be " a school for practical instruction, open to both sexes, for such as proposed to follow art as a profession; and to awaken and cultivate a taste for the Fine Arts among the undergraduates and others." For this department of Fine Arts Yale received about the same

---

46 First Annual Catalogue of Vassar Female College. 1865–66.
47 *Vassar College. Its Foundation.* 1873.
48 Welch, L. S. and Camp, W. *Yale.* Boston. 1899.

sum which was available for the entire founding of Smith College.

For a department of music Yale waited until the eighteen-nineties, the first suggestion coming in 1888. Previous to this time the college organist had given private lessons to students interested in music.

Columbia [49] was not alive to the need of young men for music and art until the nineties; and it was not until 1902 that the department of music, an infant of eight years, was separated from the department of philosophy; and the slightly older school of architecture from the faculty of applied sciences.

Harvard,[50] however, had early realized the place of the fine arts in the curriculum. In 1869 Charles W. Eliot became president of Harvard and began a policy which created from the old college the modern great university. In 1872 he instituted the plan whereby students might, if they chose, pass off certain requirements by examination, thereafter substituting elective courses for the required work thus disposed of. Under this expansive elective system, new courses of study were demanded, and provided. Immediately a department of Fine Arts was called for, and created in 1872 when an instructor of drawing was appointed, and a lecturer, Charles Eliot Norton. Norton's task was to present the history of Fine Arts and to explain their relationship to literature. One year later Norton was made professor of Fine Arts. At this time (1873) a professor of music was appointed.

It is therefore Harvard, in all probability, as well as

[49] *A History of Columbia University.* New York. 1904.
[50] Gardiner, J. H. *Harvard.* New York. 1914.

Vassar and the seminaries, which influenced Seelye in his emphasis upon the arts.

The differences, then, between the newly founded women's colleges and the men's colleges lay in two fields: in the academic field, the somewhat freer choice of electives and the emphasis upon the arts; in the field of living, closer attention to housing and food, closer attention to manners. Vassar had sewing hours; Smith had lady heads of houses, to supervise their charges and keep their feminine grace unharmed by the masculinity of most of their studies. While Durant and Vassar lived they personally kept watch, visualizing themselves perhaps as gardeners of the finest flowering of feminity.

In the curriculum, Vassar and Wellesley were later to fall in line with Smith, and require Greek for entrance. For President Seelye of Smith this requirement was more than a dusty custom. Men who had succeeded in life were those, for the most part, who were firmly grounded in the classics. Women who were to succeed in life needed to be firmly grounded in the classics. For this learning there was no substitute.

Nevertheless the study of the classics was not without its serious critics who doubted not only the absolute value of Latin and Greek, but the possibility of transfer of training. The growing sciences had for these critics far more potency. The sciences were the wisdom of the younger generation; they had practical applications. Once Greek and Latin had been practical studies: they had furnished ammunition for the minister, the lawyer, the orator; they had formed the style of the speaker and the writer. That the periodic sentence should pass into desuetude; that the simile should be drawn from scientific laboratory rather than from Homer or Virgil or Juvenal; that a race of educated men should rise up who knew not Horace, that a commentator should be needed to explain to college students Browning's now cryptic line, " He settled Hoti's business " — this would have seemed beyond the bounds of credence to the very men who challenged the classics as the indispensable core of the curriculum.

In 1870 there was published in America a volume edited by E. L. Youmans called *The Culture Demanded by Modern Life.* " The organization of a scheme of study adapted to American wants is the educational problem immediately before us," stated the editor in an able preface which pointed out that America by establishing schools rapidly had shown an appreciation of the need of education before she really knew exactly how that need ought to be satisfied.

Traditionally, just as there were " seven cardinal virtues, seven deadly sins, seven sacraments, seven days in the week, seven metals, seven planets, and seven apertures in a man's head," the study of liberal arts occupied seven years, and consisted of seven arts. The Trivium (grammar, logic, and rhetoric) and the Quadrivium (arithmetic, geometry, astronomy, and music, as an arithmetical art) had been passed down by the Romans and in 1870 were still predominant.

Mr. Youmans believed that the mind could be as

well disciplined by scientific studies as by this antique and now artificial division. Grammar, it had long been held, trained the memory, mathematics the reason. But the best Latin writers were ignorant of grammar, both of their own tongue and of the Greek they read with so much understanding; Dante, Petrarch, and Boccaccio were ignorant of Italian grammar; Shakespeare, Milton, Dryden, Addison, Pope, Young, Thomson, Johnson, Burns passed their childhood untainted by English grammar. The list of names, Greek, Roman, French, Italian, and English, who produced great writings without knowledge of grammar, who protested the introduction of the study of grammar is encyclopedic.

The study of mathematics, while admittedly of value, possessed no exclusive hold upon the development of reasoning; indeed all it gave could be given by the study of philology; moreover, what it gave was not of the value it once had been. Mathematics begins with " the unquestioning acceptance of data — axioms, definitions, rules " and therefore tends to " habituate to the passive acceptance of authority " — which was " the highest mental desiratum in the theological ages and establishments which gave rise to the traditional curriculum."

Nevertheless, the women's colleges felt — and probably correctly — that unless they planted themselves firmly under the prevailing masculine standard of education, they would not be granted an equal place in the procession. If Harvard and Yale and Dartmouth and Amherst were not to accept women, the colleges which wished to be on their level felt it necessary to abate no jot of classical training. When Martin Vassar broke with Milo Jewett, he ended the chance of innovation. The new president of Vassar felt himself on safer ground when he formed a course of study closer to that prevailing in the eastern men's colleges.

The women's colleges, then, offered as compulsory studies those subjects which had been the privilege of the ambitious few in the seminaries. Otherwise the change was not radical. Quiet hours, chapel once or twice a day, correct conduct were all in the foreground, though the years had brought a more mature point of view on the part of both instructors and instructed. Students seem no longer to have been lined up to report their infractions of petty rules, though they still retired to their rooms for regular hours of study. Even in earlier days little girls and boys had been known to have prayer meetings as games; and in the sixties and seventies young ladies were no longer as constantly concerned with their souls as earlier generations had been. "The sermon at chapel this morning," wrote one college girl, "was so solemn that we had to do something quick; so we ordered ice cream." Of the three colleges, Wellesley was the most firmly religious, having been founded by a man at a time of spiritual awakening. Sophia Smith's will, however, left no doubt in her belief in religious training; and at Vassar the president himself was charged with the moral and religious instruction of the pupils. Travellers in the sixties spoke truly when they called Americans a religious, church-going people, " prone to acknowledge the goodness of God in all things." [51]

Finding woman's rights " a very favorite subject in America " one traveller suggested that, since from his foreign point of view women seemed to have the best of it in the United States, men go out for the rights of men. Suggestions for the widening of woman's sphere were much more modest in England than in America. In England as in America there was argument as to whether that work of the world which had hitherto been done chiefly by men should be divided between men and women. In America, but not in England, there was the further question how far the political working of the world, as yet entirely in the hands of men, should be divided.

In 1860 William Hovey delivered the address at the annual exhibition (modern graduation or commencement) of the English High School in Boston and thought well enough of his speech to publish it afterwards. He openly advocated the franchise for women, since otherwise America would still have taxation without representation. [52]

Much earlier Thomas Wentworth Higginson had pointed out the abilities and rights of women, had cited the example of successful women captains of sailing vessels, lawyers, doctors, business women, astronomers, sculptors, speakers, preachers, editors, even soldiers — and Harriet Beecher Stowe.

[51] Trollope, Anthony. *North America.* Philadelphia. 1862.
[52] Hovey, William A. *Woman's Rights.* Boston. 1860.

The woman's rights movement had kept pace with the female schools, gathering strength as they did. The first American book on the subject came in 1816 from the pen of a female member of the famous Mather family.[53] Here was a plea, not for the vote, but for equal opportunities of education that men and women might work together for the common good.

In the eighteen-thirties the women who spoke in the cause of abolition began to include woman's rights in their pleas for liberty. By the middle of the century or soon after the movement counted among its famous adherents William Lloyd Garrison, William Henry Channing, Wendell Phillips, Bronson Alcott, Gerrit Smith, Theodore Parker, George William Curtis, Henry Ward Beecher, John Greenleaf Whittier, Ralph Waldo Emerson.[54] In the eighteen-fifties Lucy Stone publicly protested the marriage laws, and in marrying her Henry Blackwell agreed to her retention of her maiden name, the children to assume the names of both father and mother.

In the eighteen-sixties women in New Jersey defiantly cast votes — which were not counted. In 1869 Wyoming and Utah granted the vote to the women in their sparsely inhabited regions.

The decades slowly improved the legal position of women, various states insuring to them the right to their own property, their own earnings; and divorce laws became more favorable.

[53] Crocker, H. Mather. *Observations on the Real Rights of Woman*. Boston. 1816.
[54] *History of the National Woman's Rights Movement*. New York. 1871.

The Civil War had done much for the advancement of women, partly because new privileges always result for all classes in a post-war era; partly because women during the war had profited by their opportunities. A surplus of women, from the point of view that marriage is their only career, is a tragedy; but such a surplus from the point of view that women have a place in the world even if they are not to be mothers, has its advantages. Woman's voice may be ever soft and low, but a numerical increase does add to its volume. Young women, cried Anthony Trollope, want to get married; even if they did not, men do! All the wanting in the world could not produce enough husbands to go around after the Civil War. It was fortunate that there were educational institutions to take care of young ladies during the years that Trollope would have had devoted to courtship.

It was fortunate for the young ladies that in the sixties and seventies they had new colleges to grow up to; not that they might not have secured an adequate education at the existing seminaries; but that newness had its value; as did also the exact emulation of their brothers' college course. It is perhaps fortunate, too, that they were not always satisfied. " I came here to take a *college course,* and not to dabble in a little of every insignificant thing that comes up. More than half of my time is taken up in writing essays, practicing elocution, trotting to chapel, and *reading poetry* with the teacher of English Literature, and it seems to make no difference to Miss Howard and Mr. Durant whether the Latin, Greek, and Mathematics are well learned or not." [55] But soon the disgruntled young lady is writing home of her great satisfaction with her Latin and Greek — which to her represented the true college training.

For young ladies were not interested in enlarged curricula; they were not concerned with the arguments for or against discipline, transfer of training, the ascendency of the sciences, the practical application of all studies. They were interested in the fact that with Vassar here was " something new under the sun "; and a decade later with Smith here was " something new under the sun." No longer could their fathers and brothers tease them when they asserted that their seminaries were as good as colleges; they could now have the right to call themselves college graduates; they could flourish a degree — something which their mothers had, for the most part, never wanted; but they did not need to have a degree to become mothers. Not all girls cared to go to college — in spite of the preponderance of the sexes, men have maintained the preponderance of masculine attendance at colleges — but for those who cared, colleges were ready in abundance long before the close of the nineteenth century.

Yet there were many who deplored the passing of " the good old days when children were children still, and husbands and wives walked hand in hand, and there were no . . . questions of rights at all. In those days books were not written to prove to women that their husbands were their enemies, or others for babies

[55] Converse, F. *The Story of Wellesley.* Boston. 1915.

that it takes grown folks to understand; and little girls wore ' pantalettes ' until they were far on in their teens, and flirted not until they were out of them; and little boys wore short pants and forebore tobacco, and hung up their stockings on Christmas Eve, and pelted each other with sugar plums and comfits with quite as much of affectionate energy as that with which their prototypes of to-day fling bouquets at the dancing blondes." In those good old days, writes an editor in the sad days of post-war licence, parents could still expect obedience and honor. Hopefully he predicts the return: " And perhaps, after going through changes brought about by our insatiate national curiosity to test all things . . . we may quietly resume a social condition in which children shall again be children, whose best rights shall once more consist in the love and protection of those whose dearest privilege it will be to extend them." [56]

So, too, were the colleges deplored, schools which tended to remove young girls from the love and protection of their natural guardians, which tended to teach them that they could, perhaps, unaided drive a nail, construe a Greek sentence, and cast a vote.

In the early days of their seminaries Emma Willard, Catharine Beecher, Mary Lyon no less than Mrs. Wheaton, would have indignantly repudiated the idea that any education could be a better preparation for life than that which they offered. Mary Lyon died in 1849 before the establishment of Northern colleges for women. Mrs. Willard, living on until 1870, and

[56] Editorial. *New York Times.* Sunday, December 26, 1869.

Catharine Beecher until 1878 watched the new schools rise, actually possessing the organization " on the college system " for which they had both pleaded.

But only Mrs. Wheaton lived to see the complete change. She saw the classics lose their supremacy; she saw Butler's *Analogy* driven from the curriculum; she saw the rise of modern languages, the re-evaluation of the men's colleges with the new emphasis upon contacts and football replacing piety and discipline, the growth of the social sciences, the inception of the scientific approach to the Bible, the divorce of philosophy and the Bible, the shift of heresy from the department of philosophy or religion to the department of economics.

In 1905 when Mrs. Wheaton died, it was the minority of women who went to college, even as it had been the minority who went to the seminaries in 1835. Neighbors still commiserated mothers whose daughters, going to college, would probably never marry; or perhaps it was only the predestined old maids who went to college. Substituting college for seminary, woman for female, the doubters persisted — in the face of empirical proof that the marrying type of girl married whether she were educated or not.

In 1905 no one talked of training for eternity. There was as much doubt then of men's having souls as ever there had been of women's. No one quoted Milton's views on women and few produced the Bible as a yardstick of feminine virtues. Not only were there many women's colleges, but men's colleges had come to make provision for women students. Mary

E. Woolley, a Wheaton Seminary graduate, had, with a companion won a degree from Brown University, and the Women's College in Brown University was created, later to change its cumbersome title to Pembroke College. Even Harvard, reluctantly and none too graciously, had established a woman's annex. No one now believed that the receiving of degrees unsexed a woman, though no college, except perhaps one, believed that they added abnormally to her stature.

Woman had received education, first at the seminaries, then at the colleges, without becoming horsey, or walking with a cane (canes came much later), or wearing trousers (and when trousers did appear on feminine legs they were the means of preserving modesty), or smoking a pipe (woman's smoking in America was a result of the war of 1914–1918), or ceasing to have babies. She still curled her hair, played the piano — even occasionally the harp — sang sentimental ditties, flirted, had due regard for a well-hung mirror, read novels openly instead of covertly, and was as ready as ever a young lady of the eighteenthirties to receive an eligible proposal of marriage.

Observing that the seminaries had not injured feminine delicacy, the founders of the colleges moved forward with unhesitating steps. Henry Fowler Durant visualized Wellesley in broader fashion than any woman's college has yet followed, a university with schools of science and of medicine. It is significant, however, that from his bequest of his private library to Wellesley, he omitted his law books.

Women doctors were already a reality — Vassar had included a woman physician in her original faculty — but Durant's liberality did not extend to feminine law.

The cult of the genteel female had indeed dwindled. Young ladies were none too sure that they ought to be educated for motherhood, to become more entertaining wives, more ably teaching mothers. They seemed not to regard their chief design for living the impress upon a baby son. It may even have seemed a more desirable fate to be Madame Schumann-Heink than the mother of Liszt, Sarah Bernhardt than the mother of Henry Irving.

Through the dull decades, the years when life seemed standardized in Victorian rightness, through the gaiety of the Spanish-American War, through the idealisms and disillusionments of the World War, the women's colleges have continued, never accumulating great wealth, never receiving the stupendous gifts that have fallen unsolicited into the laps of the men's colleges; never becoming the universities Durant pictured in his imaginative views of Wellesley, but unswervingly holding to their early belief that higher education is as fitting for women as for men. Gradually the supervision of morals and manners has been superseded by a belief in the ability of an intelligent student, male or female, to guide his own private life. Harvard and Yale in their magnificent housing plans have, on a luxury scale, followed the housing plans which were an essential of the women's seminaries and colleges. Æsthetic elegance of surroundings, which would have seemed peculiarly feminine to Vassar,

Durant, and Sophia Smith, which would have added to feminine delicacy and grace, is found in Harvard and Yale rather than in the women's colleges. Yet in their more restricted quarters, women students have preserved the democracy valued by their founders. In most of the women's colleges wealth buys no privileges.

If the women's colleges to-day offer a less richly spread table for intellectual delight than the men's universities, it is the fault of endowment, not of feminine restriction. If they have ceased to require Latin or Greek for either degree or entrance,[57] it is because the modern preparatory school is too often impatient of a requirement in the classics, not because women are less able than men to construe Virgil. If they are no longer sure of the aims of education, it is not because they are less wise than their brother institutions, but that they are faced with even greater problems.

With statistics granting only a fraction of a child to college graduates, it is futile to talk of education for motherhood. With nursery schools, kindergartens, and country day schools, the modern mother is soon relieved of the exclusive care of the two or three children she is at most likely to have. Early in the nineteenth century labor-saving devices came to the aid of the housewife, and in 1934 they reduce the day's work of a modern home-maker to the minimum number of hours.

Moreover, not all women marry. Even when they

[57] Mount Holyoke, Smith, and Wellesley announced in the newspapers of Nov. 27, 1934 their willingness to accept modern languages in substitution for the classics.

do, they are no longer sure of being supported. Modern life makes many demands upon the purse that were undreamt of in the days before automobiles, telephones, radios, and electrical appliances.

Should, then, the aim of education be that of self-support? During the depression years it has been made increasingly evident that the world thinks a woman entitled to a position only so long as no man wants it — or would take it at the same salary. In newspaper editorials, in magazines, in speeches, women to-day are reminded that their place is in the home — where some men can afford to keep them. In any case women are again and again forced to choose between marriage and a position. "It is the price they must pay for professional success." [58]

In the co-educational colleges women have won a small proportion only of the places on the faculty, with promotion ever difficult — and the presidency beyond their reach. In the women's colleges as often as not a man is president, the faculty half women, half men.

Women in large numbers teach in high schools, and the squirming grades are granted them without competition. The discovery of the eighteen-thirties, that women were peculiarly fitted to teach little children, has never met with dispute — at least from men. Not yet, however, is a college degree a prerequisite for these positions in the lower schools, filled usually by graduates of the normal schools which were first started in 1839.

[58] Editorial in the *Boston Herald,* December 6, 1934.

To-day women may enter any of the professions once secured exclusively to men, yet the number of professional women who can be absorbed in any given year is necessarily small, smaller as yet than the number of professional men. Business is open to women, again with fewer positions of higher rank than for men.

Statistics cannot provide an answer to the question, how many women graduating each year from women's colleges or co-educational colleges, really desire positions. Marriage is still the easiest way for a woman to earn her living; a husband, a home, and a child still the natural desire. Yet in the face of actual conditions, it is impossible to ignore the lack of this opportunity for large numbers.

The problem before the women's colleges, then, must be to work out a program of education that will fit students for marriage, if they should marry; for a career, if that is possible for them. No longer do brothers have large enough families or roomy enough houses to have a niche by the fireplace for unemployed, unmarried sisters; hence it is marriage or a " job," in some cases marriage and a " job," to which the modern student looks forward. Modern marriage is so different from marriage in the nineteenth century, that the chemistry of breadmaking would help as little as Butler's *Analogy* — indeed, a great deal less.

Colleges for women, as well as for men, have found vocational training less satisfactory in practice than in theory. In a country unregulated by Fascism or Communism, there is no central organization to determine what field of activity shall receive a student. Specially talented students will, in the future as in the past, find vocational training in the studies they most enjoy. For the student of ordinary talent, the path is as yet dark.

Reliance upon the men's colleges to point the way is no longer expedient. Women have less faith in man's wisdom than they did in " the good old days "; 1929 taught them that the new god of economics was not fashioned of the finest clay. But the æsthetic values, once believed the peculiar province of women, have remained. Art, music, literature — these have been unharmed by the depression years. The Winged Victory is as profoundly stirring to-day, as ever it was when the first flattering group gathered about the sculptor; *Prometheus Unbound* still has power to call forth all the latent idealism of young students though they may not share Shelley's poetic belief in the perfectibility of mankind.

Perhaps the women's colleges will re-evaluate their curricula and endeavor to find out what of the wisdom of the past is still of value; what of the practical studies have application for women of to-day; what of woman's needs is like to man's or different from his. Of recent years committees surveying women's education have been all too ready with suggestions of education for motherhood. It may be old-fashioned to feel that an unused course in domestic science or the care of an experimental baby is of less help in adversity or prosperity than an unused course in Greek or art or music or English or philosophy, but a belief in the æsthetic value has, in the past which must ever be the guide to the future, shortened many of the long miles of life.

That woman's education needs new direction would seem fairly obvious. Women have successfully followed the education of a gentleman for a century; they have proved themselves capable of mastering any subject in a masculine catalogue. They have not learned through this emulation to direct the world any more wisely than their brothers.

For the prosperity years any education seemed satisfactory. For the depression years, which are recurrent, more wisdom is needed.

If women's colleges are to have any part in solving the problem of woman's place in the world as it is to-day, as it is going to be to-morrow, they must be given the means to investigate and to experiment.

"What the end is, who can say?"

BIBLIOGRAPHY

Abdy, E. S. Journal of a Residence and Tour in the United States. 3 vols. London. 1835.

Adams, C. F., ed. Letters of Mrs. Adams, the Wife of John Adams. 2 vols. Boston. 1840.

Adams, Hannah. A Memoir of Miss Hannah Adams, Written by Herself, with Additional Notices, By a Friend. Boston. 1832.

Adams, J. T. The Adams Family. Boston. 1930.

Alcott, A. Bronson. His Life and Philosophy, by F. B. Sanborn and W. T. Harris. Boston. 1893.

Alcott, William A. Young Woman's Guide to Excellence. Boston. 1849.

American Lady's Preceptor, The. A Compilation of Observations, Essays, and Poetical Effusions, Designed to Direct the Female Mind. Baltimore. 1818.

Ames, M. C. A Memorial of Alice and Phoebe Cary. New York. 1873.

Andrews, E. Benjamin. History of the United States. Vol. III. New York. 1926.

[Astell, Mary]. A Serious Proposal to the Ladies, For the Advancement of their True and Greatest Interest. London. 1697.

Baker, R. P. A Chapter in American Education. New York. 1925.

Baker, R. P., ed. Sam Slick. New York. [1923].

Banister, Mrs. (Z. P. Grant). Hints on Education. Boston. 1856.

Barnes, G. H. The Antislavery Impulse, 1830–1844. New York. [1933].

Barrows, J. H. Henry Ward Beecher. New York. 1893.

Barry, W. A History of Framingham. Boston. 1847.

Bartlett, W. A. History of the United States. Vol. VI. London. n.d.

Bayles, R. M. History of Providence County. New York. 1891.

Beard, Mary R., ed. America Through Women's Eyes. New York. 1933.

Beecher, Catharine E. An Essay on the Education of Female Teachers. New York. 1835.

The True Remedy for the Wrongs of Woman. Boston. 1851.

Treatise on Domestic Economy. Boston. 1843.

v. also under Harveson.

Beecher, C. E. and Stowe, H. B. The American Woman's Home, or Principles of Domestic Science. New York. 1870.

Bell, Margaret. Margaret Fuller. New York. 1930.

Benedict, Clare. Voices Out of the Past. London. n.d.

Best, M. A. Thomas Paine. New York. [1927].

Birney, C. H. The Grimke Sisters. Boston. 1885.

Bleyer, W. G. The History of American Journalism. Boston. [1927].

Bowen's Picture of Boston. Boston. 1838.

Boynton, H. W. James Fennimore Cooper. New York. [1931].

Brackett, A. C., ed. The Education of American Girls. New York. 1874.

Brady, C. T. The True Andrew Jackson. Philadelphia. 1906.

Branagan, T. The Excellency of the Female Character Vindicated. Philadelphia. 1808.

Bronson, W. C. History of Brown University, 1764–1914. Providence. 1914.

Brown, J. F. The American High School. New York. 1917.

Brubacher, J. S., ed. Henry Barnard on Education. New York. 1931.

Burton W. The District School as It Was. Boston. 1852.

Bush, G. History of Higher Education in the United States. Washington. 1891.

C., Olympia de. School Life Fifty Years Ago. London. 1882.

Carman, H. J. and McKee S., Jr. A History of the United States. Boston. [1931].

Child, Mrs. D. L. (Lydia Maria). Biographies of Good Wives. New York. 1846.

The History of the Condition of Women. 2 vols. Boston. 1834.

Letters from New York. Boston. 1850.

Contributions Towards a Bibliography of the Higher Education of Women. Boston. 1897.

[Cooper, J. F.] Notions of the Americans: Picked Up by a Travelling Bachelor. 2 vols. London. 1828.

Counsels to Young Men. Title page wanting.

Cousin, M. Victor. Report on the State of Public Instruction in Prussia. New York. 1835.

Crawford, Mary C. Old Boston Days. Boston. 1909.

Creevy, C. A. S. A Daughter of the Puritans. New York. 1916.

Dall, C. H. The College, the Market, and the Court. Boston. 1867.

Davies, Emily. The Higher Education of Women. London and New York. 1866.

Davis, Paulina W. History of the National Woman's Rights Movement for Twenty Years 1850–1870. New York. 1871.

Dewey, M. E. Life and Letters of Catherine M. Sedgwick. New York. 1871.

Dexter, E. G. A History of Education in the United States. New York. 1914.

Dickens, Charles. American Notes. London and New York. n.d.

Discussion, The, or The Character, Education, Prerogatives and Moral Influence of Woman. Boston. 1837.

Dwight, Margaret Van Horn. A Journey to Ohio in 1810. New Haven. 1920.

Dwight, Theodore, Jr. The History of Connecticut. New York. 1841.

Eastman, Julia. Schooldays of Beulah Romney. Dover, N. H. [1872].

Edgeworth, Maria. Belinda. London. [1848].

    Moral Tales. London. [1848].

    Life and Letters. A. J. C. Hare, ed. London. 1894.

Emerson, George B. Reminiscences of an Old Teacher. Boston. 1878.

    His Life and Times, by P. C. Waterston. Cambridge. 1884.

[Farrar, Eliza]. The Children's Robinson Crusoe. Boston. 1830.

    Young Lady's Friend. Boston. 1837.

Fénelon, F. Treatise on the Education of Daughters. Boston. 1831.

Finley, R. E. The Lady of Godey's. Philadelphia. 1931.

Fish, C. R. The Rise of the Common Man. New York. 1927.

Fordyce, James. Sermons to Young Women. 2 vols. London. 1767.

Fuller, Margaret. Women in the Nineteenth Century. Boston. 1860.

    Memoirs of Margaret Fuller Ossoli. 2 vols. Boston. 1852.

    Life, by M. Bell. New York. 1930.

    Life, by Thomas Wentworth Higginson. Boston. 1887.

Furness, S. J. The Genteel Female. New York. 1931.

Gallaudet, Thomas. The Child's Book on the Soul. Hartford. 1847.

    Life, by E. M. Gallaudet. New York. 1888.

Garrison, William Lloyd. The Story of his Life, Told by his Children. 2 vols. New York. 1885.

    Life, by Archibald Grimke. New York. 1891.

Gilman, Caroline, ed. The Lady's Annual Register for 1838. New York.

Gisborne, T. An Enquiry into the Duties of the Female Sex. London. 1797.

Goldsmith, J. A General View of the Manners, Customs, and Curiosities of Nations. 2 vols. New Haven and Charleston. 1825.

Goodsell, W. Pioneers of Woman's Education in the United States. New York. 1931.

Graves, Mrs. A. J. Woman in America. New York. 1843.

Grimke, Sarah. Letters on the Equality of the Sexes and the Condition of Woman. Boston. 1838.

Grizzell, E. D.   Origin and Development of the High School in New England.   New York.   1922.

Haight, G.   Mrs. Sigourney, Sweet Singer of Hartford, New Haven.   1930.

Hale, Mrs. Sarah J.   Juvenile Miscellany.   vols. 2, 3, 4. Boston.   1836.

    Poems for our Children.   Boston.   1830.

    Traits of American Life.   Philadelphia.   1835.

    v. also under Finley.

Hall, S. P.   Lectures on School-keeping.   Boston.   1830.

Hall, T. C.   The Religious Background of America. Boston.   1930.

Hallowell, A. D.   James and Lucretia Mott.   Boston. 1884.

[Hamilton, Thomas].   Men and Manners in America. 2 vols.   Edinburgh.   1833.

Harper, I. H.   Life and Work of Susan B. Anthony.   2 vols.   Indianapolis.   1899.

Harveson, M. E.   Catharine Esther Beecher, Pioneer Educator.   Philadelphia.   1932.

Hervey, James.   Meditations Among the Tombs; Tending to Reform the Vices of the Age and to Promote Evangelical Holiness.   Windsor, Vt.   1814.

Higginson, Thomas Wentworth.   Cheerful Yesterdays. Boston.   1898.

    Contemporaries.   Boston.   1900.

    Life of Margaret Fuller Ossoli.   Boston.   1887.

    Woman and Her Wishes.   Boston.   1853.

History of the Bible.   24mo.   Cooperstown, N. Y. 1839.

History of the United States.   Title page wanting. [1847].

Holland, F. M.   Frederick Douglass, the Colored Orator.
New York.   [1891].
Howe, Julia Ward, ed.   Sex and Education.   A Reply to
Dr. E. H. Clarke's " Sex in Education."   Boston.   1874.
Howe, Julia Ward.   Reminiscences.   Boston.   1900.
Howe, M. A. DeW.   Life and Letters of George Bancroft.
New York.   1908.

Inglis, A.   Principles of Secondary Education.   Boston.
1918.
Irwin, I. H.   Angels and Amazons.   New York.   1933.

Jex Blake, Sophia.   A Visit to Some American Schools
and Colleges.   London.   1869.
Journal of the Proceedings of a Convention of Literary
and Scientific Gentlemen Held in New York October
1830.   New York.   1831.   (Facsimile reprint.)

Kandell, I. L.   History of Secondary Education.   Boston.
[1930].
Kemble, Frances A.   Journal of a Residence on a Geor-
gian Plantation 1838–1839.   New York.   1863.

Ladies' Companion, The.   Carefully Selected and Re-
vised by a Lady.   2d ed.   Brookfield.   1826.
Ladies' Diary, The: or Woman's Almanack 1749–1761.
Larcom, Lucy.   A New England Girlhood.   Boston.
1889.
    Poems.
    Life, Letters, and Diary.   Boston.   1879.
Library of Useful Knowledge.   London.   1829.
Linn, W. A.   The Story of the Mormons.   New York.
1923.

Livermore, Mary A. The Story of My Life. Hartford. 1897.

Locke, R. A. The Moon Hoax. New York. 1859.

Macy, J. The Anti-Slavery Crusade. New Haven. 1919.

Mann, Horace. Life of, by His Wife. Boston. 1891.

Manual of Happiness for Persons of Both Sexes, A. Philadelphia. 1842.

Manual of Politeness, A. Comprising the Principles of Etiquette and Rules of Behaviour in Genteel Society for Persons of Both Sexes. Philadelphia. 1842 (first published 1837).

Marryatt, Capt. [Frederick]. A Diary in America. Philadelphia. First series. 1839. Second series. 1840.

Martin, G. H. The Evolution of the Massachusetts Public School System. New York. 1902.

Martineau, Harriet. Society in America. 2 vols. New York and London. 1837.

McIntosh, M. J. Woman in America, Her Work and Her Reward. New York. 1850.

More, Hannah. Coelebs in Search of a Wife. 2 vols. London. 1809.

    Strictures on Female Education. Salem. 1809.

    Life, by Charlotte M. Yonge. Boston. 1888.

Moreau de Saint-Méry, M. L. E. Voyage aux États-Unis de l'Amérique, 1793–1798. New Haven. 1913.

Mott, F. L. A History of American Magazines. New York. 1930.

Muzzey, A. B. The Young Maiden. 10th ed. 1848.

Nevins, A. American Social History as Recorded by British Travellers. New York. 1923.

Palmer, G. H. Life of Alice Freeman Palmer. Boston. 1908.

Phelps, Mrs. Almira H. Lincoln. Lectures to Young Ladies, Comprising Outlines and Applications of the Different Branches of Female Education. Boston. 1833.

Podmore, F. Robert Owen. New York. [1906].

Reisner, E. H. The Evolution of the Common School. New York. 1932.

Schlesinger, A. M. Political and Social History of the United States, 1829–1925. New York. 1930.

Sears, C. E. Days of Delusion. Boston. 1924.

[Sedgwick, Catherine M.] A New-England Tale or, Sketches of New England Character and Manners. New York. 1822.

Married or Single? 2 vols. New York. 1857.

Hope Leslie or Early Times in the Massachusetts. New York. 1827.

Life and Letters. New York. 1871.

Shaw, Anna Howard. The Story of a Pioneer. New York. [1915].

Sigourney, Lydia Howard Huntley. Letters to My Pupils. New York. 1860.

Letters to Young Ladies. Title page missing.

Lucy Howard's Journal. New York. 1860.

The Faded Hope. New York. 1859.

Traits of the Aborigines of America. A Poem. Cambridge. 1822.

v. also under Haight, G.

Simpson, James. Necessity of Popular Education. Edinburgh. 1834.

Slosson, E. E.   The American Spirit in Education.   New Haven. 1921.

Stanton, Elizabeth Cady.   Eighty Years and More, 1815–1897. New York. 1898.

Stanton, T. S. and Balch, H. S., eds.   Elizabeth Cady Stanton as Revealed in Her Letters. 2 vols. New York. [1922].

Stowe, Harriet Beecher.   Life Compiled from her Letters and Journals. By C. E. Stowe. Boston. 1891.

Stowe, Lyman Beecher.   Saints, Sinners and Beechers. Indianapolis. 1934.

Thompson, D'Arcy W.   Wayside Thoughts; Being a Series of Desultory Essays on Education. New York. 1868.   (Lowell Institute Lectures.)

Thwing, C. F.   A History of Higher Education in America. New York. 1906.

Tiffany, F.   Life of Dorothea Lynde Dix. Boston. 1890.

Tileston, M. W., ed.   Caleb and Mary Wilder Foote, Reminiscences and Letters. Boston. 1918.

Todd, John.   The Daughter at School. 3d ed. Northampton. 1854.

Tolman, W. H.   History of Higher Education in Rhode Island. Washington. 1894.

Trollope, Anthony.   North America.   Philadelphia. 1862.

Trollope, Mrs. Frances M.   Domestic Manners of the Americans. 2 vols. 1832.

Vanderpoel, E. M.   Chronicles of a Pioneer School (1792–1833). Cambridge. 1903.

[Wakefield, E. G.]   England and America.   New York. 1834.

Walker, A. Woman, Physiologically Considered, as to Mind, Morals, Marriage, Matrimonial Slavery, and Divorce. New York. 1847. (1st ed. 1839).

Washburn, R. C. The Life and Times of Lydia E. Pinkham. New York. 1931.

Werner, M. R. Barnum. New York. [1923].

Willard, Emma. Advancement of Female Education. 1833.

Willard, Frances E. Glimpses of Fifty Years. Chicago. 1889.

Winship, A. E. Great American Educators. New York. [1900].

Wollstonecraft, Mary. A Vindication of the Rights of Woman. London. [1891].

Wood, Samuel. Letters from Boston. Nov. 1837. Title page missing.

Woody, T. A. A History of Women's Education in the United States. 2 vols. New York. 1929.

Wortley, Lady Emmeline Stuart. Travels in the United States. London. 1851.

Youmans, E. L., ed. The Culture Demanded by Modern Life. New York. 1870.

ADDRESSES, REPORTS, ETC.

American Woman's Educational Association circular. [1852].

An Appeal to the Wives, Mothers, and Daughters of Our Land in the City and in the Country. New York. 1836.

Annual Report of the Directors of the American Education Society. 1832.

Bailey, Rev. G. H. An Address on the One Hundredth

Anniversary of Mary Lyon's Birth. Ashland, Mass. 1817.

Barnard, F. A. Education and the State. New York. 1879.

Burroughs, Charles. An Address on Female Education. Portsmouth, N. H. 1827.

Embury, Mrs. Emma C. Address on Female Education. New York. 1831.

Emerson, Rev. Joseph. Discourse Delivered at the Dedication of the Seminary Hall in Saugus. Boston. 1822.

Gallaudet, Thomas. An Address on Female Education. Hartford. 1828.

Gardiner, Spring. The Excellence and Influence of the Female Character. New York. 1825.

Hamill, S. M. Address to the Lawrenceville (N. J.) High School and Female Seminary. Philadelphia. 1836.

Hovey, W. A. Woman's Rights: An Essay Delivered at the Exhibition of the English High School. Boston. 1860.

Ladies' New York Anti-Slavery Society. First Annual Report. 1836.

Neef, Joseph. Sketch of a Plan and Method of Education. Printed for the Author. 1808.

Willard, Emma. Address. Albany. 1819.

Young, Samuel. Suggestions on Promoting Civilization and Improvement or The Influence of Woman in the Social State. New York. 1825.

MAGAZINES AND NEWSPAPERS

Advocate and Family Guardian. New York. 1835.
American Annals of Education. Boston. 1835.
American Ladies' Magazine. Boston. 1829–1837.

Boston Courier, Post, and Transcript. 1834–1836.

Cabinet, vols. I, II, III. 1829–1830.

Comic Token. New York. 1835.

Hive, The, A Paper for Young Persons and Others. Salem. 1830.

Knickerbocker Magazine. New York. 1835.

Ladies' Cabinet of Fashion, Music, and Romance. London. 1835.

Lady's Book (Godey's). Philadelphia. 1834–1840.

Liberator. Boston. 1834–1836.

Massachusetts Teacher. Boston. 1849.

New England Magazine, vols. I–IV. Boston. 1831–1835.

New York Herald. 1835, 1836, 1861.

New York Post. 1860–1861.

New York Times. 1860, 1869.

New York World. 1861.

North American Review. Boston. 1835.

Parley's Magazine. For Children and Youth. New York. 1834.

Penny Magazine of the Society for the Diffusion of Useful Knowledge. London. 1835.

Providence Daily Journal. 1835, 1836.

Providence Free Press and Pawtucket Herald. April 22, 1836.

Quarterly Journal of Education. London. 1833.

Rose Bud, 1832; Southern Rose Bud, 1833–1835; Southern Rose, 1835–1839. Mrs. Caroline H. Gilman, ed. Charleston, S. C.

Select Journal of Foreign Periodicals. Boston. 1833–1834.

Something. Nemo Nobody, ed. Boston. 1809–1810.

Youth's Companion. Boston. 1833.

SCHOOLS AND COLLEGES

Listed under the present name when still existent.
The term " female " has been omitted from all names.

I.

Catalogues of seminaries and colleges, and the histories of
the towns in which they were founded.

II.

School Histories, Prospectuses, Anniversary volumes, and
Biographies of their founders:

Abbot Academy

McKeen, Philena and McKeen, Phebe M. History of
Abbot Academy. Andover. 1880.

Semicentennial Catalogue, 1829–1879.

Adams Academy

[Guildford, L. T.] The Use of a Life. New York.
[1885].

Parker, E. S. History of Londonderry, N. H. Boston.
1857.

Albany Academy for Girls

Material supplied by Miss Margaret Trotter, Principal.

Amherst College

Exercises at the Semicentennial. Springfield. 1879.

Bates College

Bates College, Its Work and Aims. [1885].

Bradford Junior College

Memorial of Bradford Academy. Boston. 1870.

Pond, J. S. Bradford, a New England Academy. Bradford. 1930.

Brown University

Bronson, W. C. History of Brown University. Providence. 1914.

Memories of Brown. Providence. 1909.

Bryn Mawr College
    Circular No. 2, 1884.
    Inauguration of Bryn Mawr College, 1885. Philadelphia. 1887.
    President's Reports to the Board of Trustees 1884 and 1885.
Byfield Seminary
    Emerson, Ralph. Life of Rev. Joseph Emerson. Boston. 1834.
Columbia University
    History of Columbia University. New York. 1904.
Derby Academy
    A Deed of Lease and Release . . . to the Trustees. Boston. 1806.
Elmira College
    Catalogues 1861–1874.
Emma Willard School (Troy Seminary)
    Lord, John. Life of Emma Willard. New York. 1873.
    Lutz, Alma. Emma Willard, Daughter of Democracy. Boston. 1929.
Hartford Seminary.
    Ms. letters and v. also under Beecher, C. E. and Harveson, M. E.
Harvard University
    Commencement programs various dates.
    Gardiner, J. H. Harvard. New York. 1914.
    Proceedings of the Overseers Relative to the Late Disturbances in that Seminary. August 25, 1834.
    Reports of the President to the Overseers 1832–1838.
    Quincy, Josiah. History of Harvard University. 2 vols. Cambridge. 1840.
Ipswich Seminary
    [Guildford, L. T.] Use of a Life. New York. [1885].

Felt, Joseph. History of Ipswich. Cambridge. 1836.
Ipswich in the Massachusetts Bay Colony. Ipswich. 1917.
Leicester Academy
Centenary. Worcester. 1884.
Festival on Seventy-first Anniversary. Worcester. 1855.
Washburn, A. H. Address at the Dedication of the Academy Hall. Boston. 1853.
Washburn, Emory. Brief Sketch of the History of Leicester Academy. Boston. 1885.
Wright, Luther. Address Before the Trustees and Students of Leicester Academy, Convened to Dedicate the New Edifice, Dec. 25, 1833. Worcester. 1834.
Massachusetts Institute of Technology
A History of the Departments of Chemistry and Physics at the M.I.T. 1865–1933. Cambridge. [1934].
Miss Pierce's School, Litchfield, Connecticut
Vanderpoel, E. N. Chronicles of a Pioneer School, 1792–1833. Cambridge. 1903.
Moses Brown School
Mount Holyoke College
Fisk, Fidelia. Recollections of Mary Lyon. Boston. [1866].
Gilchrist, Beth. Life of Mary Lyon. Boston. 1910.
Hitchcock, E. Power of Christian Benevolence, Illustrated in the Life and Labors of Mary Lyon. New York. 1852.
[Stowe, Mrs. S. D. L.] History of Mount Holyoke Seminary, 1837–1887. 1887.
The Seventy-Fifth Anniversary. South Hadley. 1912.
v. also Ipswich and Wheaton, etc.
Pembroke Academy, Pembroke, New Hampshire
Catalogue for the 34th year. 1854.

Phillips Exeter Academy
  Crosbie, L. M. The Phillips Exeter Academy. 1923.
Rensselaer Polytechnic Institute
  Baker, R. P. A Chapter in American Education. New
    York. 1925.
  Ricketts, Palmer C. History of Rensselaer Polytechnic
    Institute. New York. 1895.
  Letters from President Ricketts.
Ripley College
  Prospectus for 1864.
  A Quarterly Journal Devoted to Female Education.
Smith College
  Greene, H. F., ed. Foreshadowings of Smith College.
    Privately printed. 1928.
  Hanscom, E. D. and Greene, H. F. Sophia Smith and
    the Beginnings of Smith College. Northampton.
    1925.
  Rhees, H. S. Laurenus Clark Seelye. Boston. 1929.
  Scribner's Monthly, May 1877. Article, Smith Col-
    lege.
  Seelye, L. C. The Early History of Smith College.
    Boston. 1923.
  Celebration of the Quarter Centenary of Smith College.
    Cambridge. 1900.
Topsfield Academy
  Perley, M. V. B. History of the Topsfield Academy,
    1828–1860. Topsfield. 1899.
  Chapman, G. T. Alumni of Dartmouth.
Vassar College
  Vassar College. Its Foundation, Aims, Resources, and
    Course of Study. 1876.
  Historical Sketch of Vassar College. New York. 1876.
  Vassar College. Fiftieth Anniversary. 1910.

Letters from Old Time Vassar. Written by a Student in 1869–1870. Poughkeepsie. 1915.

Lossing, B. J. Vassar College and its Founder. New York. 1867.

Norris, M. H. Golden Age of Vassar. Poughkeepsie. 1915.

McFarland, Rev. W. H. What Are They Doing at Vassar? New York. 1871.

Taylor, J. M. Before Vassar Opened. Boston. 1914.

Taylor, J. M. and Haight, E. H. Vassar. New York. 1915.

Wellesley College

Converse, Florence. The Story of Wellesley. Boston. 1915.

Wheaton College, Norton, Massachusetts

Larcom, Lucy. Wheaton Seminary; A Semi-Centennial Sketch. Cambridge. 1885.

Paine, H. E. The Life of Eliza Baylies Wheaton. Cambridge. 1907.

Manuscripts, note books, and letters in Wheaton archives.

Yale University

Camp, W. and Welch, L. S. Yale, Her Campus, Classrooms, and Athletics. Boston. 1899.

INDEX

AMERICAN EDUCATION:
ITS MEN, IDEAS, AND INSTITUTIONS
An Arno Press/New York Times Collection

Series I

Adams, Francis. **The Free School System of the United States.** 1875.

Alcott, William A. **Confessions of a School Master.** 1839.

American Unitarian Association. **From Servitude to Service.** 1905.

Bagley, William C. **Determinism in Education.** 1925.

Barnard, Henry, editor. **Memoirs of Teachers, Educators, and Promoters and Benefactors of Education, Literature, and Science.** 1861.

Bell, Sadie. **The Church, the State, and Education in Virginia.** 1930.

Belting, Paul Everett. **The Development of the Free Public High School in Illinois to 1860.** 1919.

Berkson, Isaac B. **Theories of Americanization: A Critical Study.** 1920.

Blauch, Lloyd E. **Federal Cooperation in Agricultural Extension Work, Vocational Education, and Vocational Rehabilitation.** 1935.

Bloomfield, Meyer. **Vocational Guidance of Youth.** 1911.

Brewer, Clifton Hartwell. **A History of Religious Education in the Episcopal Church to 1835.** 1924.

Brown, Elmer Ellsworth. **The Making of Our Middle Schools.** 1902.

Brumbaugh, M. G. **Life and Works of Christopher Dock.** 1908.

Burns, Reverend J. A. **The Catholic School System in the United States.** 1908.

Burns, Reverend J. A. **The Growth and Development of the Catholic School System in the United States.** 1912.

Burton, Warren. **The District School as It Was.** 1850.

Butler, Nicholas Murray, editor. **Education in the United States.** 1900.

Butler, Vera M. **Education as Revealed By New England Newspapers prior to 1850.** 1935.

Campbell, Thomas Monroe. **The Movable School Goes to the Negro Farmer.** 1936.

Carter, James G. **Essays upon Popular Education.** 1826.

Carter, James G. **Letters to the Hon. William Prescott, LL.D., on the Free Schools of New England.** 1924.

Channing, William Ellery. **Self-Culture.** 1842.

Coe, George A. **A Social Theory of Religious Education.** 1917.

Committee on Secondary School Studies. **Report of the Committee on Secondary School Studies, Appointed at the Meeting of the National Education Association.** 1893.

Counts, George S. **Dare the School Build a New Social Order?** 1932.

Counts, George S. **The Selective Character of American Secondary Education.** 1922.

Counts, George S. **The Social Composition of Boards of Education.** 1927.

Culver, Raymond B. **Horace Mann and Religion in the Massachusetts Public Schools.** 1929.
Curoe, Philip R. V. **Educational Attitudes and Policies of Organized Labor in the United States.** 1926.
Dabney, Charles William. **Universal Education in the South.** 1936.
Dearborn, Ned Harland. **The Oswego Movement in American Education.** 1925.
De Lima, Agnes. **Our Enemy the Child.** 1926.
Dewey, John. **The Educational Situation.** 1902.
Dexter, Franklin B., editor. **Documentary History of Yale University.** 1916.
Eliot, Charles William. **Educational Reform: Essays and Addresses.** 1898.
Ensign, Forest Chester. **Compulsory School Attendance and Child Labor.** 1921.
Fitzpatrick, Edward Augustus. **The Educational Views and Influence of De Witt Clinton.** 1911.
Fleming, Sanford. **Children & Puritanism.** 1933.
Flexner, Abraham. **The American College: A Criticism.** 1908.
Foerster, Norman. **The Future of the Liberal College.** 1938.
Gilman, Daniel Coit. **University Problems in the United States.** 1898.
Hall, Samuel R. **Lectures on School-Keeping.** 1829.
Hall, Stanley G. **Adolescence: Its Psychology and Its Relations to Physiology, Anthropology, Sociology, Sex, Crime, Religion, and Education.** 1905. 2 vols.
Hansen, Allen Oscar. **Early Educational Leadership in the Ohio Valley.** 1923.
Harris, William T. **Psychologic Foundations of Education.** 1899.
Harris, William T. **Report of the Committee of Fifteen on the Elementary School.** 1895.
Harveson, Mae Elizabeth. **Catharine Esther Beecher: Pioneer Educator.** 1932.
Jackson, George Leroy. **The Development of School Support in Colonial Massachusetts.** 1909.
Kandel, I. L., editor. **Twenty-five Years of American Education.** 1924.
Kemp, William Webb. **The Support of Schools in Colonial New York by the Society for the Propagation of the Gospel in Foreign Parts.** 1913.
Kilpatrick, William Heard. **The Dutch Schools of New Netherland and Colonial New York.** 1912.
Kilpatrick, William Heard. **The Educational Frontier.** 1933.
Knight, Edgar Wallace. **The Influence of Reconstruction on Education in the South.** 1913.
Le Duc, Thomas. **Piety and Intellect at Amherst College, 1865-1912.** 1946.
Maclean, John. **History of the College of New Jersey from Its Origin in 1746 to the Commencement of 1854.** 1877.
Maddox, William Arthur. **The Free School Idea in Virginia before the Civil War.** 1918.
Mann, Horace. **Lectures on Education.** 1855.
McCadden, Joseph J. **Education in Pennsylvania, 1801-1835, and Its Debt to Roberts Vaux.** 1855.
McCallum, James Dow. **Eleazar Wheelock.** 1939.
McCuskey, Dorothy. **Bronson Alcott, Teacher.** 1940.
Meiklejohn, Alexander. **The Liberal College.** 1920.
Miller, Edward Alanson. **The History of Educational Legislation in Ohio from 1803 to 1850.** 1918.

Miller, George Frederick. The Academy System of the State of New York. 1922.

Monroe, Will S. History of the Pestalozzian Movement in the United States. 1907.

Mosely Education Commission. Reports of the Mosely Education Commission to the United States of America October-December, 1903. 1904.

Mowry, William A. Recollections of a New England Educator. 1908.

Mulhern, James. A History of Secondary Education in Pennsylvania. 1933.

National Herbart Society. National Herbart Society Yearbooks 1-5, 1895-1899. 1895-1899.

Nearing, Scott. The New Education: A Review of Progressive Educational Movements of the Day. 1915.

Neef, Joseph. Sketches of a Plan and Method of Education. 1808.

Nock, Albert Jay. The Theory of Education in the United States. 1932.

Norton, A. O., editor. The First State Normal School in America: The Journals of Cyrus Pierce and Mary Swift. 1926.

Oviatt, Edwin. The Beginnings of Yale, 1701-1726. 1916.

Packard, Frederic Adolphus. The Daily Public School in the United States. 1866.

Page, David P. Theory and Practice of Teaching. 1848.

Parker, Francis W. Talks on Pedagogics: An Outline of the Theory of Concentration. 1894.

Peabody, Elizabeth Palmer. Record of a School. 1835.

Porter, Noah. The American Colleges and the American Public. 1870.

Reigart, John Franklin. The Lancasterian System of Instruction in the Schools of New York City. 1916.

Reilly, Daniel F. The School Controversy (1891-1893). 1943.

Rice, Dr. J. M. The Public-School System of the United States. 1893.

Rice, Dr. J. M. Scientific Management in Education. 1912.

Ross, Early D. Democracy's College: The Land-Grant Movement in the Formative Stage. 1942.

Rugg, Harold, et al. Curriculum-Making: Past and Present. 1926.

Rugg, Harold, et al. The Foundations of Curriculum-Making. 1926.

Rugg, Harold and Shumaker, Ann. The Child-Centered School. 1928.

Seybolt, Robert Francis. Apprenticeship and Apprenticeship Education in Colonial New England and New York. 1917.

Seybolt, Robert Francis. The Private Schools of Colonial Boston. 1935.

Seybolt, Robert Francis. The Public Schools of Colonial Boston. 1935.

Sheldon, Henry D. Student Life and Customs. 1901.

Sherrill, Lewis Joseph. Presbyterian Parochial Schools, 1846-1870. 1932 .

Siljestrom, P. A. Educational Institutions of the United States. 1853.

Small, Walter Herbert. Early New England Schools. 1914.

Soltes, Mordecai. The Yiddish Press: An Americanizing Agency. 1925.

Stewart, George, Jr. A History of Religious Education in Connecticut to the Middle of the Nineteenth Century. 1924.

Storr, Richard J. The Beginnings of Graduate Education in America. 1953.

Stout, John Elbert. **The Development of High-School Curricula in the North Central States from 1860 to 1918.** 1921.
Suzzallo, Henry. **The Rise of Local School Supervision in Massachusetts.** 1906.
Swett, John. **Public Education in California.** 1911.
Tappan, Henry P. **University Education.** 1851.
Taylor, Howard Cromwell. **The Educational Significance of the Early Federal Land Ordinances.** 1921.
Taylor, J. Orville. **The District School.** 1834.
Tewksbury, Donald G. **The Founding of American Colleges and Universities before the Civil War.** 1932.
Thorndike, Edward L. **Educational Psychology.** 1913-1914.
True, Alfred Charles. **A History of Agricultural Education in the United States, 1785-1925.** 1929.
True, Alfred Charles. **A History of Agricultural Extension Work in the United States, 1785-1923.** 1928.
Updegraff, Harlan. **The Origin of the Moving School in Massachusetts.** 1908.
Wayland, Francis. **Thoughts on the Present Collegiate System in the United States.** 1842.
Weber, Samuel Edwin. **The Charity School Movement in Colonial Pennsylvania.** 1905.
Wells, Guy Fred. **Parish Education in Colonial Virginia.** 1923.
Wickersham, J. P. **The History of Education in Pennsylvania.** 1885.
Woodward, Calvin M. **The Manual Training School.** 1887.
Woody, Thomas. **Early Quaker Education in Pennsylvania.** 1920.
Woody, Thomas. **Quaker Education in the Colony and State of New Jersey.** 1923.
Wroth, Lawrence C. **An American Bookshelf, 1755.** 1934.

Series II

Adams, Evelyn C. **American Indian Education.** 1946.
Bailey, Joseph Cannon. **Seaman A. Knapp: Schoolmaster of American Agriculture.** 1945.
Beecher, Catharine and Harriet Beecher Stowe. **The American Woman's Home.** 1869.
Benezet, Louis T. **General Education in the Progressive College.** 1943.
Boas, Louise Schutz. **Woman's Education Begins.** 1935.
Bobbitt, Franklin. **The Curriculum.** 1918.
Bode, Boyd H. **Progressive Education at the Crossroads.** 1938.
Bourne, William Oland. **History of the Public School Society of the City of New York.** 1870.
Bronson, Walter C. **The History of Brown University, 1764-1914.** 1914.
Burstall, Sara A. **The Education of Girls in the United States.** 1894.
Butts, R. Freeman. **The College Charts Its Course.** 1939.
Caldwell, Otis W. and Stuart A. Courtis. **Then & Now in Education, 1845-1923.** 1923.
Calverton, V. F. & Samuel D. Schmalhausen, editors. **The New Generation: The Intimate Problems of Modern Parents and Children.** 1930.
Charters, W. W. **Curriculum Construction.** 1923.
Childs, John L. **Education and Morals.** 1950.

Childs, John L. **Education and the Philosophy of Experimentalism.** 1931.
Clapp, Elsie Ripley. **Community Schools in Action.** 1939.
Counts, George S. **The American Road to Culture: A Social Interpretation of Education in the United States.** 1930.
Counts, George S. **School and Society in Chicago.** 1928.
Finegan, Thomas E. **Free Schools.** 1921.
Fletcher, Robert Samuel. **A History of Oberlin College.** 1943.
Grattan, C. Hartley. **In Quest of Knowledge: A Historical Perspective on Adult Education.** 1955.
Hartman, Gertrude & Ann Shumaker, editors. **Creative Expression.** 1932.
Kandel, I. L. **The Cult of Uncertainty.** 1943.
Kandel, I. L. **Examinations and Their Substitutes in the United States.** 1936.
Kilpatrick, William Heard. **Education for a Changing Civilization.** 1926.
Kilpatrick, William Heard. **Foundations of Method.** 1925.
Kilpatrick, William Heard. **The Montessori System Examined.** 1914.
Lang, Ossian H., editor. **Educational Creeds of the Nineteenth Century.** 1898.
Learned, William S. **The Quality of the Educational Process in the United States and in Europe.** 1927.
Meiklejohn, Alexander. **The Experimental College.** 1932.
Middlekauff, Robert. **Ancients and Axioms: Secondary Education in Eighteenth-Century New England.** 1963.
Norwood, William Frederick. **Medical Education in the United States Before the Civil War.** 1944.
Parsons, Elsie W. Clews. **Educational Legislation and Administration of the Colonial Governments.** 1899.
Perry, Charles M. **Henry Philip Tappan: Philosopher and University President.** 1933.
Pierce, Bessie Louise. **Civic Attitudes in American School Textbooks.** 1930.
Rice, Edwin Wilbur. **The Sunday-School Movement (1780-1917) and the American Sunday-School Union (1817-1917).** 1917.
Robinson, James Harvey. **The Humanizing of Knowledge.** 1924.
Ryan, W. Carson. **Studies in Early Graduate Education.** 1939.
Seybolt, Robert Francis. **The Evening School in Colonial America.** 1925.
Seybolt, Robert Francis. **Source Studies in American Colonial Education.** 1925.
Todd, Lewis Paul. **Wartime Relations of the Federal Government and the Public Schools, 1917-1918.** 1945.
Vandewalker, Nina C. **The Kindergarten in American Education.** 1908.
Ward, Florence Elizabeth. **The Montessori Method and the American School.** 1913.
West, Andrew Fleming. **Short Papers on American Liberal Education.** 1907.
Wright, Marion M. Thompson. **The Education of Negroes in New Jersey.** 1941.

Supplement

The Social Frontier (Frontiers of Democracy). Vols. 1-10, 1934-1943.